The California Gold Rush and the Coming of the Civil War

The California Gold Rush and the Coming of the Civil War

LEONARD L. RICHARDS

ALFRED A. KNOPF

New York
2007

THIS IS A BORZOI BOOK
PUBLISHED BY ALFRED A. KNOPF

Copyright © 2007 by Leonard L. Richards

www.aaknopf.com

Knopf, Borzoi Books, and the colophon are
registered trademarks of Random House, Inc.

Library of Congress Cataloging-in-Publication Data
Richards, Leonard L.
The California Gold Rush and the coming of the Civil War /
Leonard L. Richards. —1st ed.
p. cm.
Includes bibliographical references and index.
ISBN 0-307-26520-X
1. Califonia—Gold discoveries.   2. California—History—1846–1850.
3. California—Politics and government—1846–1850.   4. Politicians—California—
History—19th century.   5. Politicians—United States—History—19th century.
6. Sectionalism (United States)—History—19th Century.   7. United States—
History—Civil War, 1861–1865—Causes.   8. Slavery—Political aspects—
United States—History—19th century.   9. United States—Politics and
governement—1815–1861.   I. Title.
R865.R53 2006
979.4'04—dc22
2006048728

Manufactured in the United States of America
First Edition

For Samuel, Eliza, and Hadleigh

Contents

Preface

The roots of this book go back to my childhood. Although I was raised in Berkeley, my father grew up in Grass Valley, the heart of the California gold country. The youngest of four sons, he was the first male in the family to get out of the mines. Before he left home, however, my grandfather had insisted that he learn the family trade. So Dad knew a lot about quartz mining, including how to blow up a rock wall so that all the pieces fell neatly into one pile. I always hoped to see a demonstration, but never did. Instead, I had to settle for a diagram of a standard twenty-two-hole blasting pattern. Four or five times a year, we journeyed back to Dad's old hometown, to "Grandma's house," and there I was literally surrounded by hard-rock miners. From these experiences, I picked up bits and pieces about gold rush California. I also learned that hard-rock mining was a skill that had to be honed to near perfection and not something that could be mastered in a weekend.

These childhood experiences, however, didn't trigger the writing of this book. That decision came much later and more or less through a back door. In the 1980s, while doing research for a book on John Quincy Adams's congressional career, I dipped into pamphlets, letters, and reminiscences written by his slaveholding adversaries. As expected, I learned that most of them regarded the former president as an able but nasty old man. To my surprise, however, I also discovered that shortly after his death in 1848, many of them fantasized about taking their slaves to California and getting rich mining gold. None of them, as far as I could tell, knew the first thing about mining, much less hard-rock mining. They all seemed to think it was easy, something any slave could do. And nearly all of them deemed the slaveholding South's "loss" of California a major turning point in North-South relations. Had they gained control of the gold fields, they contended, their lives and the lives of their fellow slaveholders would have been golden.

A few years later, while studying free-state politicians who sided with the South in North-South struggles, I discovered that some of the more noteworthy came from my home state. Somehow I had missed learning that fact. Somehow I had gone through the California schools from kindergarten through graduate school and never realized that many of the state's early leaders had been "Northern men with Southern principles," that several might as well have been representing Mississippi or Alabama in national affairs, and that the state's entire congressional delegation on the eve of the Civil War had supported John C. Breckinridge, the pro-slavery candidate for president. Either such details had been omitted from the curriculum, or I simply had not been paying attention. In any event, one reason for writing this book has been to bring myself up to speed—to learn material that I should have learned forty or fifty years ago.

In the process, I've had plenty of help. The Bancroft and Huntington libraries were central. They are literally gold mines for California scholars, and the staff at both institutions alerted me to documents that I would probably never have found on my own. Also helpful were archivists at the state library, the California Historical Society, the Nevada County Historical Society, the Placer County Historical Society, the Empire Mine, and other depositories I visited over the years. As in the past, the librarians at my home institution, the University of Massachusetts, have been diligent in getting me the microfilm and obscure books that I needed. And, as in the past, I have relied heavily on my colleagues in the history department for advice and direction, especially Bruce Laurie and Barry Levy, who on more occasions than I can count listened patiently to my ramblings. I have also taught four writing seminars on the gold rush and the coming of the Civil War, and some of the students in those classes have been computer whizzes, finding facts and figures on the Internet that I never knew existed. Finally, I owe a big thanks to Jennifer Bonin for creating the maps and to Jane Garrett, Emily Molanphy, Leslie Levine, and the staff at Alfred A. Knopf for shepherding the manuscript through publication.

The California Gold Rush and
the Coming of the Civil War

Prologue

———◆◆◆———

TODAY THE LAKE IS SURROUNDED BY GOLF COURSES—ONE PUBLIC, three private—all scrambling to get their share of its water. To conservationists the courses are a nuisance, a curse on the environment and a danger to the waterfowl, but the fairways and clubhouses have been San Francisco landmarks since the 1920s and have too many patrons to be uprooted. One of the private clubs—the famous Olympic Club—has hosted four U.S. Opens. Ben Hogan played and lost there to an unknown golfer named Jack Fleck. Thousands of lesser golfers, meanwhile, have taken their clubs to the nearby public course at Harding Park.

Of the men and women who trudge the fairways of these four courses, eat and drink in the clubhouses, tell stories and lie about their handicaps, many are well aware of the Hogan-Fleck match. A few even saw it happen. Only a handful, however, are aware that just to the east of the southern tip of the lake is the place where a U.S. senator was shot to death, the last U.S. senator to be killed in California before Bobby Kennedy. Scarcely one in a thousand knows that story.

One can't blame them. It happened long ago, sixty years before any of the courses were built, before the Civil War, actually, September 13, 1859, to be precise.

At that time Lake Merced was a very popular dueling ground. Dueling was illegal in San Francisco, but the area just behind the barn at Lake House Ranch was remote enough that a duel could still be carried out in relative privacy and isolation from the law. Also, there were certain to be some technical difficulties determining jurisdiction, had the authorities tried to interfere. For the lake is not in San Francisco proper, but south of the city, on the border between San Francisco and San Mateo counties.

The duel was between David S. Terry, the chief judge of the state supreme court, and Senator David Broderick.[1] They were both Democrats, but from hostile ends of their party. Broderick, the senator, opposed the expansion of slavery, and Terry, the judge, was part of what was then called the Chivalry wing of the California Democratic Party. The Chivs were pro-South and pro-slavery. They were also determined to eliminate Broderick and other California free-soilers from positions of power. At the time of the duel the Chivs had the upper hand and seemed to be just on the edge of victory.

The judge pushed matters to a head. He probably couldn't help it. Even his friends described him as "truculent." He was young for a judge, just thirty-six, but had been on the state supreme court for four

David S. Terry, chief justice of the California Supreme Court. Reprinted from Jeremiah Lynch, A Senator of the Fifties: David C. Broderick of California *(San Francisco, 1911), 130.*

years, chief judge for two years. He was a big man, six feet three and over 220 pounds, with a noticeably flat face and a large bulbous nose. He was clean shaven except for chin whiskers. He wore his hair long, in the "Southern" style.

The judge was a Southern man and proud of it. He had been born in Kentucky and lived in Texas before migrating to Stockton in December 1849. In 1852 he had returned briefly to the South and married Cornelia Runnels, the niece of the Mississippi governor. He had assured her that he would never accept California's decision to outlaw slavery. As a supporter of "the doctrine of the ultra states' rights men of the South," he was determined "to change the Constitution of the state by striking out that clause prohibiting slavery . . . or, failing in that, to divide the state and thus open a portion of California to Southerners and their property."[2]

The judge was also a well-known knife fighter. Three years earlier, during his second year on the bench, he had tried to stop Sterling Hopkins, a member of the San Francisco Vigilance Committee, from making an arrest. He hated vigilantes and vigilante justice. In the fracas he had pulled out a bowie knife, his favorite weapon, and severely wounded Hopkins. The Vigilance Committee then had him arrested. Ironically, to his defense had come David Broderick, whose followers had been the committee's chief targets. Broderick paid three newspapers to put the judge's behavior in the best possible light.

In June 1859, however, the help of Broderick was history. The Vigilance Committee was all but dead, and the judge now saved his sharpest barbs for the free-soil wing of the Democratic Party. He called them "black Republicans" and "negro lovers." At one point he also said that they were an unprincipled "remnant of a faction" owned "heart and soul" by Broderick, whose only guidance came from "the banner of the black Douglass, whose name is Frederick." Those were code words. Everyone at the time understood that the judge was referring to Frederick Douglass, the black abolitionist, and essentially saying that Broderick took his cues from a black man.[3]

On June 26 Broderick learned of the judge's remarks in the morning newspaper while having breakfast at the International Hotel in San Francisco. He, too, was a warrior. He had made his reputation in New York City taking on the city's toughest prizefighters—Eli Hazleton, Seth Douglas, Abe Bogart, John Williamson, Mose Cutter, Sam Baisely, and Johnny Baum. Victory had never been his, but he had gained fame for never backing down. He had also gained fame as a bouncer at his New York saloon. He had a powerful build and gnarled hands, thanks partly to his years as a stonemason, and thus usually had little trouble keeping order. He also bore a knife scar that ran down his cheek into his beard. That,

David Broderick, senator from California. Reprinted from Elijah R. Kennedy, The Contest for California in 1861 *(Boston, 1912), 64.*

along with his piercing dark blue eyes and dark eyebrows, made him even more menacing.[4]

True to form, Broderick responded to Judge Terry with nasty remarks of his own. He proclaimed Terry to be a "damned miserable wretch" who was as corrupt as President James Buchanan and William Gwin, California's other senator. "I have hitherto spoken of him as an honest man—as the only honest man on the bench of a miserable, corrupt Supreme Court—but now I find I was mistaken. I take it all back. He is just as bad as the others."[5]

That was all it took. The judge challenged the senator to a duel. Both men then chose seconds to handle the details, and the seconds made arrangements for the duel to take place one week after the September election, September 13, 1859, behind the barn of the Lake House Ranch on Lake Merced.

On learning about the time and location, James J. Ayers drove a horse-drawn carriage most of the night to get there. The place was mobbed. He counted seventy-three spectators.[6] Two sets of weapons had been brought to the dueling grounds. Terry won the toss and selected the ones his side had provided: Belgian-made eight-inch barrels, with hair triggers. Terry had practiced with these pistols, Broderick had not.

The hair trigger proved deadly to Broderick. He was a skilled marksman, practiced regularly, and could handle any pistol that necessitated a quick, firm pull. But a pistol that necessitated a light touch was beyond him. He thus fired too quickly, and his shot went wildly into the ground. The judge's pistol worked perfectly. He took careful aim and shot Broderick in the lung.

Broderick died three days later. His followers never regarded the duel as just a duel. To them it amounted to an assassination. The Chivs, as they saw it, were out to get Broderick, and if Judge Terry hadn't pulled the trigger, someone else would have. Declared the Republican Edward Dickinson Baker, at Broderick's funeral service: "His death was a political necessity, poorly veiled beneath the guise of a private quarrel . . . What was his public crime? The answer is in his own words: 'I die because I was opposed to a corrupt administration and the extension of slavery.' "[7]

Echoing this sentiment was Elisha Crosby, a New Yorker who had represented Sacramento at the state constitutional convention and knew both men well. The problem, wrote Crosby, was that Broderick was as "brave as a lion" and thus a menace to Senator William Gwin and his followers. These men wanted to put California in Southern hands, colonize the southern portion of the state with Southern people, and get the state legislature to divide the state, making the southern part of it slave. Surmised Crosby: "Broderick's denunciation of this scheme, I have no doubt brought on the conflict which led to his assassination. It was pretty well understood that he was to be assassinated anyway. If Terry failed, somebody else was to kill him."[8]

1

———◆◆◆———

THE CHAIN OF EVENTS THAT LED TO THE KILLING BEGAN IN THE foothills of the Sierra Nevada on a cold morning in late January 1848. That morning, as every morning for the past several months, Jennie Wimmer had been working over a hot woodstove. Her task at the moment was making soap. Technically, she was the cook and laundress for a crew of white men, mainly Mormons, who were building a sawmill on the south fork of the American River. In fact, however, she had so alienated the Mormons that they no longer ate at her table.

Initially the men had welcomed her. Tired of their own cooking and eager to have a woman in the kitchen, they had even accepted the fact that she always served the choice portions of pork and mutton to her husband, Peter, and her seven children. But she had treated them shabbily and worn out her welcome. Whenever she rang the dinner bell, she had expected them to appear at once, and on Christmas morning, when they had taken extra time washing up, she had bawled them out, telling them that "she was Boss" and that they "must come at the first call" or go without breakfast. With that, they had "revolted from under her government" and decided to build their own separate cabin and cook for themselves.[1]

What had made matters worse was that Jennie Wimmer wasn't an old tyrant. She was a young one, just twenty-six years old, much younger than some of the men. She also cursed, and, like most white women in California at this time, she had been around.

Christened Elizabeth Jane, but always called Jennie, she was the daughter of a Virginia tobacco farmer who in 1838 had moved his family to Lumpkin County, Georgia, to mine gold. There she and her mother had run a boardinghouse for local miners, and there she had met a young miner named Obadiah Baiz. They had married and moved to Missouri in 1840. He had died in 1843, leaving her a widow with two children. She then married Peter Wimmer, a thirty-three-year-old widower from Cincinnati with five children. In the spring of 1846 the Wimmers decided to leave the United States and head west to Mexican California. They joined a wagon train of eighty-four migrants, trekked across the Rockies and Sierras, and arrived at Sutter's Fort, in what is now Sacramento, on November 15, 1846.[2]

The following spring the owner of the fort, Johann Sutter, decided to build a sawmill for his rapidly expanding agricultural empire. He, too, had been around. He had fled Switzerland for New York in 1834, leaving behind a wife and four children, large debts, and a warrant for his arrest. He then went to Missouri, New Mexico, Oregon, Hawaii, and Alaska before he reached California in 1839. Since then he had become a Mexican citizen and persuaded the governor of California to grant him a huge tract of land in the Sacramento valley, which he had dubbed New Helvetia. He was now forty-four years old and saw nothing but glory days lying ahead.

The site Sutter picked for his sawmill was some forty miles from his home base, on the south fork of the American River, in a place that came to be known as Coloma.[3] Had Sutter been in his native Switzerland, he could have found plenty of millwrights who knew how to tap the power of falling water. But in the Sacramento valley finding a skilled millwright or even a millwright's apprentice was next to impossible. So to oversee the operation Sutter turned to James Marshall, a thirty-seven-year-old

Johann Sutter, owner of New Helvetia. Reprinted from Frank Soulé et al., The Annals of San Francisco *(New York, 1854), 765.*

New Jersey carpenter who had tried his hand at ranching in the Sacramento valley and failed miserably.

Sutter assigned thirteen of his Mormon hands to work under Marshall. They were part of a larger contingent of eight hundred Mormons who had been sent by Salt Lake City to earn money fighting in the Mexican War. This contingent in 1847 had come to Sutter's Fort on their way back to Utah. About eighty had stayed to work, not for wages, but for horses and cattle to take home with them. Sutter still had nearly fifty Mormon hands. He thought that they were the best workers he had ever encountered. The men he assigned to Marshall had agreed to stay until the following spring. Then they planned to head east across the mountains to join Brigham Young and their fellow Saints on the shores of the Great Salt Lake. They, too, had been around. One of their leaders, Henry Bigler, had survived the anti-Mormon wars in Missouri and Illinois and now was an elder in the Mormon church.

Sutter also employed Maidu Indians. He essentially rented them from tribal leaders. He had for years, using some as personal servants, others to dig irrigation ditches and plant his orchards. He didn't think much of their work habits, but they cost him much less than the Mormons, and so he decided to have one Maidu crew dig the race for his sawmill. To oversee them he hired Jennie Wimmer's husband, Peter. The camp also needed a cook and a laundress, and for those duties Sutter hired Jennie, not knowing that her dictatorial ways would drive Henry Bigler and his fellow Mormons to the point of rebellion.

As luck would have it, however, Jennie Wimmer had one skill that the others lacked. Thanks to her time in Georgia, she knew how to tell the difference between gold and fool's gold. That knowledge proved helpful when Peter brought to her kitchen a pebble that James Marshall had found earlier that morning in the freshly dug tail race. The find had excited Marshall, so much so that he ran back to his Mormon crew, shouting: "Boys, by God I believe I have found a gold mine!"[4]

James Marshall, discoverer of gold. Reprinted from Frank Soulé et al., The Annals of San Francisco *(New York, 1854), 767.*

The workers, however, had been skeptical. They had tested the metal, biting and hammering it to see if it was brittle, and found that it was malleable. But they still had doubts. So, too, did Marshall. The chips he found just didn't have enough luster, he thought, to be gold. Didn't gold glisten? He wasn't certain. Nor was Peter. But Jennie knew what to do with the pebble Peter handed her. She tossed it into a kettle of soap she was making, knowing that it would corrode if it was fool's gold. She then finished making the soap and set it off to cool. The next morning one of the hands asked her about the pebble. "I told him it was in my soap kettle. . . . A plank was brought for me to lay my soap onto, and I cut it in chunks, but it was not to be found. At the bottom of the pot was a double handful of potash, which I lifted in my two hands, and there was my gold as bright as could be."[5]

James Marshall then braved a drenching rain to take the news to Sutter. He found Sutter writing at his office desk, totally surprised to see him. Hadn't Marshall just received all the supplies he needed? To Sutter's further surprise, Marshall then insisted that the door be locked and asked for two pails of water and a scale. He then showed Sutter what he had found, and the two men spent the next couple of hours consulting the *American Encyclopedia* and doing one experiment after another. They bit and hammered the metal to see if it was malleable. They doused it with nitric acid to see if it would tarnish. They weighed it against silver. They weighed it a second time—and then a third. They immersed the scales into a pail of water to see if it had greater specific gravity and sunk to the bottom. Finally, after again consulting the *American Encyclopedia*, they pronounced it gold.

Sutter decided that the discovery must be kept secret. The next day he rode up to Coloma. "I had a talk with my employed people all at the Sawmill" and asked "that they would do me the great favor and keep it a secret." But he forgot to silence Jennie Wimmer and her sons. They told all who came by, including a teamster, Jacob Wittner, who carried the news back to Sutter's Fort. Sutter himself also had loose lips, and by March the news had reached San Francisco.

The first reports were dismissed as nonsense. Legends, talk, and boasts of gold had been heard many times before. Just six years earlier, in 1842, gold had been found in the mountains just north of Los Angeles, but the find played out quickly. Maybe Coloma would just be more of the same. The two weekly San Francisco newspapers, *The Californian* and *The California Star*, treated the first reports with casual indifference.

In downplaying the reports, the *Star*'s owner had an ulterior motive. The newspaper belonged to Sam Brannan, a dapper and friendly man who seemingly spent half his time serving God, the other half serving mammon.[6] A twenty-nine-year-old Maine native, Brannan had been a Mormon leader for most of his adult life. When he was fourteen years old, his sister had married a Mormon missionary, and he tagged along with the honeymoon couple to what was then the Mormon headquarters in Kirtland, Ohio. He had converted to the faith, helped build the first temple, and become a printer. He was then sent to New York City as the East Coast publisher of Mormon literature. He made valuable commercial contacts there and by age twenty-five had become a rich man.

Then, in 1844, when anti-Mormonism erupted into a full-scale war in Illinois and the killing of the church's founder, Joseph Smith, in a Carthage jail, Brannan was ordered to move the East Coast Mormons out of the United States to safer ground. Brannan bought a schooner, the *Brooklyn*, to transport seventy men, sixty-eight women, and a hundred children. They sailed south, around Cape Horn, to what was supposed to be a sparsely populated haven in northern Mexico. They arrived in Yerba Buena, soon to be renamed San Francisco, on the last day of July 1846. The town was a sleepy place, a shack town of maybe five hundred residents.

Sam Brannan, Mormon entrepreneur. Reprinted from Frank Soulé et al., The Annals of San Francisco *(New York, 1854), 748.*

There, to Brannan's disgust, he saw an American flag flying, signaling that California was about to become U.S. property.

Brannan didn't bring just his people to California. He also brought his entrepreneurial skills. On the *Brooklyn* he had loaded a printing press, the makings of a sawmill and a flour mill, and tools of every sort. Once in San Francisco, he had the press and two mills working within weeks, and with the help of his fellow Mormons began to build a commercial empire from San Francisco to Sacramento, where he established a retail store outside the walls of Sutter's Fort. Among his new enterprises was *The California Star*, one of the two newspapers that treated rather casually James Marshall's finding of gold.

All through March and April, the *Star* made light of Marshall's discovery. It was no big deal, nothing to get excited about. Meanwhile, the *Star*'s owner expanded his holdings in the gold fields. As a deputy of Brigham Young, he went there to collect tithes. But instead of sending the money to Salt Lake City, he used it to open a store at Mormon Island and Coloma and to build a hotel in Sacramento. He also stocked his Sacramento store with everything a gold seeker might need and gained a monopoly on steamboat landings at Sacramento. Then, on May 12, Brannan returned to San Francisco with a bottle of gold dust. Holding it high at the corner of Portsmouth Square, he shouted: "Gold! Gold! Gold from the American River!" By month's end, almost the entire male population of San Francisco had left town for the gold fields.

The U.S. military, especially, was hard hit. In San Francisco, sailors abandoned their ships, soldiers deserted by the hundreds. In Monterey, three seamen ran away from the *Warren*, thus forfeiting four years' pay, and "a whole platoon of soldiers" fled the fort and "left only their colors behind." The situation became so bad that the fort's commanding general and the ship's captain "had to take to the kitchen" and cook their own breakfast. Imagine, wrote one lieutenant, "a general of the United States Army" and "the commander of a man-of-war . . . in a smoking kitchen, grinding coffee, toasting a herring, and peeling an onion"![7]

A deserter from the fort at Monterey. Reprinted from Walter Colton, Three Years in California *(New York, 1852), 71.*

Joining the deserters were scores of former soldiers who had recently been discharged. Out of the disbanded Mormon Battalion came several hundred. In California to acquire horses and cattle before heading to the Great Salt Lake, they now stayed to mine gold. Several hundred more gold seekers came out of the New York Volunteers, a regiment of some seven hundred men who had been recruited in New York by Colonel Jonathan Drake Stevenson, a well-heeled Democratic politician, to fight in the war against Mexico. They had been mustered into the army in August 1846, and after training for six weeks, they had been sent around Cape Horn to occupy California. Most had finished their military obligation and were now awaiting a ship home. On hearing the news of "gold on the American River," the vast majority instead headed for the Sierras.[8]

A month after the news broke, the American consul in San Francisco, Thomas Larkin, reported the situation to the American secretary of state. Not only had a "large portion" of the sailors and soldiers stationed in San Francisco and Sonoma deserted, but the navy had put out to sea to keep more men from joining them. In addition, three-quarters of the city's houses were now deserted, "every blacksmith, carpenter and lawyer" was now leaving, the "brick-yards, saw-mills and ranches" had no one left to run them, both of the city's newspapers had stopped publishing, the city had "not a justice of the peace left."[9]

The mammon half of Brannan's nature thus triumphed. His businesses profited, and he became a millionaire. He acquired large holdings in both Sacramento and San Francisco. He gave up the Mormon church, never joined Brigham Young in Utah, never forwarded the tithes he received from gold-mining Mormons. Not all was rosy, however. His wife who had accompanied him to California discovered that he was a bigamist, that without her knowledge the Mormon church had given him permission to take her as a second wife, and that he was still legally married to another woman, whom he had callously abandoned along with their child. The divorce suit cost him much of his fortune. So did a lawsuit that he later filed against the railroad entrepreneurs who eventually came to dominate California. Drink finally ruined him.

The news that Brannan parlayed into a fortune traveled mainly by sea. It thus reached ports in the Pacific Ocean months before it reached New York or Boston. New York and Boston were fourteen thousand nautical miles from San Francisco, while Acapulco and Honolulu were just two thousand, Callao four thousand, Valparaiso six thousand, Sydney and Canton seven thousand.

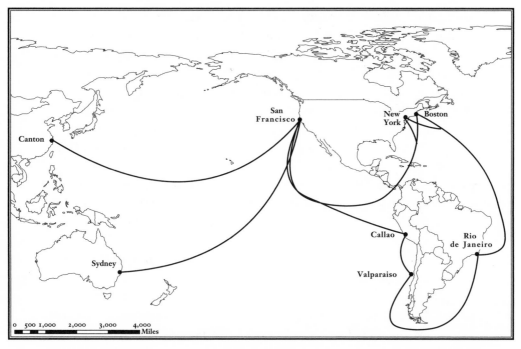

Sea routes to San Francisco

Among the ships docked in San Francisco in May 1848 was a brig owned by José Ramón Sánchez of Valparaiso, Chile. While loading the ship with hides and tallow, California's principal exports, the supercargo heard about gold on the American River and purchased some gold dust at $12 per ounce. On June 14 the brig set sail for Chile and arrived in Valparaiso on August 19. Within days the rush was on. Two dozen hopefuls bought passage on the *Virjinia*, which was just about to head north, and Chilean merchants began outfitting other ships.[10]

Among those who lined up for passage was forty-one-year-old Vicente Pérez Rosales, a restless intellectual who already had had a colorful career as a gold miner in the Chilean Alps and a cattle rustler in Argentina. Along with his three brothers, a brother-in-law, and two servants, Rosales got passage on a French bark bound for San Francisco. The ship was jammed. All told, there were ninety male passengers, two females (including a prostitute named Rosario), four cows, eight pigs, and three dogs, along with a crew of nineteen men. The ship left Valparaiso in December 1848. Fifty-two days later, after much boredom and a few near disasters, Rosales and his shipmates reached the mouth of the Golden Gate, which, he wrote, "inspired awe but at the same time smiled, seeming to open wide to receive us."[11]

Meanwhile, far across the Pacific, *The Sydney Herald* broke the news of gold on the American River in December 1848. Among those who took notice was thirty-three-year-old Edward Hargraves, "a corpulent bull-calf of a man" who had worked as a sailor, publican, and shopkeeper. After settling his affairs at home, Hargraves formed a small group of gold seekers and bought passage on the *Elizabeth Archer*, an English bark out of Liverpool. On board were at least one hundred passengers. Leaving Sydney on July 17, 1849, the ship reached San Francisco eighty-one days later. As it entered the harbor, Hargraves's hopes skyrocketed. Everywhere he looked he saw abandoned ships, "a complete forest of masts—a sight well calculated to inspire us with hope, and remove the feelings of doubt." The next day the *Elizabeth Archer* joined them, as the whole crew, excepting one officer and three apprentice boys, jumped ship.[12]

Hargraves's high hopes soon dimmed, however. Heading well east of San Francisco, he hoped to make a fortune prospecting on the Stanislaus River. He learned the craft of prospecting with pans, cradles, and excavation, but he found little gold and nearly froze to death at night. During the day, however, he noticed that the California terrain showed similarities to that of his Australian home. Hadn't he seen similar rocks and geological formations in New South Wales, within three hundred miles of Sydney? He was certain he had. Unsuccessful in California, he decided to return to Australia and discover gold there. Arriving in Sydney in January 1851, he proceeded to the interior, and on February 12 found gold in Lewis Ponds Creek, a small tributary of the Macquarie River. The impact was instantaneous. In 1852 Australia produced sixty million in gold, and Hargraves became a national hero.[13]

Simultaneously, while the news of California gold was enticing Edward Hargraves and other readers of *The Sydney Herald*, ship brokers spread the word in southern China, especially throughout the Canton region. Why Canton? That has become a matter of dispute. According to one school of thought, the region had been devastated by civil war, floods, droughts, typhoons, and famine. Families were thus desperate, looking for a way out. According to another interpretation, the area was more market-oriented than most of China and thus had more than its share of risk takers.[14]

Whatever the explanation, ship brokers saw the Cantonese as fair game. Playing on their hopes and fears, one enterprising Hong Kong broker concocted an illustrated pamphlet that promised "big pay, large houses, and food and clothing of the finest description" for all those who went to California. The broker also claimed that California was "a nice country, without mandarins or soldiers," that the Chinese would be welcomed there with open arms, and that the "Chinese god" was already there.[15]

Accompanying such fabrications were word-of-mouth reports that allegedly came from the Chinese who were already in California. According to S. E. Woodworth, the agent and consul for the Chinese in California, two Chinese men and one woman had reached California before news of gold had reached China. They had arrived on the brig *Eagle*, from Hong Kong, in February 1848.[16] One man named Chum Ming supposedly heard many stories about gold on the American River and traveled to the gold country to see for himself. He then wrote a friend in Canton who immediately set sail for "Gum Shan," or "Gold Mountain," as California was called. This tale, and many like it, made its way around the crowded streets of Canton.

The combination of lies, hope, and desperation caused thousands of young Chinese to mortgage their futures and board boats to "Gum Shan." It was a dangerous gamble, but many probably had little to lose. Most had to work off the cost of their passage (between $30 and $50), and nearly all were told that it would be easy to accomplish once they reached the land of gold. By February 1849, according to Woodworth, 54 Chinese men and one Chinese woman had successfully crossed the Pacific. By the following January, his tally had climbed to 789 men and two women.[17]

Not much is known about any of the men. But one of the two women became both rich and famous. Her name was Ah Toy. Allegedly, she had to pay off a debt and pay for her passage by serving the Chinese male population as a prostitute. But once she got to San Francisco, she quickly attracted the attention of wealthy white men. As a result of their favors, she purchased her freedom and became the owner of two of the most profitable brothels in San Francisco, at 34 and 56 Pike Street, later Waverly Place and now Walter U. Lum Place, which she stocked with girls she bought and imported from China. For several years, Madam Ah Toy was one of the principal dealers in Chinese prostitutes throughout California. In addition, she operated a chain of saloons in San Francisco, Sacramento, and other boomtowns. Years later, she sold out and returned to China a wealthy woman. Only a precious few did as well in Gold Mountain as she did.[18]

As word of gold on the American River was making its way around the Pacific, the U.S. military dispatched several couriers to carry the message to Washington, D.C.

The first and most famous was Christopher "Kit" Carson. A thirty-nine-year-old Kentuckian who had been raised in Missouri, Carson had already gained fame as a mountain man and scout for John C. Frémont, the nation's most celebrated explorer. Frémont, in his reports, had made much of Carson, his horsemanship, his marksmanship, his daring, his Indian fighting. Frémont even told how, when he fell into an ice-cold Sierra stream, Carson saved not only his life but also his precious rifle. Thanks to Frémont, Carson became a national folk hero, the epitome of the Wild West, the illiterate, quiet, unassuming, and plainspoken frontiersman with broad shoulders and a barrel chest and clear blue eyes.[19]

In May 1848, Carson's military superiors gave him several letters about the discovery and a copy of *The California Star* to take to Washington. Saddling up in Los Angeles, he made his way to Santa Fe, his home in Taos, then on to Missouri, where he boarded a steamboat, and then on to Washington. He arrived there on August 2, after three months on the road. Along the way, newspapers made much of his presence but omitted mention of the gold, as did the Washington, D.C., *Daily Union*, when he arrived in the nation's capital.

Also dispatched to Washington was the navy lieutenant Edward Fitzgerald "Ned" Beale. Sent on July 27, roughly three months after Carson, Beale went by way of Mexico, bearing some gold and the navy's report to Secretary of State James Buchanan and Secretary of the Navy John Y. Mason. He arrived in Washington on September 18 and two days later had an audience with President James K. Polk. He told Polk about what Marshall had found. But Polk didn't believe him.

In July, the acting military governor of California, Colonel Richard B. Mason, decided to heed the advice of his aide Lieutenant William Tecumseh Sherman that they go to the Sierras and "see with their own eyes" exactly what was happening. So, leaving Monterey, the two officers toured the gold country. They met with Sutter. They also encountered Sam Brannan, who as a "high priest" was busy collecting tithes from Mormon miners. The miners, in turn, were obviously finding gold. Upon returning to Monterey, Mason had Sherman draft a glowing report for him to sign. Calculating the value of the gold at $16 an ounce, the report claimed that men could earn more in a day than soldiers made in a month. It also predicted that gold from the Sierras would "pay the cost of the war with Mexico a hundred times over." Along with the report, Sherman convinced Mason to send a tea caddy with over two hundred ounces of gold.[20]

Mason's messenger, Lieutenant Lucien Loeser, left California on August 30, via Panama. Two weeks later Mason decided the news was too important to be entrusted to just one man. So he sent a second messenger, with a duplicate copy of the report, via Mexico. The second messenger arrived first, on November 22.

By this time, even President Polk had begun to believe that something important had occurred in California. The president, moreover, needed all the good news he could get. The war against Mexico had gone well militarily, but not politically. One army under General Zachary Taylor had invaded northern Mexico and scored a smashing victory over superior Mexican forces at Buena Vista. Another army under General Winfield Scott had captured Mexico City, the enemy capital. Still another army under Colonel Stephen Watts Kearny had taken Santa Fe and then California. The fighting had lasted hardly a year, cost the nation less than two thousand lives on the battlefield and some eleven thousand from disease, and made heroes by the dozen.

To Polk's dismay, however, most of the glory fell to Whig generals, who were using the war to gain the presidency. Moreover, Whig newspapers and Whig politicians, while extolling the gallantry of Whig generals, had lambasted him for leading the nation into an unjust war. He indeed had pushed for war, claimed that Mexico had invaded Texas, shed American blood on American soil. But the documents he had provided Congress justifying his call for war hadn't supported his interpretation of events. Dissent had been unrelenting. What, critics asked, was the president up to? What was his hidden agenda? Was the war just another subterfuge to expand slavery? In the House the fledging congressman Abraham Lincoln of Illinois had called on him to pinpoint where blood had first been shed—was it on American or Mexican soil?

Indeed, Lincoln and others had treated him as a war criminal, and Horace Greeley of the *New-York Tribune* had labeled him the "Father of Lies."

So it was fortuitous that just nine days before Mexico had been forced to sign the Treaty of Guadalupe Hidalgo, which officially ended the war, a carpenter from New Jersey found several pieces of gold in the Mexican Cession. Polk on December 5 thus made the most of Mason's report in his annual message to Congress, repeatedly emphasizing the "abundance of gold" and predicting that California and the other territories taken from Mexico would "add more to the strength and wealth of the nation" than any previous acquisitions. And two days later, when Loeser finally arrived, Polk put the gold, tea caddy and all, on display at the War Office.

By this time, people from all over the world were pouring into California. Some five thousand Mexicans had already marched across the Sonora to California. Thousands of Chileans and Peruvians had journeyed northward. Hawaiians and Tahitians had also come. So had dozens of British convicts, sentenced to labor in Australia. The word had even reached France, where within the year thirty-six ships would be outfitted and deliver some two thousand Frenchmen, and where Louis Napoleon, hoping to get rid of malcontents, would establish a national lottery and succeed in eliminating four thousand of his subjects.[21] Above all, the Chinese came on the credit-ticket system, crossing the Pacific on clippers, often in as little as thirty days. Within five years, some forty thousand had arrived in San Francisco.

Polk's message added to the hubbub and spurred thousands of his countrymen to join the rush to California. From mid-December to mid-January, sixty-one sailing vessels, averaging fifty passengers each, left New York, Boston, Salem, Norfolk, Philadelphia, and Baltimore for the gold region. Many more left New Orleans, Charleston, and other ports. In February 1849, another sixty ships set off from New York, seventy from Philadelphia and Boston, eleven from New Bedford. In Massachusetts alone, 124 gold rush companies were formed. And by year's end, some eight hundred ships, barks, brigs, schooners, and steamers, carrying forty thousand passengers, left the East Coast for the gold country.[22]

Most initially went by way of Cape Horn. It was the old, established way. It was also the Massachusetts way. Boston and Salem seamen had been doing it for forty years. Handling transport for some six thousand migrants, all but 22 of the 124 Massachusetts companies chose to go around the Horn. To meet the demand, Boston and Salem merchants rapidly put together a fleet of old, patched-up whalers, schooners, brigs, and steamers. The largest was the *Edward Everett*, which weighed seven hundred tons and carried 150 passengers. The smallest was the schooner *Toccao*, which weighed twenty-eight tons and carried only 5 passengers.[23]

The trip was harrying. It was over well-charted water, but getting around the Horn was still the "dread of all mariners." Lieutenant William Tecumseh Sherman, among others, learned that the hard way. In 1846–47, it took him 196 days to get to California. The New York Volunteers made better time, reaching California in 161 days. Not much had changed by 1849. The passengers on the *Leonore* were the luckiest. They got to California in 149 days, the fastest time yet recorded. More typical was the *Edward Everett*, which took 174 days. The 30 men who booked passage on the brig *Pauline* had no luck whatsoever. It took them 40 grueling days just to get around the Horn, and by the time they reached San Francisco, they had been at sea for 241 days.[24]

Nearly all the passengers were men with deep pockets. Women and children were a rarity, and on most ships the only poor men aboard were the members of the crew. The cost of a berth on every ship was steep, as much as most Americans made in a year, and on some ships more than they made in two or three years. To get onto a ship, a workingman thus had to have financial help from family and friends. Then he had to buy into one of the many gold rush companies that were formed. Usually called trading and mining companies, and sometimes mining and trading companies, they were generally run by men who knew a lot about trading, nothing about mining. The cost of joining was sometimes as low as $300, but more often $400, $500, $600, or $700, as the demand for passage ebbed and flowed. One Boston company, the North Western Trading and Mining Company, charged its members $1,000 each.[25] Then, once the organizers collected enough money, they purchased a boat and supplies and hired a captain and crew, and off the company sailed.

In joining a company, the gold seeker also had to agree to abide by the company's bylaws. One basic rule was to heed the dictates of the officers of the company, who were usually listed by name and title and sometimes elected by the members. Another was to regard the company

FOR
CALIFORNIA!
Mutual Protection
Trading & Mining Co.

Having purchased the splendid, Coppered and very fast Sailing

Barque EMMA ISIDORA,

Will leave about the 15th of February. This vessel will be fitted in the very best manner and is one of the fastest sailing vessels that goes from this port.

Each member pays 300 dollars and is entitled to an equal proportion of all profits made by the company either at mining or trading, and holds an equal share of all the property belonging to the company. Experienced men well acquainted with the coast and climate are already engaged as officers of the Company. A rare chance is offered to any wishing a safe investment, good home and Large profits.

This Company is limited to 60 and any wishing to improve this opportunity must make immediate application.

An Experienced Physician will go with the company.

For Freight or Passage apply to 23 State Street, corner of Devonshire, where the list of Passengers may be seen.

JAMES H. PRINCE, Agent,
23 State Street, corner of Devonshire St., Boston.

For further Particulars, see the Constitution.

Propeller Power Presses,
142 Washington St., Boston.

Advertisement, barque Emma Isidora. *Courtesy, American Antiquarian Society.*

as "a band of brothers" and to always back each member in a crisis. Still another was to behave "like a gentleman," to act honorably, and to never partake in such shameful acts as drinking excessively, gambling, fighting, or frequenting prostitutes in South American ports. The latter prohibitions, in the judgment of one historian, probably were just boilerplate, written to reassure wives and loved ones back home.[26]

Whether boilerplate or not, the rules gave way quickly once the men hit the high seas. One company, which consisted of twenty-five Harvard men, paid no attention to the rules whatsoever. They treated the whole trip as a time to frolic. According to their own records, they drank excessively, fought frequently, and chased after prostitutes in Rio de Janeiro. Twelve of these hell-raisers managed to get themselves into serious trouble. Four missed the boat in Rio, and eight had a falling-out with the ship's captain and were left behind. Only thirteen of the original twenty-five reached San Francisco.[27]

Other gold seekers reached San Francisco only because of their captain. That was true of passengers on a New York ship, the *George Washington*. While the boat was docked off the Brazilian coast, some thirty men went ashore, irritated the locals, and got into a drunken brawl. When it was over, two passengers were dead, one had a broken leg, and ten were wounded. The Brazilians suffered even heavier casualties, two dead and fourteen wounded. Some three thousand Brazilians then surrounded the rest of the passengers and wouldn't let them go. Finally, three days later, the ship's captain threatened to "resort to arms" and got their release.[28]

More often, when faced with unruly passengers, the captain simply left them to fend for themselves. The most famous incident of this sort involved not drunken men but a woman, one of the few to travel around the Horn in 1849. The woman was Eliza Farnham, a well-connected New Yorker who had written extensively on female superiority and had been the head of the women's division at Sing Sing prison. In late 1848, Farnham learned that her husband had died in California and had left her a farm. She quickly decided to go to California with her two children and her maid. Then, while mulling over travel plans, she had an inspiration. What California needed, she surmised, was "real" women. The place was becoming a hellhole without them. So she created her own company, the California Association of American Women, and tried to recruit 130 "intelligent, virtuous and efficient" women "not under twenty-five years of age" to accompany her. The cost for each would be $250, a bargain price. Once in California, they would marry miners and thus civilize the place.²⁹

To carry out this mission, Farnham had the help of some of New York's leading reformers and politicians. Horace Greeley, the editor of the *New-York Tribune*, backed her. So did William Cullen Bryant, the editor of the *New-York Evening Post*, as did Henry Ward Beecher, the pastor of Brooklyn's Plymouth Church. In all, thirteen prominent New Yorkers supported her undertaking. They, too, saw it as an opportunity to "accomplish some greater good." Yet the only women she could get to go were three of her friends, and two of them were married.

Despite this failing, Farnham and her friends left New York in July 1849 on the ship *Angelique*. Once at sea, Farnham locked horns with the ship's captain. Deeming him a brute, she refused to accept his authority and battled him constantly. When was he going to do something about the "dreadful quality" of the ship's drinking water? Why did he allow his steward, "a lazy, lying, worthless creature" and "a mulatto" to boot, to take up with her maid? Who was to look out for her children? The battle continued around the Horn. Finally, when the ship docked in Valparaiso, the captain let her go ashore to find a replacement for her lovesick maid. Then off he sailed, taking with him her two children and leaving her "destitute, in a city of strangers."³⁰

Farnham's friends predicted that the captain would pay for this treachery. They were wrong. Instead, her sad tale provided fodder for scores of barroom jokes—and a reminder that it was dangerous to run afoul of a sea captain.

In sailing around the Horn, Eliza Farnham, the Harvard men, and most trading and mining companies opted to take the old, established way to California. In 1849, however, there was another route that cut months off the total trip if all went well. Some six thousand gold seekers took it.

Eliza Farnham, New York reformer.
Courtesy of The New-York Historical Society.

That entailed taking a steamer from New York or New Orleans to the town of Chagres on the Atlantic side of the Isthmus of Panama, then traveling across sixty miles of land to reach the Pacific port of Panama City and catching another steamer to San Francisco. The total distance was about five thousand nautical miles, whereas the trip around the Horn was fourteen thousand nautical miles. With any luck, going by way of Panama cut travel time in half, maybe a third.[31] In 1849, however, there was a major bottleneck. The steamers on the Atlantic side were both bigger and more plentiful than the ones on the Pacific. Thus getting to the isthmus was much easier than getting out the other side.

On the Atlantic side the major steamers belonged to George Law, a forty-three-year-old New Yorker who two years earlier had formed the U.S. Mail Steamship Company and taken over a federal contract from A. G. Sloo to provide biweekly mail service between New York, Havana, New Orleans, and Chagres. Under this contract, Law had to have five steamers, each of fifteen hundred tons, working the Caribbean. He did and was able to move about five hundred gold seekers per ship to Chagres. Once they got there, they never stayed long, for Chagres was much like a garbage dump, with rotting hides, bullocks' heads, fish, cattle, and the remains of other animals lining the thresholds and interiors of huts and putrefying the damp, tropical air. "No one remained in Chagres more than one night, but at the risk of a malignant fever."[32]

Once they got across the isthmus to the Pacific side, however, conditions improved dramatically. Panama City was "relatively healthy." It was an old Spanish town known for its quaint church, narrow sun-shaded streets, cracking walls, mandolins and guitars, monkeys, bananas, cockfights, and bullfights. Unfortunately, finding a ship in Panama City for the last leg of the trip was a major problem. Sometimes the waiting list exceeded two thousand. The more fortunate stayed in hotels, on cots, ten to a room, at eight dollars per week. The less fortunate camped outside city walls.[33] Ships that came up the coast were usually full, and the government's contract with the Pacific mail carrier called for only three steamers, two weighing a thousand tons and one, six hundred tons.

These belonged to another New Yorker, William H. Aspinwall. One year younger than Law, Aspinwall looked and dressed like a typical Wall Street businessman. By nature, however, he was a riverboat gambler. He also had an uncanny knack for making the right bet at the right time. In the early 1840s, he talked his partners into backing a radically new design of clipper ship. That had paid off. And in November 1847, he did something that his fellow merchants considered even more radical. He purchased a contract to carry mail between Panama, San Francisco, and Oregon by steamship. How was he going to make money on this deal? No one thought he could—in 1847—and deemed the contract "Aspinwall's folly."[34]

Authorized and subsidized by Congress, the contract obligated Aspinwall and his partners to have three ships on their way to the Pacific in October 1848. By the time they got there, Panama City was packed with people who wanted to get to San Francisco. Three ships were not enough to handle the crowd that had poured through the isthmus. No one had anticipated that the quaint old Spanish town would suddenly become a boomtown, a jumping-off point for thousands who wanted to get to San Francisco. No one had anticipated that San Francisco, once a sleepy village, would suddenly become a major attraction.

Aspinwall's "folly" thus became a gold mine. His three ships could only handle about three hundred passengers each. So while Law's fleet was bringing about twenty-five hundred passengers to Chagres, Aspinwall on the other side had room to move out only about nine hundred. To make matters worse, the route north was not easy. A direct path was impossible because of the prevailing winds and currents that came down the coast. Ships therefore had to head out into the Pacific to about the longitude of the Hawaiian islands, and then catch a westerly and make their way to San Francisco. The time lag and lack of berths created a major bottleneck.[35]

Ticket prices thus surged. The original price was $250 for first cabin, $200 for lower cabin, $100 for steerage. But with scalping, steerage went as high as $1,000. So, in July 1849, Aspinwall jacked up his rates: $300 in cabin, $150 for steerage. He was well on his way to becoming one of the richest merchants in Manhattan.[36]

Among those who added their mite to Aspinwall's fortune in the spring of 1849 was David Broderick. For him the long wait in Panama City was a nightmare. He suffered continually from a tropical fever, an unwanted souvenir of a night in Chagres. Accompanying Broderick was his future business partner, Frederick Kohler. At first glance the two men had little in common. At age twenty-nine Broderick was nine years younger than Kohler. He was also of Irish Catholic stock, while Kohler was of German descent. Kohler was a native New Yorker, having grown up on Staten Island, while Broderick had spent the first five years of his life in the District of Columbia, where his father, a stonecutter, had worked on the ornamentation of the Senate chamber. Broderick's hands were gnarled from his years as a stonecutter and bouncer in New York saloons. Kohler had been a jeweler by trade.[37]

Broderick's rough looks, however, were deceiving. He was a book-worm by nature. He had dropped out of school at age fourteen, on the death of his father, and helped support his mother and brother by apprenticing at a stonecutter's yard on the corner of Washington and Barrow streets. But he continued to study on his own. He was also befriended by two men who more or less served as his tutors. One was Townsend Harris, a China importer and Tammany Hall member who opened his personal library to Broderick. He later relieved Broderick from the long hours of stonemasonry, finding him work as a saloon keeper, first at the Subterranean at age twenty, later at the Republican. From all reports, Broderick used the time well. He never drank; instead, he spent all his spare time poring over books. The other tutor was George Wilkes, a man with a gifted pen who later founded the *National Police Gazette*. To make ends meet, Wilkes often wrote and published "trash." At heart, however, he was an intellectual and an insatiable reader of all the eminent authors of the day. He encouraged Broderick to broaden his reading habits, to master the great works of the English language, and to study political theory.[38]

Broderick, moreover, had known Kohler for years. Both were old New York firemen, Broderick as a member of Howard Engine Company No. 34 and Kohler as an assistant engineer of the New York Volunteer Fire Department and a member of Protection Engine No. 5. In New York, as well as other eastern cities, volunteer fire companies did more than fight fires. They were also the premier social clubs in working-class neighborhoods. They were essentially fraternal orders with their own badges, mottoes, and initiation procedures. They tried to outdo one another in staging prizefights, dogfights, dances, parades, and an occasional formal ball. They had also been political organizations since the 1830s, initially used by elite politicians to get out the vote, but now used as a voice for men like themselves. Out of their ranks would come six mayors of the city.[39]

For Broderick, as well as many others, service as a fireman had been a stepping-stone to a political career. Shortly after he joined the

Howard Company, one of the oldest in New York, he had been elected foreman, even though he was not yet old enough to vote. Among his associates was Mike Walsh, who had become a master in roughhouse politics. A fellow Irishman but a Protestant, Walsh was ten years Broderick's senior. He also had a gift that Broderick never acquired. He was a "naturally gifted" speaker, one who could raise crowds to a fighting pitch, and in 1840 he had founded the Spartan Association, a gang of Bowery boys who at his bidding frequently took to the streets, often in support of workingmen's rights, but also to rough up "regular" Tammany Hall and Albany Regency Democrats.[40] In 1842, on Election Day, Walsh's troops got into a street fight with Tammany Democrats that resulted in a full-scale riot.[41]

Along with Walsh, Broderick and his friend Wilkes established a political constituency that challenged Tammany Hall from below. As spokesmen for some of the poorest neighborhoods in Manhattan, they sided initially with the Locofocos, a radical Tammany faction that wanted to widen the Democratic Party's "Bank War" into a crusade against all bankers, local as well as national, Tammany allies as well as Tammany enemies.

Broderick and Wilkes also embraced George Henry Evans's radical politics. The editor of *The Working Man's Advocate* and later *The Radical*, Evans was primarily concerned with the plight of free white labor, the growing subjugation of white labor, which he termed "white slavery." He thought all slavery was a disgrace, black as well as white, but that Northerners ought to set an example for slaveholders of the South by tending to their own problems first. He blamed the unequal distribution of wealth, the growing gap between the rich and the poor, first on banks and monopolies, and then on land speculation. To bring about equality, Evans and his followers originally advocated land confiscation. Later, however, they downplayed this radical demand and championed free distribution of public lands to actual settlers. That proposal eventually made its way into national politics through the homestead movement and the Free-Soil Party.[42]

In going up against Tammany Hall, Broderick invariably came out on the losing end. In 1841, without Tammany's blessing, he got a federal patronage job as one of seventy-six inspectors at the New York Custom House. That was largely because the incumbent president, John Tyler, was desperate. A renegade Democrat, Tyler had run for vice president in 1840 on the Whig ticket because the Whig chieftains thought his presence might help them carry Virginia. They miscalculated. Not only did they lose Virginia; they also had to cope with Tyler when William Henry Harrison, their choice for president, died after one month in office. As president, Tyler quickly proved that he was still a Democrat at heart and vetoed one Whig bank bill after another. He so irritated Whig leaders that they read him out of the party. But Tyler was still a young man, at age fifty-one the youngest to yet hold the presidency, and he had high hopes of creating a new party, mainly from disaffected Democrats.

Thus Broderick got his Custom House appointment. He loved it, especially the fact that it gave him the power to bestow favors on his friends. But it wasn't his for long. Once the Democrats regained the presidency in 1845, they made sure that all seventy-six jobs went to "regular" Tammany men.[43]

Broderick, however, was not one to "wait his turn." That earned him a host of enemies later that same year when Tammany Hall hosted the new president. The leaders selected forty party members, half old guard, half youngsters, to go to New Jersey and escort President Polk to Manhattan. Broderick, at age twenty-five, was one of the youngest chosen. After reaching New Jersey by steamer, most of the forty waited silently outside the house where Polk was staying. Broderick, however, refused to be humble and silent. Instead, he went inside and returned with the president on his arm. He then told the men, in a loud, commanding voice, to form a circle and "give attention to the President." Then, after Polk said a few words, Broderick told the men to "form a line of march," took Polk by the arm, and led him to the steamer that was to bring him to New York. Polk, naturally, thought Broderick was in charge and acted accordingly.[44]

Many Tammany graybeards were furious. Not only was Broderick a youngster. He was also an Irish Catholic, a member of the ethnic group that had shaken much of old New York. More than 300,000 half-starved Irish tenant farmers had descended upon the city since the War of 1812, and many thousands more were coming. Desperate for living space, they had helped turn Five Points into a major slum. Through sheer numbers and terrorism, they had driven blacks off the docks, taken away their jobs as hackney coachmen and draymen, stripped them of their livelihoods as ditchdiggers and domestic servants. At the same time, the skyrocketing growth of their Roman Catholic church, manned largely by Irish priests, had sparked violent opposition from white Protestants.

At first, both major parties had sought the Irish vote. But in the 1840s the Whigs had teamed up with anti-Catholic Protestants and shown some sympathy toward blacks, thus driving the Irish into the arms of Tammany Hall. The Tammany chieftains thus had become dependent on the Irish vote. They also needed Irish brawn in bare-knuckled ward politics. They had no intention, however, of letting an upstart Irishman run their party.[45]

The graybeards got even, one year later, when Broderick ran for Congress. He was just twenty-six, one year over the minimum, but with the backing of Mike Walsh's newspaper, *The Subterranean,* and George Henry Evans's newspaper, *The Working Man's Advocate,* he won the Democratic nomination easily. That should have resulted in victory on Election Day had the Democratic Party been united. His Tammany adversaries, however, entered another Democrat, Jack Bloodgood, a hard-drinking lawyer of old Knickerbocker stock. They then directed Custom House officials to get out the vote for Bloodgood. This split the Democratic vote and led to the victory of a Whig aristocrat, Fred A. Tallmadge.[46]

The treachery of the Tammany elite left a lasting mark on Broderick. He brooded for months. He fired off angry letters denouncing the men who caused his defeat. He finally concluded that they were no different from blue bloods the world over, just another bunch of mean-spirited aristocrats who looked down on all men who worked with their hands and took pleasure in crushing them. He also condemned the Custom House workers who did the bidding of the Tammany elite, especially men of his own social class, claiming that they were jealous of him, unable to even understand why he wanted to better himself, and thus willingly did the work of his tormentors.[47]

Broderick also began considering opportunities outside New York. His mother had died in 1843. His brother, Richard, had died in 1845, thanks to a freak accident. His ties to the city were thus slight. He then received a letter from Colonel Jonathan Drake Stevenson, the commander of the New York Volunteers in California. Stevenson, although a Tammany man and a party regular, had befriended Broderick many times over the years. He had put Broderick in touch with Townsend Harris. He now urged Broderick to come to California.[48]

Short of funds, Broderick borrowed travel money from George Wilkes, his fellow "radical," and joined the Republic Company, an association of eleven New Yorkers who pooled their resources for the trip.

Securing passage on the steamer *Crescent City*, they left New York on April 17. In Panama City, they had trouble finding a steamer for the last leg of the journey. Finally, gaining berths on the *Stella*, they made their way north and passed through the Golden Gate in mid-June, thus completing a two-month journey.[49]

Their first glimpse of San Francisco stunned them. Before them were hundreds of abandoned ships, from Sydney and Singapore and Bremen and Baltimore, from literally all over the world, rotting on the tidal flats of Yerba Buena Cove. On entering the city, they encountered even more strange sights—Peruvian gold seekers in chocolate brown ponchos, Malayans with krises in their belts, Tasmanian sheepherders in cabbage tree hats and moleskin trousers, and, strangest of all, pigtailed Chinese in knee-length breeches and quilted jackets. The weather was also peculiar. In New York, June was always a warm month; in San Francisco, it was cold and foggy.

Barroom in California. Reprinted from Frank Marryat, Mountains and Molehills; or, Recollections of a Burnt Journal *(New York, 1855), 43. Marryat, like all travelers, was struck by the fact that men from all over the world had come to California.*

· · ·

Once they got their bearings, nine members of the Republic Company headed for the gold country. Broderick and Kohler remained in the city.

Broderick quickly found a place to board, the house of Emma and Tom McGuire, a couple he knew from his days in New York. The two men had much in common. Back in New York, Tom McGuire had been a saloon keeper, hack driver, fight promoter, volunteer fireman, and Tammany stalwart. Abandoning the New York Bowery for San Francisco, the couple had opened the Jenny Lind Theater, which provided a wide variety of entertainment ranging from opera to blackface minstrelsy. Broderick stayed with the McGuires until 1854. Thereafter, he lived in the better local hotels.[50]

Broderick and Kohler also got a helping hand from Colonel Stevenson. The former head of the New York Volunteers had heard numerous complaints from San Francisco businessmen who disliked dealing in gold dust. It took too much time. It led to too much squabbling. They wanted to deal in coins. But who was to mint the coins? The nearest mint was thousands of miles away. Here, Stevenson decided, was an opportunity for his fellow New Yorkers. Kohler, the jeweler, could do the assaying, and Broderick could do the hard manual labor. To get them started, Stevenson lent them $3,500.

The two men then formed F. D. Kohler & Company. They began striking coins with face values of $5 and $10, but with an actual gold content of $4 and $8. They made huge profits. Other private mints sprang up, and within the year Kohler and Broderick decided to sell out to Baldwin & Company. Kohler became the state assayer and the chief engineer of the San Francisco Fire Department. Meanwhile, with his profits, Broderick began speculating in San Francisco waterfront properties. He made a fortune.[51]

Simultaneously, and more important to Broderick, he became a force in San Francisco politics. Money never mattered much to him. He was a bachelor with no kin. His personal expenses were modest. He just wanted enough money so that he didn't have to worry about it. But political power was a different matter. The more he had, the better. Here again he had the help of Stevenson, along with some of Stevenson's disbanded New York Volunteers. Together, they introduced a modification of the Tammany system into San Francisco.

The system, as they fashioned it, depended heavily on volunteer fire companies. Fires were common in San Francisco, far more so than in

New York, and they were far more dangerous, as they wiped out not just a building or two but buildings, shacks, and tents in all directions. So firemen in San Francisco were heroes with plenty of work to do. Broderick did more than his share and in one fire, in particular, distinguished himself by his bravery. But he never regarded his company and others as just firefighters. He made sure that they functioned also as political clubs, getting out the vote on Election Day and providing a training ground for up-and-coming politicians.

Even more important to building a political machine was having a steady source of revenue. Never doubting the proposition that money was the "mother's milk of politics," Broderick contributed much of his own income to his fledgling organization. He also tapped the earnings of elected officeholders. Some elected offices, such as sheriff, tax collector, and assessor, were lucrative. Indeed, they were worth a lot of money. Instead of receiving salaries, the men who held these offices got to keep all or a portion of the fees they collected. The totals sometimes were staggering, more than $50,000 per year, more than most Americans made in a lifetime. To a would-be candidate, Broderick offered a deal: the backing of the local Democratic machine for half the fees. His half then went to pay for election banners, to rent meeting halls, to hire musicians and other entertainers, to aid the sick and needy, and to support less affluent party operatives.[52]

By December 1849, only six months after Broderick arrived in San Francisco, the nucleus of the system was in place. Not only had he become a rich man. He was also well on his way to controlling San Francisco politics. That January the incumbent state senator, Nathaniel Bennett, quit to become a justice on the state supreme court. In the election that followed, Broderick ran as Bennett's replacement. It was no contest. He polled 2,508 votes, ninety-nine times as many as his closest competitor, winning all but 101 of the votes that were cast.[53]

2

AT THE SAME TIME THAT DAVID BRODERICK DECIDED TO LEAVE New York for California, a maverick Virginia politician, Henry Wise, began fantasizing about California. Now in his forty-second year and razor-thin, Wise had two "children" who planned to take off for the gold country. They weren't his children exactly. They were actually his sister Margaret's children, but she was a widow, and he deemed them his responsibility.

Wise took special pride in being the family patriarch. It was not a unique characteristic. It was one that many Virginia gentlemen shared. But in his case, suggests one of his biographers, it was writ large because Wise himself had never had a caring father. His father, a wealthy planter-politician on Virginia's Eastern Shore, had died when Wise was five. Moreover, in a long and carefully written will, his father had purposely discriminated against Wise and Wise's younger siblings, leaving the lion's share of the estate to Wise's older brothers and the "least productive portion" to Wise. Raised largely by relatives, Wise had subsequently done well. He had gone to Washington College in Pennsylvania, studied law in Virginia under Henry St. George Tucker, and become a prominent lawyer, briefly in Tennessee, then on Virginia's Eastern Shore. But he never forgot his father's will.[1]

Wise's family in 1849 was extensive. He had fathered thirteen children, four by his first wife, nine by his second. Only seven had survived infancy. One of his sons was now away at college; the other six were at home. Unable to afford a tutor, Wise himself taught them mathematics and English composition, and his wife, Sarah (who would soon die giving birth to still another child), taught them Greek, Latin, Spanish, and French. In addition to his own children, Wise also supervised the education of two of his invalid brother John's sons as well as his sister Margaret's offspring. Wise also owned nineteen slaves whom he regarded as his "responsibility," if not as his "children." To all, he gave advice and expected obedience.

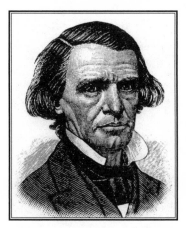

Henry Wise, Virginia. Reprinted from Ben: Perley Poore, Perley's Reminiscences, *2 vols. (Philadelphia, 1886), 1:279.*

As a family man, Wise was dependable, but the same could not be said about his politics. He had switched parties—and seemingly his principles—more than once. He had been a supporter of Andrew Jackson in his youth and had even honeymooned at the Hermitage, Jackson's Tennessee mansion. In 1833, the Jacksonians had backed him for a seat in the House of Representatives. Over the next decade, he gained fame nationally as a powerful defender of slavery and Virginia against Northern criticism. He was also a powerful advocate for the annexation of slaveholding Texas. In an age of oratory, he was a star performer, often deemed one of the Old South's best, capable of even matching wits with the wily John Quincy Adams of Massachusetts.

But when Jackson in 1836 chose Martin Van Buren of New York to be his successor, Wise had refused to go along. Saying that he preferred "any decent *white* man in the nation" to Van Buren, he threw his support to Hugh Lawson White of Tennessee, one of three Whigs to run against Jackson's choice for president.[2] Then, after the death of his first wife, Ann, in 1837, Wise married Sarah Sergeant, the daughter of a wealthy Whig congressman from Philadelphia. By 1840, all observers thought Wise was firmly entrenched in the Whig camp.

That, however, was short-lived. In 1841, upon the death of William Henry Harrison, the Whig Party faced a crisis. The presidency went to John Tyler, who vetoed one Whig bank bill after another. Whom would

Wise support? His party or the president? Wise chose to side with Tyler, his fellow Virginian, over his party. He became the leader of "the corporal's guard," a handful of House members who backed the president. For his loyalty, Tyler made Wise minister to Brazil in 1844.

Over the next three years, Wise then made a new name for himself, not as a spokesman for slavery but as a vehement opponent of American involvement in the slave trade between Africa and Brazil. The trade, he said, was barbarous and cruel. It was bad for the future of Brazil. It was the work mainly of "hypocritical Yankees." And it was against American law. His harsh words eventually destroyed his usefulness in Brazil, and in 1847 he was virtually kicked out of the country.

Wise's harsh words also raised some concern among his fellow slaveholders. In saying that the slave trade was bad for Brazil, he often came close to saying that black bondage was a curse rather than a blessing. That had been said many times in old Virginia. It was commonplace when Wise was a youth. His legal mentor, Henry St. George Tucker, had never bothered to conceal his disdain for slavery. But those days had long passed. Most informed Virginians now believed that such talk was dangerous, and many echoed the remarks of South Carolina's John C. Calhoun and spoke of slavery as a "positive good." The Old Dominion still had more blacks in bondage than any other state. Moreover, many Virginians were busy selling their surplus slaves to slave traders.

Returning to Virginia, Wise thus had fences to mend. He again switched parties. He formally rejoined the Democratic Party, hoping that Democrats in the Virginia legislature would choose him to represent the state in the U.S. Senate. At the same time, he also tried to refurbish his family fortune. He now had nineteen slaves, one shy of the magic number twenty, the number that one needed to officially qualify as a "planter." But they were not earning him much money. He made far more from his law practice than he made from his nineteen slaves. And that was not just his problem. It was indicative of a problem that bedeviled every farmer on Virginia's Eastern Shore.

Slavery, as Wise viewed the institution, was just not profitable on the worn-out fields of Virginia. His farm consisted of some four hundred acres. About half was productive. On his best soil he grew corn and oats. On less fertile land he grew sweet potatoes, raised livestock, and maintained peach and pear orchards. All told, he probably grossed no more than $500 per year. He was better off, however, than all but a handful of his Accomac County neighbors. Their forefathers had done well with tobacco, but that was in the distant past. Most farms had abandoned tobacco for cereal grains even before the American Revolution.[3]

Throughout Accomac County, farms and slaveholdings were stagnant. In 1830, slaves made up about 28 percent of the population, the lowest of any Tidewater county. By 1849, the percentage hadn't changed any, but the total population hadn't changed, either. The growth rate was near zero.[4] To make money, Wise's neighbors had to take their slaves elsewhere—to the cotton states of Alabama and Mississippi, to the sugar belt of Louisiana, or to the new virgin lands of Texas. Another alternative was to rent their slaves to Richmond manufacturers, or to sell them to slave traders who roamed the county, buying up the surplus, and then shipped them off to New Orleans.

And California? No place, in Wise's judgment, came close to matching California. It was the solution to his—and every Virginia slaveholder's—problem. A slave worth $1,000 in Virginia would be worth $3,000 to $5,000 in the gold mines of California. Indeed, if California ended up in Southern hands, the future for him and his neighbors would be golden. Every cornfield on the Eastern Shore, he predicted, would soon be empty of black laborers. They would all be off in California, digging gold. Indeed, every cornfield in Virginia, North Carolina, Maryland, Kentucky, Tennessee, and Missouri would soon be empty of black laborers. The demand for slave labor would be so great that even the cotton and sugar plantations of the Deep South would be depleted of black laborers. Masters would make so much money that in just five years they could afford to colonize their slaves in "Polynesia." Yes, if they wanted, he and his neighbors could get out of slavery—and at a huge profit.[5]

If Wise had an active fantasy life in 1849, so, too, did William McKendree Gwin. He, too, had high hopes about California. He, too, saw the gold rush as the answer to his dreams.

Physically, the two men were exact opposites. Wise was thin, wiry, emaciated. Gwin looked much like the Hollywood version of an Old South senator. He was a large man, about six feet two, stately yet muscular, with a massive head, a strong chin, a large straight nose, sharp blue eyes, and heavy brows, all topped by a stunning head of hair, once flaxen but now at age forty-three streaked with gray, long and full, reaching the nape of his neck. Not only did Gwin look the part of a

Southern senator; he wanted to be one. Unfortunately, if he remained in Mississippi, it was not likely to happen. He had too many rivals and too many enemies.

William McKendree Gwin, Mississippi. Reprinted from Frank Soulé et al., The Annals of San Francisco *(New York, 1854), 790.*

Like his Mississippi rivals, Gwin was a major slaveholder but not a native of the state. He had grown up in Tennessee, the son of a Methodist minister. At age twenty-one, he became a lawyer, but after seeing Tennessee's established lawyers wax eloquent in court, he doubted if he could compete with them. So, after consulting his father, he sought a medical degree, graduated from Transylvania University in 1828, and moved to Clinton, Mississippi, in 1830. For the next four years, he practiced medicine. Then, in 1834, he quit to become a full-time planter-politician.

Gwin's decision to pursue politics full-time grew out of his family's ties with Andrew Jackson. Gwin's father had been one of Jackson's subordinates during the War of 1812 and had commanded fourteen hundred sharpshooters at the Battle of New Orleans. In 1831 Jackson invited his old comrade's son to live in the White House for six months and serve as his private secretary. He later looked to young Gwin and his brother Samuel to build the Jackson party in Mississippi.

The brothers, however, needed a power base in Mississippi. To facilitate that, Jackson decided to make William the U.S. marshal for southern Mississippi and Samuel head of the federal land office. But Jackson couldn't get these appointments through the Senate. His problem was Senator George Poindexter of Mississippi, who regarded Jackson as a tyrant and had no desire to share political power with Jackson's cronies. William met secretly with Poindexter and somehow got his blessing. But Poindexter continued to block Samuel's appointment, making much of the fact that he wasn't a native Mississippian and accusing him of conniving with land speculators at the expense of the federal government and "honest God-fearing settlers." Jackson then urged the two brothers to destroy Poindexter by orchestrating his defeat in the state legislature when he came up for reelection in 1836.

As a rival candidate, the brothers settled on Robert J. Walker and helped him take Poindexter's Senate seat. In the process, they infuriated Poindexter and his backers. The two sides subsequently came together at a banquet honoring the governor. Poindexter launched into a tirade against Jackson. Samuel hissed as Poindexter spoke. Shortly thereafter, Poindexter's law partner, Judge Isaac Caldwell, challenged Samuel to a duel. The duel took place in Clinton before four hundred witnesses. It was deadly. Samuel's bullet killed Caldwell immediately. Samuel left the field with a shattered lung and, two and a half years later, died from his wound.[6]

Meanwhile, William Gwin became one of the wealthiest politicians in Mississippi. Thanks to Jackson's appointing him U.S. marshal for Mississippi, he collected $150,000 per year in fees and, after expenses, probably pocketed half that amount. Joining forces with Robert Walker, John A. Quitman, and others, he became involved in a maze of land speculations. Gwin soon had several plantations, plus three that he rented out, and almost two hundred slaves. By 1840, in Warren County alone, he owned a mansion worth $50,000, two lots in the city of Vicksburg valued at $20,000, and two thousand acres on the Mississippi River assessed at $14,000. He also temporarily went back to his old profession, the law, and represented the Chickasaw tribe in a lawsuit against the federal government. He won over $112,000 and charged the tribe half for his services. Over the next several years, some of his land deals went sour and cost him dearly. But in 1849, he was still a rich man, one of the richest in Mississippi.[7]

Politically, however, William Gwin was stymied. Elected to Congress in 1840, he had become a confidant of John C. Calhoun's. Initially, as a good Jackson man, he had deemed the eminent South Carolinian a pariah. But in Washington, he lived in the same boardinghouse as Calhoun and soon fell under Calhoun's "personal magnetism." He even tried to get Jackson to support Calhoun for president in 1844.[8] Meanwhile, he decided not to run again for Congress. He yearned for a higher office. He returned to Mississippi and from there teamed up with Robert Walker to stop Martin Van Buren from getting the Democratic presidential nomination. Successful in that effort, he enthusiastically supported James K. Polk for president in 1844. When Polk won by an eyelash, he lobbied Polk to make Walker his treasury secretary. That, too, came to pass.

With Walker's appointment, the office that Gwin had long coveted,

U.S. senator, became vacant. Walker left no doubt whom he wanted as his replacement. He campaigned hard in Gwin's behalf. But Poindexter's followers and the supporters of rival candidates rallied their troops and got the governor to oppose the appointment on the grounds that Gwin was associated with "broke speculators." The Senate seat, to Gwin's disgust, thus went to another Democrat, a less controversial one, Joseph Chalmers. Gwin then reluctantly offered himself for another term in the House. Again, however, he lost out, this time to Jefferson Davis, an up-and-coming Mississippi Democrat.

Thanks to his friend Walker, Gwin in 1846 received an appointment from the Treasury Department to oversee construction of the New Orleans Custom House. Although the post paid only $8 per day, a far cry from the fees he had received as a federal marshal, it gave Gwin valuable political contacts. But it was a patronage position, dependent totally on Democratic control of the White House. And in 1848, the Democratic candidate, Lewis Cass, lost the presidency to Zachary Taylor, "Old Rough and Ready," one of the Whig generals who had gained fame in the rout of Mexico. Gwin was thus certain to soon be out of a job.

A few months later, on March 5, 1849, to be exact, Gwin was in Washington. He watched the inauguration procession of Zachary Taylor as it passed by Willard's Hotel. Next to him stood a short but imposing man, Stephen A. Douglas, "the Little Giant" of Illinois. Like Gwin, the Illinois senator was a lifelong Democrat. He also had a vested interest in Mississippi and Mississippi slavery. The previous June his wife had inherited a Mississippi plantation of some twenty-five hundred acres and over one hundred slaves. In accordance with her father's will, Douglas himself managed the property, kept in touch with the overseers who directed the slaves and the New Orleans merchants who sold the cotton crop, and received 20 percent of the annual income.[9]

The two men spoke of the future. Douglas still had a job to do as senator from Illinois. Gwin was going to be out of political work at the end of the month. What, then, did he intend to do? Gwin allegedly told Douglas that he was going to go to California, make California into a state, and be back in a year as the new senator from California. At that time, he would ask Douglas to present "his credentials as a senator from the State of California."[10]

So, anyway, recalled Gwin many years later. It sounds apocryphal. But there is no doubt that Gwin's desire for a U.S. Senate seat prompted him to take off for California in April 1849. He went by way of Panama. He traveled the same route as Broderick, but at a faster pace, leaving later, arriving earlier. He didn't have to wait as long in Panama City. He had more clout. He gained passage on one of Aspinwall's steamers, the *Panama*, which left Panama City on May 18 and arrived in San Francisco on June 4, nine days before Broderick.

Built for mail, the *Panama* initially had accommodations for about eighty passengers. On its maiden voyage it carried four hundred. The few women on board shared a tent on the quarterdeck. Around them slept several hundred men, their places on deck marked by chalk. The passenger list included two future governors, three future senators, two future congressmen, two future state supreme court justices, seven future generals and an admiral, two future ambassadors, and one potential First Lady.

The potential First Lady was Jessie Benton Frémont. She was also the best known of the passengers. No one as yet had heard of "Fighting Joe" Hooker, destined to gain fame as a Civil War general. No one as yet had heard of Major George Derby, later known as the comic writer John Phoenix, who entertained his shipmates with nightly spoofs, skits, and plays. And only a few had heard of Gwin. Nearly everyone on board, however, had heard of Jessie Benton Frémont. Most found her charm, her wit, and especially her poise to be exceptional for a woman who was only twenty-five years old. Others took note of her dark brown eyes, dark auburn hair, and still-girlish figure.[11] Her fame rested partly on her father, partly on her husband, and partly on her pen.

Jessie Benton Frémont. Reprinted from Ben: Perley Poore, Perley's Reminiscences, *2 vols. (Philadelphia, 1886), 1:376.*

Her father, Thomas Hart Benton, had been one of the nation's most prominent senators for nearly thirty years. Elected to the Senate by the Missouri legislature in 1820, he was now in his fifth term. He was a bull of a man, five feet eleven, broad-shouldered, barrel-chested, heavily muscled. He was well known nationally both for his intellect and for his belligerent ways. His ego was enormous. Once, upon being introduced to a young man who had walked two hundred miles to hear him, he replied: "Young man, you did right." Equally enormous was his troubled past. He had been kicked out of the University of North Carolina for stealing. He had killed a man in St. Louis for calling him a puppy.[12]

Benton's senatorial career had gone through two distinct phases. In his first years in the Senate, he had savaged paper-money banks. He had blamed them for the Panic of 1819 and the hard times that followed. He had been the champion of hard money, cheap land, and a frugal government that spent money only on the military and westward expansion. He had also been "decidedly pro-slavery" and in 1829 advocated the purchase of Texas so that several more slave states might be added to the Union. At one point, he had even talked about adding nine more slave states.

Then, beginning in 1836, he shifted his focus. He began criticizing John C. Calhoun and other pro-slavery agitators, increasingly portraying them as "firebrands" and "disunionists" whose extremism endangered the South and the Union. Most Northerners, he contended, were no threat to the South. They hated blacks and loved the Union. Only a few adhered to the teachings of William Lloyd Garrison and other Northern abolitionists. In reality, Garrison and other abolitionists were just bogeymen that Calhoun and his followers used to alarm Southerners. Moreover, the Calhounites, in recklessly promoting slavery and touting it as a "positive good," were the underlying cause of one national crisis after another. Not only were they giving antislavery "fanatics" like Garrison a national forum and causing thousands of well-meaning Northerners to rethink their position on slavery; they were also making demands on the national government that could only lead to disunion.

By the late 1840s, Benton's war against the Calhounites had gotten him into trouble. No longer was he seen as promoting the interests of slaveholders. Instead, he was repeatedly identified with a number of Missouri Democrats who opposed the expansion of slavery. He also stood out as one of only two Southern senators to vote for the admission of Oregon to the Union with no slavery.

Alarmed by his behavior, Claiborne

Thomas Hart Benton, senator from Missouri. Library of Congress.

F. Jackson, a powerful force in the Missouri assembly, rallied Benton's statehouse critics. Meeting in January 1849 in a small room adjoining the Missouri Supreme Court chambers, they hammered out a series of resolutions that essentially affirmed Calhoun's position and instructed Missouri senators to act in "hearty cooperation with the slaveholding States . . . for our mutual protection against the encroachments of Northern fanaticism." In March, Jackson presented the resolutions to the Missouri assembly. The assembly endorsed them. In May, at the capitol in Jefferson City, Benton denounced the resolutions and called on the people of Missouri to join him in the battle against Claiborne F. Jackson, Calhoun, and other "disunionists."[13]

Thus, at the time that Jessie Benton Frémont made her trip west, her father was in deep political trouble. He was barely hanging on to his Senate seat. He would lose it the following year.

Also in trouble was Jessie's husband, John C. Frémont. That, too, was partly her father's doing. Among her father's beliefs was that the best route to the Pacific was straight west from St. Louis, overland through the Rockies, following roughly the 38th parallel. To prove that the 38th parallel route was workable even in bad weather, he had dispatched his son-in-law to map a trail late in the year, just before the snows fell, on October 21, 1848.

By this time, Frémont had become the nation's most famous explorer, rated by the popular press far above Lewis and Clark, almost on the same level as Columbus. Much had already been written about the first thirty-six years of his life, his slender wiry frame, his dashing good looks, his daring, and his resourcefulness. While much of it was hyperbole, Frémont undoubtedly had come a long way since his Savannah boyhood. The illegitimate son of a Virginia patrician woman who had run away from her elderly husband and taken up with a French émigré teacher, he had been raised in genteel poverty by his mother. Well aware of his origins, he grew up to be a restless loner, a proud and reserved man who was austere in his personal habits, rigorously self-disciplined, eager to prove himself, and unwilling to always play by the rules imposed from above.[14]

Frémont's disdain for authority got him into serious trouble more than once. At the same time, however, he owed much of his success to men of power. A prominent lawyer, John W. Mitchell, sponsored his early education. He got into the College of Charleston but was thrown out for poor attendance. Then an eminent South Carolina politician, Joel R. Poinsett, came to his aid. Poinsett secured a position for Frémont as a math instructor on the USS *Natchez* and then a commission in the U.S. Topographical Corps surveying a route for the Charleston, Louisville, and Cincinnati railroad. Later, as secretary of state, Poinsett arranged for Frémont to assist the eminent French explorer Joseph N. Nicollet in surveying the region between the upper Mississippi and Missouri rivers. Several months later, Frémont was commissioned as a second lieutenant in the U.S. Army Corps of Topographical Engineers. Two successive expeditions with Nicollet provided Frémont with wilderness experience and helped him become a first-rate topographer, skilled in describing fauna, flora, soil, and water resources.

Working with Nicollet also brought Frémont in contact with Thomas Hart Benton. Not only was Benton a staunch advocate of western expansion; he was also the chair of the Senate Committee on Military Affairs and thus in a position to help the two topographical engineers. Thanks to his interest in their work, the senator repeatedly invited the young lieutenant to his C Street home. One evening he gave Frémont the task of escorting his oldest daughter, Eliza, to a concert at Miss English's boarding school in Georgetown. That evening Frémont became entranced with the second of Benton's four daughters, sixteen-year-old Jessie, who attended the same school.

Jessie Benton by no means shared Frémont's hardscrabble background. Her upbringing had always been one of comfort. Nor did she share his reserved, often brooding temperament. She was far more open, optimistic, and outgoing. Like him, however, she tended to be impetuous and headstrong.[15]

That proved decisive. As the romance blossomed, her parents tried to stop it. They wanted their daughter to marry up in society, not down. They set up all sorts of roadblocks to keep their daughter from seeing Frémont. All failed. Without their approval—indeed, against their wishes—the couple eloped. No Protestant minister dared to marry them. But with the help of another senator's wife, they found a Catholic priest willing to make them husband and wife. When Benton learned about it, he exploded. He fumed and hollered. He made dire threats. He threw the newlyweds out of his house.

In time, however, Benton's love of his daughter overcame his ire. Not only did he invite the couple back to his C Street home; he also became his son-in-law's patron. In 1842, when Nicollet was too ill to travel, Benton arranged for Frémont to take his place. At the senator's urging, the U.S. Army appointed Frémont to head a twenty-five-man, four-month expedition to survey and map the Oregon Trail as far as the South Pass over the Continental Divide. He did that and more. He climbed to what he thought was the highest peak in the Wind River Range and raised a homemade eagle flag and declared all the nearby country American territory. When he returned home, he dictated his report to Jessie. She put it into lively, memorable prose. Congress then printed it by the thousands, and overnight Frémont became a hero, known popularly as the Pathfinder.

John C. Frémont, "the Pathfinder." Reprinted from Ben: Perley Poore, Perley's Reminiscences, 2 vols. (Philadelphia, 1886), 1:305.

Frémont became even more famous in 1843–44 when he led a band of men all the way over the Oregon Trail, then south along the mountain range bordering California, and then across the Sierras into California. Later, he "circumnavigated" the whole West. Out of these expeditions, his Prussian cartographer and constant critic, Charles Preuss, produced the first scientifically derived map of the West and the first accurate, detailed emigrant map of the Oregon Trail. Again, on returning home, Frémont dictated his report to Jessie, and she put it into vivid prose.

In the eyes of many, Frémont was also a mistreated war hero. In 1846, probably on orders from Washington, he led sixty well-armed mountain men into Mexican California, defiantly raised the American flag on a hill outside Monterey, and then headed north to Klamath Lake in southern Oregon. Then, after meeting with President Polk's secret agent Archibald Gillespie, Frémont and his men returned to the Sacramento valley, where in June 1846 they encouraged settlers to capture the little pueblo of Sonoma and proclaim the Bear Flag Republic. Shortly thereafter, when news of the war with Mexico reached California, the navy under Commodore Robert F. Stockton seized California ports. Stockton appointed Frémont commander of the California Battalion, a motley assortment of sailors, marines, soldiers, mountain men, and California residents, to finish the conquest.[16]

General Stephen Watts Kearny, in the meantime, arrived from New Mexico. Recently promoted, he immediately got into a dispute with Commodore Stockton over who was in command. Against Kearny's wishes, Stockton appointed Frémont his successor as military governor and sailed off for Mexico. Frémont, who was now a lieutenant colonel in the U.S. Army, rashly sided with the naval officer. Kearny, in turn, arrested Frémont for mutiny and marched him east, in disgrace, to face a rancorous court-martial. Despite having the public and Thomas Hart Benton on his side, Frémont was found guilty of insubordination and dismissed from the army. President Polk approved the verdict but reinstated him for "meritorious and valuable services." Frémont bitterly refused executive clemency and resigned his commission.[17]

The court-martial, thanks to vast newspaper coverage, only added to Frémont's fame. The public generally thought he got a raw deal. The College of Charleston, the school that had once thrown him out for poor attendance, offered him a teaching position on its faculty. The Charleston to Cincinnati Railroad offered him $5,000 per year to be its president.[18]

At this point, his father-in-law prevailed on him to prove to the world that the best path to the Pacific was straight west from St. Louis. With the financial backing of St. Louis businessmen who eagerly hoped to locate a central, all-weather railroad route through the Rockies, Frémont led a company of some thirty men into the rugged mountains of southern Colorado in the dead of winter. It was a disaster. Ten men, a third of the expedition, perished in the snow. Frémont blamed the guide, "Old Bill" Williams, a sixty-one-year-old mountain man, for leading the expedition astray. So did the Prussian cartographer, Charles Preuss, normally Frémont's harshest critic. Others laid the blame at Frémont's feet.[19]

Despite the failure of the 1848–49 expedition, the lively reports that Frémont and Jessie had produced a few years earlier had a life of their own. They quickly became classics in exploration literature.

Although a scientist, Frémont had an artist's eye for detail. His observations were thus often memorable, romantic. He also celebrated his men and their adventures with boyish enthusiasm. And Jessie clearly had a gift with words. The reports caught the public eye. They could be read for scientific data. They could also be read as adventure stories. Fathers and mothers read them to their children.

The impact was immense. Joaquin Miller, growing up on an Ohio farm, later recalled listening to his father read by candlelight from Frémont's report. Wrote Miller:

> I never was so fascinated. I never grew so fast in my life. Every scene and circumstance in the narrative was painted in my mind to last and to last forever. . . . I fancied I could see Frémont's men, hauling the cannon up the savage battlements of the Rocky Mountains, flags in the air, Frémont at the head, waving his sword, his horse neighing wildly in the mountain wind. . . . It touched my heart when he told how a weary little brown bee tried to make its way from a valley of flowers far below across a spur of snow, where he sat resting for a moment with his men; how the bee rested on his knee till it was strong enough to go on to another field of flowers beyond the snow, and how he waited a bit for it to go at its will. . . . I was no longer a boy . . . now I began to be inflamed with a love for action, adventure, glory, and great deeds away out yonder under the path of the setting sun.[20]

The reports were also timely. Hundreds of thousands now had their eyes on the West. How were they to get there? What might they encounter? Never before had there been maps that provided detailed directions. Never before had there been so much practical information, such as where to find water and firewood, where to graze livestock, or how to avoid Indian attacks. Never before had there been such vivid descriptions of the West.[21] The account of the Great Salt Lake basin was so animated that Brigham Young, after reading it, became convinced that he had found the promised land for his long-suffering Mormon followers. And in 1847–48, he led them west to Utah.[22]

The reports also generated derivatives. The most important was probably a series of seven maps—created by Preuss—depicting the entire length of the Oregon Trail. Issued by the U.S. Senate in 1846, the maps became for thousands of emigrants their only guide. Others carried along Frémont's detailed reports.

Typical were Josiah and Sarah Royce. Along with their two-year-old daughter, Mary, the Royces left Iowa for California on the last day of April 1849. After loading up with provisions, they set off in a covered wagon pulled by three yokes of oxen and one yoke of cows. They were guided, as Mrs. Royce later put it, "only by the light of Frémont's *Travels.*"[23]

The Royces were just three of some thirty thousand Americans who made the trek across the Oregon Trail that summer. They were unique in that two members of their party, Sarah and Mary, were females. No more than one thousand females made the trip that summer. Nearly all the emigrants were young males. Never before had the United States seen such an exodus of young men, all heavily armed, most on the road for the first time in their lives. Did they understand what they were doing? Were they prepared for the rigors that lay ahead? No one knew for certain. Cartoonists, however, had a field day making fun of greenhorns heading west.

Cartoon making fun of greenhorns going west. From H. R. Robinson, "A Gold Hunter on His Way to California, via St. Louis," ca. 1849. Library of Congress.

Only a few hardy souls traveled alone. Some traveled in small groups. Most joined pack trains or joint-stock wagon companies. These ventures involved laborious preparations, writing constitutions and bylaws, choosing captains, buying wagons and horses, studying Frémont's reports. Usually the participants shared a common background and knew their fellow travelers before they got started.[24] And usually they formed companies that were much like the ones that sailed around Cape Horn. Most were joint-stock companies in which each member paid in a certain amount for the purchase of wagons, oxen, and provisions. Most had titles that included the words "mining" and "trading." Most had "Rules of Regulation," which more often than not prohibited swearing, drinking, and violation of the Sabbath. And most had elected officers with military titles.

Initially, Josiah and Sarah Royce were not members of a large wagon company. They started out across Iowa with their own wagon and with just a few other emigrants. Traveling slowly, roughly three miles per hour, they joined up with several other "small companies." It took them a full month to cross Iowa and reach Council Bluffs, which for them was the jumping-off point, the place where the adventure began. Here they found "a city of wagons" waiting to cross the river and head off into "Indian country." And here they joined a "real" wagon train.

While Sarah Royce watched, Josiah got together with other men at Council Bluffs and helped organize a company, much like a militia company, with a captain and subordinate officers. The men also agreed to a set of bylaws. The most troublesome issue was what to do on the Sabbath. Should it be a day of rest? Or a day of travel? The majority decided it was too late in the season to spend each and every Sunday in camp. They would rest only if the weather was bad. Finally, on June 10, a Sunday, it became their turn to cross the river. They set off for the Far West.

The Royce wagon train followed the Mormon Trail, along the north side of the Platte River, to Fort Laramie. On the way, they encountered bands of Pawnees, Sioux, Cheyennes, and Poncas riding on scrawny horses back and forth across the grasslands, presumably hunting bison, although Sarah Royce never reported seeing a single buffalo. One band of nearly one hundred braves, some well armed and others carrying "indifferent weapons," demanded a tribute from every emigrant passing through their land. The Royce train, brandishing rifles, revolvers, knives, and hatchets, refused to pay the tribute and forced their way past the "sullen" braves. Many expected more trouble ahead, a night attack perhaps.

Yet while the Royces worried about marauding Indians, the natives were just a minor problem. The big problem was Asiatic cholera. It ravaged every part of the United States in 1849. It flourished in Boston and New York, on dirt farms in Missouri and Illinois, and on plantations in the Deep South. It was quick and deadly. Victims were suddenly overwhelmed with diarrhea, cramps, and spasmodic vomiting. That led to dehydration. Then their faces turned blue, their skin crinkled, their fingers and toes became dark and cold. Then, often within just a few hours, they were dead. Men and women who were robust and healthy in the morning were dead by nightfall. It was eerie, unsettling, unforgettable.

The disease thrived wherever filth and want existed. Most vulnerable, therefore, were the infant cities of the West, where transients were plentiful and the sewage and water systems were inadequate. St. Louis lost one-tenth of its population. Almost as hard-hit was Cincinnati. Even harder hit was Sandusky. No one, however, understood what caused the disease. No one realized that it was due to a deadly organism, *Vibrio comma*, entering the body through the mouth and causing an infection in the small intestine. No one realized, moreover, that the incubation period was up to five days and thus many healthy-looking people were already deathly ill. President Zachary Taylor attributed the epidemic to "the Providence of God" and set aside August 3 as a day of prayer. Others blamed it on the national diet, "soft" water, strong drink, night air, or whatever their pet peeve might be. One Harvard doctor insisted that cholera was linked to limestone in the soil. Some emigrants on the Oregon Trail blamed it on beans and got rid of their entire bean supply.[25]

The Oregon Trail was probably ideal as a breeding ground for deadly organisms spread by diarrhea, vomiting, flies, and contaminated water. The steamboats that fed the trail with emigrants came from St. Louis and other towns along the Ohio, Mississippi, and Missouri rivers where cholera was rampant. The gold seekers then carried it westward, leaving it in abandoned camps and water holes, to be passed on to the next group that followed them. As a result, the trail was soon marked with hundreds of wooden crosses bearing only a name and the word "cholera."

The Royce wagon train added two more crosses. The first victim was an older man, the oldest in the company. He complained of intense pain, and the Royces had him lie down in their wagon, as it was large and had a comfortable bed. He became worse, much worse. They rushed the man to a doctor, in another camp up ahead, and the doctor said it was cholera. A few hours later, the old man died. Sarah Royce was then left with the nasty task of cleaning the wagon. She washed and aired everything and hoped for the best. Three days later cholera struck down two more. One died that night; the other slowly recovered. They had no more cases, but they saw plenty of crosses as they moved west and heard of many deaths in the companies that followed them.

The Royces remained part of the wagon train until the last Sunday in July. On that day, they decided to honor the Sabbath, to rest and pray. Joining them was one other family, which consisted of a husband and wife and three small boys. For the next month the two families traveled together, protected by just two men, rather than the usual forty or more. Once they reached the Great Salt Lake, the two families parted. This wasn't unusual. Salt Lake was the place where companies invariably broke up, some members going one way, others another. At Salt Lake every man seemingly made new arrangements for his wagon. New companies thus were formed.

At the time the Royces arrived, there was much talk about a hotshot guide who was organizing a wagon train that was scheduled to leave a month or two later by a "new and better" southern route. The Royces decided not to wait. They also decided not to take the new southern route that was being highly touted. They chose instead to follow an old route, one that crossed the forbidding desert immediately west of the Great Salt Lake and then followed the Humboldt River to the Sierras. The only person willing to accompany them was an old man, in bad health, who was desperate to get to California. He had nothing to contribute except an ox. Nonetheless, with his help, off they went on August 30. They were soon joined by two young men who had nothing to contribute but their youth.

The Royces, moreover, no longer had Frémont's *Travels* to help them. Their only guide now "consisted of two small sheets of paper, sewed together, and bearing on the outside in writing the title 'Best Guide to the Gold Mines, 816 miles, by Ira J. Willes, GSL City.'" Put together by an old codger who had been to California and back the previous year, the handwritten document detailed the best route across the Great Salt Lake Desert and down the Humboldt River, identifying campsites, watering holes, and grazing land. But from the Humboldt Sink to the Carson River it was "all confusion."[26]

Fortunately for the Royces, as they approached the sink, they encountered a Mormon party returning from California. The leader provided them with very precise and good directions. Unfortunately, they didn't follow the directions to the letter, missed the cutoff to Mormon Meadow, and ended up in a dry, barren, and deadly desert. Just the thought of turning back appalled them. But they had to do it or die. Retracing their steps, they found the cutoff and spent several days recuperating at the meadow. But the diversion proved too much for two of their oxen. One yoke, Old Tom and his mate, had to be unhitched and left behind to die.

Farther on they encountered even more wreckage—three or four prairie schooners, huge Conestoga wagons, as tall as houses. Around them, scattered about the desert floor, were pasteboard boxes, wrapping paper, trunks and chests, pamphlets and books. In the wreckage, the young men found bacon, the first meat they had had in weeks. The only other thing worth picking up, noted Sarah Royce, was a small cloth-bound book titled *Little Ella*. She thought that her daughter would like it someday, as a "souvenir of the desert," and put it into her pocket.[27]

The next day the lead cows suddenly became excited. First one, then another sniffed the air. Water lay ahead. The Royces had survived the desert. They were so far behind schedule, however, that the next step of their journey—getting over the Sierra Nevada range—was formidable. The first snows had already fallen. Truckee summit would soon become impassable.

Fortunately, the U.S. government had sent out a relief company to help stragglers get over the summit, and a woman in a preceding party had told two of the rescuers about the Royces. The two men came down the mountain to fetch the Royces. They bore some bad news. It was too late in the year to get the wagon and all the household goods over the summit. The good news was that the rescuers had brought mules and knew what they were doing. Abandoning the wagon and half their baggage, the Royces forged ahead.

On October 24, in the evening, they finally reached their destination, the gold camp of Weaverville. They had been on the road for 178 days. Some time later, they moved on to San Francisco. Still later, they moved to Grass Valley, the heart of the mother lode, and became major figures in the community.

The misadventures of the Royces, years later, provided a gripping story when Sarah Royce put her "pilgrimage diary" into narrative form. She did it at the urging of her son, who was born in Grass Valley and had become a prominent philosophy professor at Harvard University. At the time, much was made of the hardships that Mrs. Royce had experienced. In fact, however, her story was fairly typical. Nearly every emigrant, it seems, had a similar hard-luck story. It was easy to make mistakes, to get lost in the desert.

The only way to avoid trouble, many believed, was to book passage on the right wagon train. And that, as Niles Searls learned, was no easy task. A twenty-four-year-old New York lawyer, Searls was not one who was easily fooled. He was also a prudent man. He realized that he was a greenhorn and needed the help of experts in crossing the continent. Many wagon companies offered their services. Which one should he take? The *Daily Missouri Republican*, a highly regarded St. Louis newspaper, touted an outfit called the Pioneer Line. Allegedly it had developed the "best scheme yet devised" to reach the gold fields.

The brainchild of two St. Louis entrepreneurs, Thomas Turner and a man named Allen, the Pioneer Line promised to take care of everything. All Searls had to do was bring his baggage and pay them $200. Then, in fifty-five to sixty days, he would be in California, making his fortune. On display the company had twenty-two massive freight wagons and twenty sleek carriages for Searls to inspect. All were top-of-the-line, in magnificent shape, with the company's name prominently emblazoned in big gold letters for all to see. The company had also hired a noted mountain man, Moses "Black" Harris, to "pilot" the expedition. Searls liked what he saw and signed up.

So did 160 other passengers. At first glance they seemed just like the emigrants on every other wagon train. Nearly all were greenhorns, going west to get rich. The oldest was sixty-six years old, the youngest fifteen, and the vast majority were in their twenties. That, in 1849, was the norm. Unlike the emigrants on most wagon trains, however, they didn't come from just one town, one state, or one region of the country. They came from all over. At least forty-eight were from the Mississippi valley, twenty-two from the Deep South, twenty-one from the Mid-Atlantic states, and twenty-three from New England. Most seemed to be well-off. Most seemed to be prudent, responsible men. Ten listed their occupation as doctor. That, thought Searls, was a good sign.

Searls and the other 160 passengers left for the gold fields on May 15, 1849, about half a month after the Royces. They reached Placerville on October 10, about half a month before the Royces reached Weaverville. They were on the road 138 days, thus beating the Royces' time by 40 days.

Better trip? No way. The trip was a disaster. Along with 161 passengers, the company started off with forty overloaded wagons and just three hundred mules to pull them. The initial pace was hectic. The mules couldn't handle it. They began dying off after the first two hundred miles. Baggage and wagons had to be abandoned. The veteran guide, Black Harris, died of cholera before the trip even started. Fifteen passengers died on the trail, nine from cholera. By the time the rest reached Placerville, only a handful could still walk or stand. Seven soon died from their ailments.[28]

Searls was one of the lucky ones. He never found much gold. But his law practice did well, and he later became chief justice of the California Supreme Court.

The overland route that Searls and his fellow passengers on the Pioneer Line took to get to California was by far the most popular. Hundreds of diaries, travel books, emigrant guides, and reminiscences detailed the experience. Soon it came to be seen as "the" California trail.

The Platte-Humboldt route, however, wasn't the only one. In its shadow was the southern route, the Gila River trail. In 1849, some twelve thousand emigrants took the Gila River trail to California. Fully half came out of the Mexican state of Sonora, an area that had been ravaged both by civil war and by war with the United States. The remainder came mainly out of Texas.

From all over Texas and Sonora, a network of minor trails fed into the Gila trail. Running along the Old Spanish Trail, the Gila River trail had been upgraded to handle heavy wagons in 1846 by the Mormon Battalion under the command of Lieutenant Colonel Philip St. George Cooke. Sometimes called Cooke's road, it began on the Rio Grande and proceeded southwest into northern Mexico and then north through Tucson to the Gila River. It then followed the river to its juncture with the Colorado River and crossed the arid Colorado desert to the coastal plains of San Diego.[29]

The Gila trail was generally flatter and wider than the more popular northern trail. Large Conestoga wagons thus found it easier to nav-

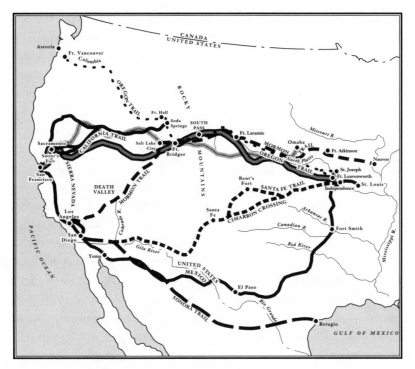

Trails west

igate. It was also possible to hook up two lighter wagons in tandem, something that was next to impossible on the northern trail. But the Gila trail led into southern California, not northern California. So, at trail's end, the prospector still had four hundred miles to go before reaching the gold fields.

West of Tucson, moreover, the trail was even drier and hotter than the northern trail west of Salt Lake City. Finding firewood and pasture was thus even more of a problem. Travelers loaded up on buffalo chips, which burned well, and often journeyed at night to avoid the heat of the day. Water was an even bigger problem, especially on the ninety-mile stretch of wasteland west of the Colorado River. Here, to be short of water meant certain death.

The greatest disadvantage of the southern route was the danger of Indian attack. Tribes along the northern trail were relatively peaceful, but the Gila trail ran through Apache country, and the Apaches were anything but peaceful. They were few in number, roughly six thousand people, but along with the Comanches, they had long been regarded as the scourges of the Southwest. No government as yet had been able to subdue them. Veterans of 250 years of guerrilla war, first with the Spanish and then with Spanish-speaking Mexicans, they had long lived in a world where stealing livestock, enslaving enemies, and scalping and torturing captives were the norm.[30] How did it start? Some scholars would later claim that the Apaches learned the fine art of torture and mutilation from the Spanish. Others would attribute it to Apache culture. Regardless of how it began, it was well established by the time English-speaking Americans pushed their way into Texas.

The Apaches at first saw the newcomers as potential allies in their ongoing struggle against Mexico. That was largely wishful thinking. From the outset the Texans regarded the Apaches as savages and treated them accordingly. In 1849, however, the biggest problem the Apaches faced was still Mexico. As in years past, the Mexican government in Chihuahua offered tempting rewards to anyone who was willing to butcher Apaches. All along the Gila trail, the news was the same: $2,000 for Chief Gómez's head, $200 for each dead warrior's scalp, $100 for each dead squaw's scalp, and a lesser but undisclosed amount for each papoose's scalp. Did the bounties increase the danger? Or lessen it? No one was certain.[31]

Among those who added to the danger was John Joel Glanton. Now thirty years old, Glanton was a native of South Carolina. He had spent his boyhood in Tennessee working with outlaws, then migrated to Texas in 1835, where he rose quickly, becoming a captain of the Texas Rangers at age sixteen. Then, after his girlfriend was scalped by Lipan Apaches, he became a notorious scalp hunter. Yet despite his notoriety, he remained a Ranger, rubbed shoulders with "respectable" people, and in 1846 married into a prominent Mexican family.

Thanks to his father-in-law, Glanton then became the commander of a Mexican military company that hunted down "hostile" Indians. Operating out of Chihuahua, Glanton and eighteen fellow Texans went after Chief Gómez. After several failed attempts, they somehow managed to penetrate Gómez's camp, hack off his head, and scalp many of his followers. With their trophies, they then beat a hasty retreat to Chihuahua, fighting Apache warriors all the way. After collecting their reward, they became indiscriminate butchers, scalping friendly Indians as well as hostile ones. They then turned to scalping Mexican peons for a profit. With that, the Mexican government declared them outlaws.

No longer welcome in Chihuahua, Glanton and a larger gang of thirty men moved farther west. At the juncture of the Gila River and the Colorado, they spotted a moneymaker, a ferry run by Yuma Indians. Overpowering the Yumas, they took over the ferry, lured gold seekers aboard, and then killed them for their money and possessions. Finally, in 1850, the Yumas got revenge. They attacked the ferry, "brained" Glanton and most of his men, and took Glanton's scalp.[32]

Thanks to Glanton, Chief Gómez, and hundreds like them, "the land of little rain" was a war zone. To get through it, wagon trains on the Gila River route tended to convoy. Thus, they typically were much longer than those on the northern route. Nothing fewer than a hundred wagons was considered safe. Each convoy was usually made up of three to five separate wagon trains plus a few individual stragglers. During the day the convoy usually had outlying guards to make sure the livestock did not graze too far away from the wagon train and fall into Indian hands. At night the convoy circled the wagons and herded the cattle into the "corral" for protection against Indians.

Among the Texans who took the Gila trail to California in 1849 were many slaveholders. Nearly all left their wives and children behind. Most also left their slaves behind, given the unknown circumstances that lay ahead. A few were less cautious and brought some of their slaves with them. How many? No one knows for certain, but definitely more than a handful.

Perhaps the least cautious was Colonel Thomas Thorn. He had moved many times in his forty-three years. Born in New Jersey, he had migrated to the Deep South in the 1820s, first to Mississippi, then to Tennessee, where he married Mary Sherman, the daughter of a prominent North Carolina slaveholder. The couple then moved on to Arkansas, where the oldest of their five children was born, and then on to Texas. Thorn was an organizer, and during the war with Mexico he raised and commanded troops. In 1849 he got gold fever and organized two hundred wagons to take the Gila trail to California. Unlike most gold seekers, Thorn brought along his wife and children. He also brought thirty slaves.

Not all thirty reached the gold fields. In southern California, several of Thorn's slaves bolted. He caught two and had them severely beaten. But the local sheriff refused to help and even protected some of the runaways. Most got away. Then, upon reaching Mariposa, Thorn encountered more trouble. The miners didn't want to compete with slave labor. They encouraged more slaves to flee. By 1850, Thorn had only ten slaves left. Among the remaining slaves were Diana and Lewis Caruthers and their three children. Diana Caruthers and two of her daughters helped Mary Thorn run a boardinghouse, which soon gained fame locally as one of the few places a miner could get a decent meal. Also among the remaining slaves was Peter Green, who for $1,000 would buy his freedom from Thorn in 1855.[33]

Thorn's impact on California history was minimal. Far more important was another Texas slaveholder, Thomas Jefferson Green. Born in North Carolina in 1802, the second year of Jefferson's presidency, Green grew up in a slaveholding family. As a young man, he went to West Point and served in the North Carolina legislature. Then, in the mid-1820s, he moved to Florida, became a plantation owner, and served in the Florida legislature. After his wife, Sarah, died in 1835, Green organized the Texas Land Company, a land colonization project, and moved to Texas. On reaching Texas, he abandoned the colonization project to serve in the Texas revolutionary army. Commissioned brigadier general, he returned to the United States to raise volunteers, money, and ammunition for the Texas cause. Simultaneously, he won a seat in the Texas House of Representatives, where he became a strong opponent of General Sam Houston.

In December 1842, Green made his mark in Texas history. He was second in command of the Mier expedition, the last of the Lone Star Republic's raiding expeditions into the area south of the Nueces River. The brainchild of some of Houston's harshest critics, the campaign was a disaster. The Texans were overwhelmed by superior Mexican forces. Green and his men had to surrender to General Pedro de Ampudia. Held at Perote Prison, in the Mexican state of Veracruz, many of the men subsequently died from malnutrition, wounds, disease, or execution. Green, however, escaped and made his way back to Velasco, Texas, where he was again elected to the legislature.[34] And again he attacked Sam Houston, this time for not helping to get the prisoners released. Houston later said Green had all the characteristics of a dog except fidelity.[35]

When news of gold on the American River reached Texas, Green was among the first to go. Along with several other Texans, he set off for California in the spring of 1849. Determined to make the gold diggings into slave country, they brought fifteen slaves. By July, Green and his fellow Texans had reached the Yuba River. There, at Rose's

Bar along the east bank of the river, they appropriated a large number of claims under both their names and their slaves' names. Altogether, they staked out about one-third of a mile of the riverbank. The other miners were furious. They objected vehemently. Green and his friends refused to budge. They decided instead to test the mettle of the miners.[36]

During the same spring that Green and Thorn made their way to California, so did Broderick's future nemesis David Terry. He was much younger than Green and Thorn, having turned twenty-six that March, but just as determined to bring slavery to the gold country.

While Kentucky-born, Terry was essentially the product of the Texas frontier and the teachings of his mother's family. Named after his maternal grandfather, David Smith, he had been taken out of his father's hands when he was a small boy living on a large cotton plantation in Hinds County, Mississippi. For reasons that aren't entirely clear, his mother decided that his father wasn't a fit father and husband. Leaving her husband behind, she took Terry and his three brothers to Texas to live with her mother, Obedience Fort Smith, first on a plantation that belonged to her brother Benjamin Fort Smith, then on a 4,606-acre plantation that her mother acquired on the southwestern edge of Houston. She herself then obtained a land grant on Oyster Creek, twenty-five miles west of Houston, and began raising cotton on a large scale.[37]

Three years later, Terry's mother died. Terry was only thirteen at the time, and his oldest brother, who had been named after Benjamin Franklin, had just turned sixteen. Technically, the sixteen-year-old was now head of the family. In reality, his grandmother and his mother's siblings were in charge. By 1841, all of the grandmother's offspring had moved to the Houston area, and all seemingly took orders from her. With their input, Terry came of age and absorbed the customs prevalent among the wealthy planters of south Texas. Becoming a Texas Ranger, treating women with respect, following the "code of honor"—all became important to him. He developed only one peculiarity that was not widely shared in his family. With respect to weapons, he came to prefer the bowie knife, because unlike a revolver it never misfired.

As for slavery, Terry never doubted the wisdom of it. Not only did he become "a strong believer in African slavery," noted one acquaintance, he "had little patience with anyone who was not."[38] His family, for several generations past, had owned slaves. His grandmother owned slaves. His uncles and aunts owned slaves. His uncle Benjamin not only owned slaves but illegally imported slaves from Africa. His older brother, also named Benjamin but called Frank, soon became one of the biggest slaveholders in Texas, owning 105 slaves on the eve of the Civil War.[39]

Terry spent a decade on the family plantation. Then, in 1843, he went to Houston to work in the law office of his uncle Colonel T. B. J. Hadley. Admitted to the bar in November 1845, Terry practiced law in both Houston and Galveston. In 1846, when war with Mexico broke out, he enlisted for three months in the Texas Rangers, thus fulfilling one of his boyhood dreams, and fought in the Battle of Monterey. After the battle, he sought an appointment as district attorney of Galveston. He didn't get it. Shortly thereafter, he became convinced that the love of his life, a distant cousin, had lost interest in him.

So in 1849, when the opportunity arose to go to the gold fields, Terry took it. His brother Frank made arrangements to be part of a mining company. But apparently Frank was needed at home. Terry persuaded his brother to let him go instead. The company consisted of twenty or thirty "substantial citizens," mainly from the Houston area, and "five able bodied negro men."[40] When the men passed through Austin in mid-April, Colonel W. J. Kyle appeared to be in charge. By the time they reached El Paso, in late June, Terry was in command.

Getting through Apache country proved difficult. First, Apache warriors stole several animals. Terry's men pursued them, recaptured the stolen property, and took some Apache horses in revenge. The warriors, to no avail, demanded their horses back. Then, a day or two later, on approaching a rocky pass, John A. Alexander, the former state auditor of Texas, was sent ahead. Two Apaches came toward him, making peace signs, asking for tobacco. As he reached in his pouch for tobacco, they shot him. Terry's men then chased the two killers, only to discover that they had been led into an ambush. The battle lasted several hours. Terry didn't lose any more men. But the braves had the upper hand. They were well entrenched in the rocky pass. And in the end, Terry had to retreat.[41]

After this incident, Terry's party made their way to California with no further trouble. Arriving on September 3, they broke up and went their separate ways. Terry tried his hand at gold mining in Calaveras County. He had little luck. By December, he had decided to leave "shovel and rocker" behind. He moved to Stockton, the principal distributing center for the southern mines, and opened a law office.

What became of the five slaves? No one knows for certain. They didn't accompany Terry to Calaveras County. Maybe they went with one of the other Texans. Or maybe they learned, as Terry did to his disgust, that California had just outlawed slavery.

3

———◆◆◆———

THE DECISION TO OUTLAW SLAVERY CAME TO A HEAD WHEN DAVID Terry's fellow Texans Thomas Jefferson Green and his friends staked out claims on the Yuba River under the names of their slaves. Until that time there had been rumblings against slavery throughout the gold country, but no decisive action had been taken.

No action, in fact, had been needed if Mexican law was still in effect. Unlike the Louisiana Territory, where slavery had been legal before it became U.S. property, slavery had been banned in California for nearly twenty years. It had been abolished in all of Mexico in 1829. Was that ban still in effect? Thousands of gold seekers seemed to think so.

Men like Terry thus looked to Congress to override Mexican law. To their chagrin, however, there was now a concerted effort in Congress to make sure that didn't happen. It began before gold was discovered, in August 1846, when President Polk sprang on the House of Representatives a last-minute request for $2 million to facilitate peace negotiations with Mexico and to buy California and New Mexico.

The request came at the end of the congressional session, just hours before Congress was to adjourn. The members, wilting from the August heat, had been in session since December. They were anxious to get home. At the time, nearly every Northern Whig thought the president was a scoundrel who had led the country into war on false pretenses. And many believed that Polk, a Tennessee slaveholder, was part of a Slave Power conspiracy to extend slavery. At the same time, some Northern Democrats, especially those who took their cues from the ex-president Martin Van Buren, worried about being identified with a war that appeared to have been "waged for the extension of slavery." That, said their mentor, was tantamount to committing "political suicide with their eyes open."[1] They were also upset by the way Polk handled patronage. Too many choice appointments had gone to Southerners and not enough to men they supported.

Now faced with the president's last-minute request, nine Van Buren Democrats decided to take a stand. They got together during a House recess and worked out an amendment to the Two Million Bill that would prohibit slavery in any territory obtained by virtue of the appropriation. To present this amendment, they looked to David Wilmot, an obscure thirty-two-year-old Pennsylvania Democrat who was known mainly as a good-natured man who cussed a lot, dressed sloppily, and always had a wad of chewing tobacco in his mouth. Wilmot had backed all the key party measures—the annexation of Texas in 1845, Polk's decision to split the vast Oregon country with Great Britain, and Polk's tariff reduction program—when some of the others had not. As a good party man who was friendly with the House's Southern leadership, they thought he had the best chance to gain the floor.

They expected fireworks once Wilmot presented the amendment. That didn't happen. Instead, half of the House members seemingly had their minds elsewhere, on catching a train home and getting away from Washington's unbearable heat. Debate was perfunctory. The proviso then passed the House, 85 to 79, but neither the proviso nor the Two Million Bill got through the Senate in the few hours before adjournment.[2]

Debate heated up in the next session of Congress. Again Polk requested money, this time $3 million. To this request, Preston King, a New York Democrat, added a tougher version of the proviso, one that prohibited slavery in "any" territory "hereafter" acquired by the United States. In debate, Wilmot called on Congress to join him in bettering the lives of white settlers. "I have no squeamish sensitiveness upon the subject of slavery," he declared, "nor morbid sympathy for the slave. I plead the cause of white freemen. I would preserve for free white labor a fair country, a rich inheritance, where the sons of toil, of my own race and own color, can live without disgrace which association with negro slavery brings upon free labor."[3]

Wilmot's "white only" appeal was potent. It had wide support, especially among Northern Democrats. Hence, more than ever, the proviso was a threat to the South. The Polk administration worked frantically to defeat it and succeeded in getting eighteen Northern Democrats to join the South in opposition. Nonetheless, on February 15, the measure passed the House, 115 to 106. Four days later, in the Senate, John C. Calhoun of South Carolina lambasted the proviso. Its passage, he declared, would give the North overwhelming power in the future, and such a destruction of sectional balance would mean "political revolution, anarchy, civil war, and widespread disaster." As a Southern man, a cotton planter, a slaveholder, he would never acknowledge inferiority. "The surrender of life is nothing to sinking down into acknowledged inferiority."[4]

Shortly thereafter, the Senate rejected the proviso and passed its own Three Million Bill without a word about slavery. This bill came before the House on March 3, the last day of the session. Again, antislavery forces tried to attach the proviso. This time the Polk administration stepped up its efforts to kill the proviso and succeeded in getting twenty-two Northern Democrats to vote with the South and six more to miss the crucial vote. The proviso thus went down to defeat, 97 to 102, and Polk got his $3 million with no strings attached.

Yet even though the proviso failed to become law, the idea didn't die. It was added to one bill after another, and David Wilmot, once an unknown congressman, became a celebrity in antislavery circles. Southern hotspurs, meanwhile, realized that they had a problem. No longer could they sit idly by and hope that the concept of "free soil" would fade away like the setting sun. They had to do something. They especially had to rally all Southerners in opposition. Accordingly, John C. Calhoun and several close associates perfected a counterargument. They insisted that the Wilmot Proviso was not just wrong. It was also unconstitutional.

On January 5, 1847, Robert Barnwell Rhett of South Carolina explained the pro-slavery position to the House of Representatives. The Wilmot Proviso, said Rhett, rested on the false assumption that lands acquired by the United States belonged to the federal government. That was dead wrong. The federal government was a creation of

Go it, ye Cripples! Ya-a-up!

WILMOT, THE WIZARD.

Southern cartoon accusing the "wizard" David Wilmot of trying to "swallow the South at a gulp." Reprinted from The John-Donkey, *January 8, 1848.*

the states. Thus land acquired by the United States belonged to the states, and only as an agent of the states did the federal government have any authority over the territories. And, as an agent of the states, the federal government could not discriminate against the citizens of any state. It therefore must enable citizens of the slaveholding states to enter the territories freely and on equal terms with the citizens of the free states. In short, wherever the American flag went, so did slavery. Six weeks later, on February 19, Calhoun made the same argument in the Senate.[5]

In doing so, the two South Carolinians introduced into debate what came to be known as the common-property doctrine. It soon had a wide following in the South, especially among Democrats. Northerners, however, generally dismissed it as "just a lawyer's argument."

Thanks to the furor over the Wilmot Proviso, Congress in 1848 was incapable of dealing with the California question. Gold had been discovered. Thousands of people from all over the world were on the move to the Sierras. Nine out of ten were young males. Lawlessness was certain. Yet no legal resolution was in sight.

In the 1848 presidential election, the losing Democratic candidate, Lewis Cass, offered a solution. Instead of having Congress decide the slavery issue, he proposed leaving it in the hands of the people who settled the territories. Dubbed "squatter sovereignty," it appealed to Northern Democrats who hoped to sidetrack the slavery issue. On December 11, Senator Stephen A. Douglas, who was making a name for himself as "a man who got things done," introduced a bill in the Senate to bring the entire Mexican Cession into the Union as a single state with Congress not legislating on the slavery question. That delicate matter might be solved someday by the people who settled the territory, but not by Congress.

Two days later, to Douglas's dismay, the House rejected his proposal. It reaffirmed its adherence to the Wilmot Proviso, 106 to 80. Then, eight days later, the House Committee on Territories reported a bill for the organization of California with all the "conditions, restrictions, and prohibitions" of the Northwest Ordinance of 1787. That, from Douglas's perspective, was just more of the same, as the Northwest Ordinance had prohibited slavery north of the Ohio River. Southerners were livid.

Finally, on February 7, 1849, William B. Preston, a Virginia Whig, followed Douglas's lead. Introducing a bill similar to Douglas's in the House, he spoke against Congress deciding the slavery question. He likened the process to "a foreign government" making decisions for "a people abroad." It hadn't worked in 1776, said Preston, when the British parliament tried to impose restrictions on the thirteen colonies. Instead, it had driven the American people to rebellion. Did Congress want to be in the same position as the British parliament was at the time of the American Revolution? Did Congress not see the parallels between the California situation and that of the thirteen colonies in 1776?

Preston's proposal went nowhere. Antislavery Northerners attacked it as just another Southern scheme to allow slavery to enter the Mexican Cession. They proposed an amendment that explicitly banned slavery. The amendment passed, 91 to 87. That torpedoed Preston's bill. Meanwhile, in the Senate, Douglas's bill was also going nowhere. It lay dead in the water.[6]

Congress was thus paralyzed. The situation was so bad that outgoing president Polk feared that disgruntled Californians would seize the initiative and establish an independent republic. Then what would the federal government do? Send in troops? He had only a few more weeks to serve. The problem then fell to his successor, General Zachary Taylor, and the next Congress.

Meanwhile, in the gold country, rumblings against slavery were commonplace. Sam Brannan, the Mormon entrepreneur who popularized the slogan "Gold on the American River," took up the issue as early as March 1848.

In his newspaper, *The Californian*, Brannan called for an all-white California—no slaves, no free blacks—and claimed that 90 percent of the people agreed with him. Ten days later, a rival newspaper, *The California Star*, upped the estimate to 99 percent. Months later, in January 1849, Brannan again called for an all-white California, this time at a public meeting in Sacramento. Backing him was the presiding officer of the meeting, Peter H. Burnett of Missouri. It was essential to keep all blacks, free as well as slave, out of California, said Burnett. Brannan's resolutions then passed by a unanimous vote. In February, the same resolutions came before a public meeting in San Francisco and again passed easily.[7]

Then, in July 1849, miners on the Yuba River did more than talk. The year before, gold had been discovered on the river by a thirty-one-year-old Pennsylvanian, Jonas Spect. The news had brought thousands of gold seekers to the Yuba. By April 1849, the miners had decided they needed laws to handle disputed claims. Meeting at Spect's store at Rose's Bar, they had drafted a legal code. Among other provisions, it limited the size of a mining claim to what one man could work by himself. They also elected a committee of the oldest miners to enforce it.[8]

Three months later, Thomas Jefferson Green and his fellow Texans arrived. Ignoring the local rules, they took over about one-third of a mile on the left bank of the Yuba and established grandiose claims of their own measurement in their own names and the names of their fifteen slaves. The miners immediately sent a committee to inform them of the "law." Green and his friends refused to back down and threatened to fight if necessary. The miners then called a general meeting at Rose's

Bar, for Sunday, July 29. There, they voted "that no slave or negro should own claims or even work in the mines." A new committee, with some younger members, was then sent to Green's camp. Although unarmed, they "made clear their errand." The slaves were to be out of the district by the next morning. That night the slaves fled, followed the next morning by Green and his fellow Texans.

The code that the Yuba miners passed that July applied not only to Thomas Jefferson Green and his slaves. It applied to any combination of masters and slaves, and it was enforced. Three months after the Green incident, a majordomo from Chile arrived with a gang of peons to work under his authority. The miners told him to get out. He ignored the warning. They hanged him. Weeks later, another Chilean entrepreneur showed up. He, too, failed to heed their warning. They cut off his ears.[9]

Map of the gold country. The Yuba River, where Thomas Jefferson Green tried to establish slavery, is in the northern third.

Three days after passing their code, on Wednesday, August 1, the Yuba miners had the opportunity to elect someone to represent them at the state constitutional convention. They had been urged to do so first by General Bennet Riley, then by the president of the United States.

Riley had arrived in California in April 1849 to replace Colonel Richard B. Mason as military governor. A large "grim old fellow" and "fine free swearer" in his mid-fifties, Riley realized immediately that he was in no position to actually govern California. He also learned that San Franciscans for some time had been clamoring for a provisional civilian government. Rather than oppose this groundswell, Riley decided to give Congress a bit more time and then lead it. In late May he learned that there was little hope that Congress would do anything. Five days later, on June 3, Riley issued a call for an election on the first day of August to select delegates for a convention to meet in Monterey. There, the delegates would write a state constitution—or, if they wished, organize a territorial government, elect superior court judges, prefects, and sub-prefects, and fill all vacancies for alcaldes, justices of the peace, and other offices that had once existed under Mexican law.[10]

The day after Riley issued his call for a convention, T. Butler King arrived in San Francisco. He came on the *Panama*, the same ship as William Gwin and Jessie Benton Frémont. He had been sent by the new president, General Zachary Taylor, under the guise of studying the need for mail steamship lines and survey routes for a Panama railroad. In fact, King, a slaveholding congressman from Georgia, had been sent on a secret mission to encourage Californians to form a state so that Congress would have "no territory to legislate upon."

President Zachary Taylor, also a major slaveholder with at least 127 slaves in Louisiana and Mississippi, had concluded even before taking office that the long-winded congressional debate about slavery in the territories was both dangerous and unnecessary. His logic was simple. Since Mexico had abolished slavery, the institution could not be revived in territories taken from Mexico. Thus men like David Wilmot, John C. Calhoun, and Robert Barnwell Rhett were just causing trouble, just playing with fire. And since everyone agreed that states could make their own decisions regarding slavery, the solution was to make California into a state as soon as possible and get the issue off the political agenda. So in April 1849, Taylor dispatched King to California, never dreaming that the process would be well on its way by the time King got there.[11]

The Yuba miners knew exactly the type of delegate they wanted. They wanted someone who would use his influence to forever prohibit slavery in California. For that task they chose a twenty-seven-year-old lawyer, William Shannon.

At first glance, Shannon didn't appear to be up to the task. He was a man "of moderate proportions, a florid, open countenance, with a laughing devil in his eye." He was also a prankster, "ever full of fun and frolic," but never "malicious, a current of good humor ran through all his acts."[12] At the same time, however, the miners knew that they could count on Shannon. He was tougher than he looked. He was also an antislavery man.

Born in county Mayo, Ireland, Shannon had moved to Steuben, New York, at age seven. He had been admitted to the New York bar in 1846. That same year he had joined Colonel Jonathan Drake Stevenson's New York Volunteers, been elected captain of Company I, and sailed around the Horn to California on the *Susan Drew*. Stationed first in Monterey, then in San Diego, he had been discharged from the army in September 1848. He had then formed a partnership with two of his fellow officers, hired ten of his enlisted men, and sent them to Coloma to mine gold. Meanwhile, he went to Monterey to see Colonel Mason, the military governor of California, and secured an appointment as alcalde of Coloma, a position that essentially made him the region's chief legal officer—mayor, sheriff, judge, all rolled into one.

Growing up in upstate New York, Shannon had no experience with black bondage. But he had seen it firsthand on his trip around the Horn. The stopover at Rio de Janeiro had appalled him. It was bad enough, wrote Shannon, that Brazil was a "priest-ridden society." Its effects could be seen everywhere—"utter ignorance, superstition, and indolence . . . the absence of all energy and enterprise." But what made Brazil truly "loathsome" and "revolting" was slavery. "Here are not the descendents of negroes who were brought perhaps more than a century ago from their land, but the African himself, bearing all the marks of country and tribe as well in the sometimes frightful tattooing perhaps over most of the body, as well as the features. And horrible as the practice is, you almost lose your pity, in the disgust which their appearance excites."[13]

If General Riley had his way, Shannon and the other delegates were to begin work on the first day of September. That didn't happen, as some of the delegates were slow getting to Monterey. But by Monday, September 3, enough had arrived to meet the quorum requirement and officially organize for business.

It was a young group, with only four of the forty-eight delegates over age fifty and nine under age thirty. Twenty-two hailed from the free states, fifteen from the slave states, seven from California, and four from overseas.[14] The most cohesive group were the seven Californians. They already knew one another and were led by Abel Stearns, who had been born in Massachusetts but had married a Spanish woman and had lived in California for twenty years.[15]

Shannon was not the only member of Colonel Stevenson's New York Volunteers at the convention. Ten of the forty-eight delegates were New Yorkers, and seven had come to California as part of Stevenson's regiment. Of these the best known was Edward Gilbert, a thirty-year-old printer who had once been the associate editor of the *Albany Argus*, the leading Democratic newspaper in New York. Like Shannon, he had been an officer under Stevenson. Upon his discharge, he had founded the *Alta California*, now San Francisco's leading newspaper. A staunch advocate for statehood, Gilbert had run a series of editorials belittling the impotence and arbitrariness of the military regime in Monterey and helped push General Riley into calling a constitutional convention.[16]

Among the slaveholding delegates was William Gwin. On disembarking from the steamship *Panama* on June 4, he immediately launched his campaign to become a U.S. senator. On June 12, he spoke at a San Francisco meeting. There was no need, he said, for California to become a territory first and then a state at a later date. California already had more than enough people to qualify for statehood. It should immediately become a state. Later that summer, Gwin made the same pitch to meetings in Sacramento and Stockton. On August 1, he was chosen to be one of San Francisco's eight delegates.[17]

Gwin expected to be in charge. On a steamer from San Francisco to Monterey, he told a fellow delegate, Elisha Crosby, that he was the logical choice for president of the convention. He also "assumed a very haughty and dictatorial attitude," noted Crosby, and "affected that air of superiority that to the average American is offensive." Everyone "knew," moreover, that he had "in his pocket, a combination of the State Constitutions of Ohio and Iowa."[18]

At the convention, another delegate, Jacob Snyder, a thirty-four-year-old Pennsylvanian who had gained renown for his role in the Bear Flag Revolt in 1846, mocked Gwin for expecting to be president and for bringing along a constitution that he expected to have adopted. Did he think the rest of the delegates were there as "merely dummies to represent numbers and sections"? Snyder then nominated for president "Long Bob" Semple, a forty-two-year-old Kentuckian who had also partaken in the Bear Flag Revolt and was now a Monterey printer. The grizzly six-foot eight-inch redhead won easily. To Gwin's dismay, four-fifths of the delegates voted against him, even though Semple acknowledged that "he had never seen the inside of a legislative hall and knew no more about the rules of proceedings than a child does in learning the ABCs."[19]

Once Semple was elected, the delegates got to work writing a constitution. General Riley had left open the question of whether they were to create a territorial government or a state. So Gwin, who could not become a senator from a territory, moved that they form a state. Only the southern California delegates objected. Fearing that they would be saddled with heavy land taxes and have little say in the new state government, they preferred to be under the federal government. One delegate, José Antonio Carrillo of Los Angeles, floated the idea of splitting California in two, creating a state north of San Luis Obispo and letting southern California become a territory, but this proposal never got off the ground. The southern Californians were hopelessly outnumbered, and thus Gwin's motion passed easily.

The actual writing of the state constitution was largely a clerical task. Gwin was not the only one who had a copy of the Iowa Constitution in his pocket. So did others, and for those who didn't Gwin had extra copies to spare. That document had just been written in 1846. Some delegates also had the New York Constitution, which had been revised in 1846. Using those two documents and others as guides, a select committee scissored and pasted together a constitution for the other delegates to consider. Of 136 sections, at least 66 were taken out of the Iowa Constitution, 19 out of the New York.[20]

None of the sections that the select committee reported to the convention, however, barred slavery. So on Monday, September 10, Shannon moved to include another section in the California Constitution: "Neither slavery nor involuntary servitude, unless for the punishment of crimes, shall ever be tolerated in the State."

Promptly seconding Shannon's motion was William Gwin, the owner of two hundred Mississippi slaves. That surprised Elisha Crosby, who had "expected very considerable opposition from the Southern element." He also thought that the constitution that Gwin had in his pocket called for opening the southern half of California to slavery. He concluded that Gwin had probably just counted noses and realized that he was outnumbered by men from "New England and New York and Pennsylvania." In any event, noted Crosby, "Gwin with great good grace, advocated the adoption of the clause prohibiting slavery."[21]

Actually, Gwin had already counted noses earlier that summer. In his pursuit of a Senate seat, he had traveled north to the gold fields to take the political pulse of the region. He saw immediately that the gold diggings could be worked efficiently by slave labor. But he also quickly learned that the miners would have none of it. A year later, when cornered by some pro-slavery men at an evening function, he summed up the prevailing attitude:

> I can satisfy you in a few words. In California, labor is respectable. In our mines are to be found men of the highest intelligence and respectability performing daily labor, and they do not wish to see the slaves of some wealthy planter brought there and put in competition with their labor, side by side. It is from the very fact that labor is respectable that we wish to keep it so by excluding slavery from our state.[22]

Shannon's motion thus had Gwin's blessing. But it did not satisfy Morton M. McCarver, a forty-two-year-old Kentucky-born Democrat. McCarver had bounced around from one frontier to another, having lived in Louisiana, Texas, Iowa, and Oregon before coming to California. In the Deep South, he had developed a fierce hatred for both blacks and their masters.[23] To Shannon's motion, McCarver thus added an amendment: "Nor shall the introduction of free negroes under indentures or otherwise, be allowed."

Several delegates then pointed out that McCarver's amendment was out of order. Shannon's motion, they contended, had to be decided first. After a short debate, McCarver withdrew his amendment, and Shannon's proposal to outlaw slavery in California passed by a unanimous vote.

But McCarver wasn't to be put off. He raised the issue time and again. Shannon opposed it on principle; others feared that it violated the U.S. Constitution and thus would block statehood. McCarver then added a proviso to his original proposal, taken directly from the Missouri Constitution: "The legislature shall, at its first session, pass such laws as will effectually prohibit free persons of color from immigrating to and settling in this State, and to effectually prevent owners of slaves from bringing them into this State for the purpose of setting them free. . . . Provided, That nothing in this constitution shall be construed to conflict with the provisions of the first clause of the second section of the fourth article of the Constitution of the United States."

In one form or another, McCarver's desire to ban free blacks as well as slaves from the state was hotly debated for two entire days.[24] Said McCarver in defense of his proposal: "No population that could be brought within the limits of our territory could be more repugnant to the feelings of the people, or injurious to the prosperity of the community, than free negroes. They are idle in their habits, difficult to be governed by the laws, thriftless, and uneducated. It is a species of population that this country should be particularly guarded against."

In making this argument, McCarver insisted that slaveholders planned to bring blacks into California as indentured servants, work them for a short time in the mines, and then set them free. He claimed to know several men with such plans. He also said that other delegates had "received letters from the States" that confirmed his assessment. The result, said McCarver, would be disastrous. "Do the delegates suppose the white population of this country will permit these negroes to compete with them in working the mines? Sir, you will see the most fearful collisions that have ever been presented in any country. . . . The evil would be greater than slavery itself."[25]

Echoing this argument was James McHall Jones, a twenty-five-year-old lawyer from Louisiana. What made California the "epitome of free society," contended Jones, was that in the mines the individual white miner enjoyed a "vast advantage . . . over capital." But once slaveholders brought in their black indentured servants, that would no longer be the case. The servants would "enter into competition with and degrade the white labor of the miners." And would slaveholders bring in black servants? There was no doubt about it. It "had been made manifest to members of this House by private letters."[26]

Also supporting McCarver was Jacob Snyder, the onetime Pennsylvanian who had mocked Gwin's high-handedness. Snyder had lived in Missouri before coming to California. From that experience, he was convinced that a typical Missouri slave would net for his owner over a period of thirty-five years no more than $6,800. But suppose the owner made a contract with his slave, eventual freedom after four years of work in the California mines. At $4,000 a year in gold dust, the slave owner would net $16,000. "Do you suppose this will not be tried? It will, sir, and depend on it, you will find the country flooded with a population of free negroes—the greatest calamity that could befall California."[27]

To McCarver's fellow Kentuckian "Long Bob" Semple, the danger was even "greater" than most delegates imagined. He was certain that without a ban on black migration, the Southern states would dump unwanted slaves on California. "I can assure you, sir, thousands will be introduced into this country before long, if you do not insert a positive prohibition against them in your Constitution—an immense and overwhelming population of negroes, who have never been freemen, who have never been accustomed to provide for themselves. What would be the state of things in a few years? The whole country would be filled with emancipated slaves—the worst species of population—prepared to do nothing but steal, or live upon our means as paupers."[28]

This brought a sharp retort from Shannon. Semple's claim that California would become a dumping ground for eastern slaves, he said, was sheer nonsense. Why would eastern slaveholders go to the trouble and expense of sending their slaves to California? Why not simply ship them north across the Ohio River? More fundamentally, said Shannon, banning free blacks from the state was ethically repugnant. "Free men of color have just as good a right, and ought to have, to emigrate here as white men."[29]

Henry Tefft, a twenty-six-year-old New Yorker, then weighed in. He took Shannon to task for not having his priorities straight. Shannon, said Tefft, should be concerned with the thousands of intelligent, able, young white men now working in the diggings. "No new State in the Union has ever had a population so enterprising and intelligent in character. They are working willingly, and they do not consider it a degradation to engage in any department of industry which will afford an adequate remuneration. But will this state of things continue—will this class of population continue to work cheerfully and willingly if you place them side by side with the negro? They would be unable, even if willing, to compete with the bands of negroes who would be set to work under the direction of capitalists. It would become a monopoly of the worst character. The profits of the mines would go into the pockets of single individuals."[30]

Edward Gilbert, the editor of the *Alta California* who had also been one of Stevenson's Volunteers, then rallied to Shannon's defense. He first ridiculed the horror stories put forth by McCarver and his supporters. "We are told that slaveholders will manumit their slaves and bring them to this country to mine gold; that they will give up their plantations, however lucrative may be their business, and sacrifice their property to accomplish this object; that they will do all this, when they see staring them in the face, in the Constitution of California, that no slavery shall exist here. I do not believe this; it is not credible."

Then Gilbert attacked McCarver's proposal on ethical grounds. "If you insert in your Constitution such a provision or anything like it, you will be guilty of a great injustice—you will do a great wrong, sir—a wrong to the principles of liberal and enlightened freedom. . . . Are we to attempt here to turn back the tide of human freedom which has

Edward Gilbert, editor of the Alta California *and spokesman for all "freemen." Reprinted from Frank Soulé et al.,* The Annals of San Francisco *(New York, 1854), 773.*

rolled across from continent to continent? Are we to say that a free negro or Indian, or any other freeman, shall not enter the boundaries of California? I trust not, Sir."[31]

Thus it went back and forth for two full days. Again and again, the same arguments were reiterated. Free blacks were bad members of society. Black competition would degrade white labor. Slave owners would find it advantageous to bring in manumitted slaves as contract laborers. And these laborers would earn for their former masters many times their worth. Yet at the same time, many delegates found McCarver's motion troubling. A few said it was morally wrong. More feared that it might jeopardize California's becoming a state.

To this objection, McCarver insisted that his amended motion would suffice. It passed the committee of the whole. In the end, however, the convention voted it down, 8 to 31.

Shannon prevailed on two other occasions at the convention. One concerned the property rights of married women.

New York, his home state, had just reversed a long-standing legal practice, one that reigned supreme not only in New York but throughout the nation. Under this well-established system, a woman's assets and debts became her husband's on her wedding day. She no longer had any right to control property that had been hers the previous day. Nor did she have any right from that day forward to acquire property, make contracts, keep or control her own wages or any rents, transfer property, sell property, or file suit. On the plus side, she was no longer responsible for the debts she acquired before marriage or during marriage. All her rights and liabilities now belonged to her husband.[32]

The system had lent itself not only to endless debate over whether it was "divinely inspired" but also to two very different hard-luck stories. Reformers, on the one hand, liked to dredge up the sad tale of a rich widow with grown children who married a wastrel who frittered away the widow's hard-earned wealth on one harebrained venture after another. In the end, the woman and her heirs were left with nothing, and there was nothing they could do about it. The traditionalists, in turn, preferred the story of a poor widow who was being hounded by creditors and was but one step away from the poorhouse. Upon her marriage, her assets went to her husband, but so, too, did her debts, and her new husband, like any good patriarch, kept her creditors at bay and paid off the debts, and she lived happily ever after.

As time passed, men and women who wanted to change the old system gained momentum. The long depression that began with the Panic of 1837 gave them more horror stories to tell. Wealthy New Yorkers, moreover, increasingly took steps to get around the law, setting up trusts whereby only some of a beloved daughter's property fell into the hands of her husband. The various reform movements of the period—especially temperance and antislavery—provided many women with the training to agitate for change. The high point for the reformers probably came at the famous July 1848 women's rights convention at Seneca Falls, a gathering of some two hundred women and forty men at which one speaker after another called for a Married Women's Property Act.

But passing such an act would have been all but impossible had Jacksonian Democrats continued to dominate the New York state legislature. While some reformers were Jacksonian Democrats, the most notable being Thomas Herttell of New York City, the vast majority were Whigs. Only the Whigs were likely to put such a measure through. The election of 1848 made that possible. It split the old Van Buren coalition, with some Democrats running as Free-Soilers and others as "regular" Democrats, and as a result the Whigs gained an overwhelming majority in the legislature. The upshot was "an act for the more effectual protection of the property of married women." The act, passed in 1848 and amended in 1849, gave a married woman the same property rights she would have had if she had remained single.

Taking his cue from his fellow Whigs in New York, William Shannon moved to include such a provision in the California Constitution. It stated: "All property, both real and personal, of the wife, owned or claimed by her before marriage, and that acquired afterwards by gift, devise, or descent, shall be her separate property, and laws shall be passed more clearly defining the rights of the wife, in relation as well to her separate property as that held in common with her husband."

The delegates, by and large, thought this was a splendid idea. One delegate, to be sure, vehemently opposed the measure, and another wanted it to be left up to the state legislature. But such grumbling had little impact. Henry Tefft, a fellow New Yorker, said the provision was necessary to stop the husband from squandering the wife's money in California's helter-skelter speculative economy. Another New Yorker, thirty-four-year-old Kimball Dimmick, pointed out that such a law might be revolutionary back east but it was hardly revolutionary in California. For under Mexican law, the wife already owned her own property. More persuasive yet was Henry Wager Halleck, a thirty-four-year-old West Point graduate who later became famous as a Civil War general. As a bachelor, he advised all bachelors to vote for the motion, as it would induce rich women to come to California.[33]

That was the clincher. Anxious to attract women to California, the delegates endorsed the proposal by a voice vote. The state legislature then went a step further and placed the state under the Spanish law of "community property," whereby a wife jointly owns everything she and her husband acquire during marriage.

Shannon's other victory came in the debate over California's boundary. The debate was by far the most animated of the convention. It also raised the ugliest suspicions.

First, a committee decided that Mexican California, which consisted of nearly 450,000 square miles, was too vast for one state. It recommended a more manageable state with the eastern boundary at the 116th longitude line, roughly the eastern boundary of today's Nevada. As soon as this proposal reached the convention floor, debate heated up. William Gwin then reminded the delegates that they were supposed to write a constitution for "all" of California. He argued that the eastern boundary should follow the map of Charles Preuss, Frémont's cartographer, which would place it in the Rockies near the 112th degree line. Joining Gwin was Henry Halleck, who suggested that the delegates might also add a proviso authorizing Congress, if it so wished, to strip away the land east of the Sierras.[34]

Both men pushed for a big California on the grounds that in one dramatic stroke the delegates could resolve the slavery question that had so paralyzed Congress. When Halleck made this argument, Charles Tyler Botts, a forty-year-old Virginian, had trouble restraining himself. Did Halleck, asked Botts, think Southern men in Congress were asleep? Why not settle the slavery question by extending the boundary to the Mississippi River? Why not include Cuba, "a future

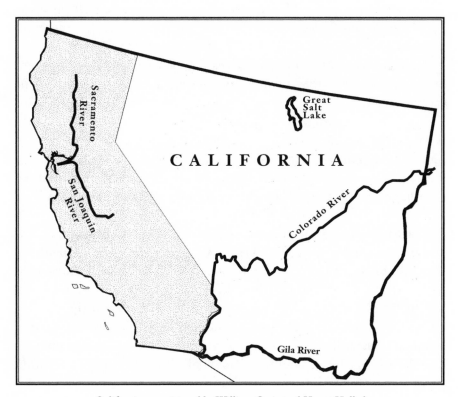

California as envisioned by William Gwin and Henry Halleck

acquisition"? Yes, slavery was a great evil, and for that reason he wanted it excluded from California. But trying to do Congress's job, trying to resolve the slavery question nationally, that was absurd and might cost California statehood.[35]

Gwin and Halleck also pushed for a big California on the grounds that in the long run, a larger domain would result in more power for the Pacific coast. Everyone knew that Texas had been admitted to the Union with the right to divide into five states. Why not the same for California? Said Gwin: "So far as I am concerned, I should like to see six states, fronting on the Pacific in California. I want the additional power in Congress . . . of twelve Senators instead of four; for it is notorious, sir, that the State of Delaware, smaller than our smallest district, has as much power in the Senate as the great State of New York . . . I want the power and the population."[36]

On September 24, during an evening meeting when only half the delegates were present, Gwin moved to substitute the Gwin-Halleck proposal for the one submitted by the boundary committee. He had the votes and won easily, 19 to 4. The maneuver, however, bred distrust. What was Gwin up to? Halleck could be dismissed as a well-meaning neophyte. No one thought that about Gwin. He was clearly a seasoned political veteran.

John McDougal, a thirty-two-year-old Ohioan, said what others believed. He accused Gwin and some of his slaveholding associates of trying to add a poison pill to the final document. Said McDougal: "They want a constitution presented to Congress so objectionable that it will be thrown back on us for another convention, it leaves them the opportunity of bringing their slaves here. It is what they desire to do, to create some strongly objectionable feature in the constitution in order that they may bring their slaves here and work them three months."[37]

Was this true? One of Gwin's admirers, James McHall Jones of Louisiana, dismissed the charge as poppycock. He had heard the same argument during a convention break. A "gentleman," he said, had told him that Gwin had orchestrated the extended boundary controversy to hamstring Congress and thus delay California's admission to the Union "for some two or three years, and thereby give to the south a chance . . . to bring in their slaves." The charge was "not worthy of con-sideration," said Jones. Everyone knew, moreover, that Gwin wanted to become a U.S. senator, and this would delay that goal by two or three years.[38]

Once the Gwin-Halleck proposal gained the upper hand, William Shannon stepped in. He offered an amendment to make the eastern border of California the Sierra Nevada. In his corner were several men who had come to California by wagon train or by foot. They pointed out that the Sierra Nevada range formed a "great natural boundary." They also brought up the "Mormon question." They had been through Salt Lake. They had seen "with their own eyes" that the Mormons marched to a different drummer. Did the delegates actually think that they could impose statehood on twenty thousand Mormons without their consent? That would violate republican principles. It would also surely lead to trouble. Finally, they joined others in arguing that an extended boundary, far from settling the slavery question, would only further inflame congressional debate and deny California statehood.

That was decisive. In the end, Shannon's motion prevailed. The final vote, recommending the Sierras, was 32 to 7.

In their effort to keep slavery out of California, Shannon and his fellow delegates championed the rights of labor. They had no choice. The state they hoped to create was now packed with miners and potential miners. In the Sierras, some forty thousand men now spent each and every day panning gold. In San Francisco, boatloads of gold seekers hoped to join them. Without question, the vast majority of these men did not want to compete with slave labor. Nor did they want to compete with peon labor or contract labor. But what about with wage labor? Men who worked for corporations?

On that question, too, there was little room for doubt. In the diggings, noted the miner Samuel Upham, labor was king. There were "no chartered institutions" that "monopolized the great avenues of wealth." They weren't tolerated. Instead, everyone had "an equal chance to rise." Hard manual labor was not only respected. It was esteemed, so much so that to have any standing in the community, a man had to work his own claim with his own hands. "Neither business nor capital," concluded Upham, "can oppress labor in California."[39]

This attitude, moreover, was reflected in mining "law." Since there were no established cities and towns in the Sierras, placer camps invariably found that they had to form their own rules and regulations. Some five hundred camps did so. Technically, these codes had no legal standing, but in fact they were the law of the land. The codes varied. Should a jury consist of six men, twelve men, or twenty men? There was no agreement. Two elements, however, were central to all of the codes. To have mineral rights, the man who "discovered" or "claimed" an area had to mark it and record the location. To retain these rights, he had to work the claim steadily, as many as twenty days a month in some camps. Most codes also limited the claim to what one man could mine alone, initially 100 to 150 square feet. The goal everywhere was to prevent absentee ownership and monopoly of mining claims.[40]

Shannon and his fellow delegates also embraced this attitude. Not one spoke in behalf of corporations. The only issue was to what extent the constitution needed to protect Californians *against* corporations. And here the delegates made a decision that was quite radical. They rejected the usual legal principle whereby a stockholder's liability was limited to the value of his stock. They made a stockholder liable instead for his proportionate share of a corporation's entire indebtedness. If he owned 10 percent of the stock, he was liable for 10 percent of all damages. If he owned 20 percent, then 20 percent of the damages. And so on.

Wouldn't that make it much harder for corporations to attract investors? Yes, and that clearly was the intention. On this issue, moreover, there was complete accord.[41] The only serious debate occurred over banks and paper money. Some delegates wanted to outlaw anything that even looked like a bank. Others wanted to permit "associations . . . for the deposit of gold and silver." The convention finally decided on the latter, while prohibiting bank corporations altogether.[42]

Were the delegates, seventeen of whom were lawyers, sincere in their hostility toward banks and corporations? William Gwin, for one, never doubted their sincerity. Years later, he recalled how he finally gained the trust of his fellow delegates. At first, only one out of five trusted him. Most of the rest assumed that he had a pro-slavery agenda, that he wanted "to resist the insertion" of an antislavery clause in the bill of rights, and that he called for large boundaries so that California might be divided into several slave states. The turning point, wrote Gwin, came when he took a stand against corporations and state debts, when he argued that the legislature should be restricted in its powers to create corporations and to charter banks and that state debts should not exceed $300,000. Only then did his detractors realize that he, too, wanted to keep California a haven for the workingman.[43]

Nonetheless, the corporations soon came. Within months of the state constitutional convention, the nature of mining in California began to change radically. Today, all the towns along Route 49, the road that takes thousands of tourists each year through the gold country, tell much the same story. They all sell replicas of a grizzly old miner panning gold. They all sell books detailing the tools he used, the hard life he lived. They all pretend that he was the key to their existence. He was, wasn't he? Yes, but only for a very short time. By late 1849, as the men in Monterey were singing his praises, he was on the way out. Despite all the delegates' fine talk about keeping "capitalists out of the mines," the capitalists came, and they came in a rush.

They especially came quickly to the two richest gold rush towns, Grass Valley and Nevada City. The two lie cheek by jowl, just four miles apart. The former was established in the summer of 1849 by two groups of overlanders. Following the Truckee route down the Sierras to Sacramento, the weary travelers stopped at the twenty-five-hundred-foot elevation to graze their animals in a small valley watered by Wolf Creek and known for its waist-tall grass. It was a beautiful place. To the east were tall pines, to the west oak trees. The animals for the first time in days were content. While they grazed, some of the men searched the gullies and streambeds. Discovering paying placers, they decided to stay. One of the two groups, men from Boston, later established a permanent camp of canvas shanties and log huts that they named Boston Ravine. That name eventually gave way to Grass Valley.[44]

Grass Valley was soon overshadowed by its northeastern neighbor, Nevada City. Rich placers were discovered there in the fall of 1849 by prospectors working their way up Deer Creek. These were "pound diggings," places where a man could get twelve troy ounces of gold per day. The word spread, and a thousand men arrived before winter. Thousands more came in the spring. Up the hill from Little Deer Creek, A. B. Caldwell set up a store in a square tent. People called the place Caldwell's Upper Store and the locality Deer Creek Dry Diggings. Later, another storekeeper, O. P. Blackman, proposed that the camp be given the permanent name of Nevada.[45]

Both Grass Valley and Nevada City began as placer camps, where individuals and small companies washed "loose" gold from riverbanks, streams, gulches, and sandbars. There were over five hundred such camps in the Sierras. The technology was simple. Placer miners relied mainly on moving water and the heaviness of gold, which caused it to settle to the bottom of whatever recovery device they used. Three devices were common. The simplest and best known was the pan. More complicated was a rocker, a wooden box with riffles on the bottom that was rocked back and forth. More sophisticated yet was a sluice, a long wooden box with cleats on the bottom that was placed in a running stream.

Sketch of a placer miner's equipment: a rocker, a pan, and a boring tool. Drawn by an early miner. Reprinted from W. R. Ryan, Personal Adventures in Upper and Lower California in 1848–9, 2 vols. *(London, 1852).*

Panning was hard work. The miner first shoveled pay dirt into a pan, preferably one that had a flat bottom and tapered sides, about three inches deep and eighteen inches in diameter. Then he submerged the pan into water, rocked it back and forth to get a whirlpool effect, and allowed the lighter dirt, sand, and gravel to wash over the lip until only the heavier gold was left. The process took some time to master, and fifty pans were considered a good day's work. Collis P. Huntington, who later became a railroad tycoon, lasted just half a day. He decided that spending all day squatting with his hands in icy mountain water was not for him. Selling shovels was a much easier way to make a living.

Placer mining became the most celebrated, the one that still gets the most attention in picture books. But its heyday didn't last long. In Nevada City and Grass Valley, entrepreneurs pooled their resources and formed seventeen mining corporations in 1851 and another sixteen in 1852. One outfit, the Manhattan Quartz Mining Company, listed none other than Horace Greeley, the editor of the *New-York Tribune*, as its secretary and treasurer. It was the proud owner of sixty-four mining claims and promised all investors "a golden harvest." Four of its trustees were also trustees of a larger company, the Grass Valley Gold Mining

Company, which was capitalized at $250,000. It held more than four hundred mining claims. Gone were the days of one claim per miner.[46]

Why the sudden change? Individual miners in both camps soon discovered that the number of gold seekers far exceeded the number of pound diggings and that pound diggings played out quickly. In Nevada City, that happened within a year. As the easy gold gave way, men spent more time looking for the source of placer gold. In doing so, they found veins of gold embedded in hard rock and in gravel ridges. In 1850, miners began sinking holes, which reminded some of coyote holes and came to be known as coyote diggings. One whole section of town soon got a new name, Coyoteville.

If the veins were near the surface, an individual miner could still handle it by himself. All he needed was a pick and shovel. But deep veins required more sophisticated and expensive equipment, more than one man could afford or handle. Open-pit mining, for example, necessitated steam shovels. More expensive yet was hard-rock mining. Perfected in Cornwall, England, and elsewhere, it necessitated digging shafts, drilling holes for blasting, blasting with black powder, mucking the loosened rock into ore cars that were transported by mules to the main shaft, then loading it into ore skips that were hoisted out of the mine, then crushing it at the stamp mill into sand-sized particles, and then chemically processing the particles.

To get at embedded gold, some miners got together with their neighbors, formed partnerships and joint-stock associations, and sometimes sought outside money. One such miner was Anthony Chabot. A thirty-six-year-old native of Quebec, he had a claim on Buckeye Hill, a ridge just above Nevada City, that he had staked out in 1849. On it he found gold impregnated in gravel. For nearly two years, he spent most of every day shoveling gravel into a sluice, cursing the hard work, and daydreaming of an easier way to get at the gold. In April 1852, he thought he had the answer. He fashioned a canvas hose to wash the gravel into his sluice. The next year Chabot joined forces with Edward Matteson and Eli Miller to construct a larger canvas hose. Then Miller, once a tinsmith by trade, made a tapered nozzle of sheet iron and attached it to the hose. Now the force of the water was sufficient to break up gravel banks. Chabot and his partners could now do in a matter of hours what previously took weeks to do with picks and shovels.[47]

Thus hydraulic mining sprang to life on the ridges above Nevada City. The new system immediately attracted attention. Could it be used elsewhere—on all the high gravel ridges above the American, the Bear, the Feather, and the Yuba rivers? Many thought so. To raise the needed capital, miners consolidated their claims and formed stock companies. The new companies quickly developed bigger and more powerful hoses, ones that dispatched huge jets of water that could kill a man two hundred feet away. Thousands of yards of gravel could now be easily removed. Hydraulicking ravaged the countryside. Soon every claim in Coyoteville belonged to one hydraulic company, and the entire village was literally washed away.

Supplying water year-round for these powerful hoses, however, proved to be a problem. Water was plentiful in the spring, just after the snows melted, but by fall often little more than a trickle. Only in 1856 was there enough river water to keep the hoses working to maximum capacity all year long. To the rescue came bigger companies with more capital. They constructed mountain reservoirs and dug hundred-mile ditch systems. They, in turn, dictated terms to the hydraulickers. Most of the ditch companies overbuilt and fell prey to still bigger companies with more capital. Soon two giant water companies dominated the

Hydraulic mining. Courtesy of The Bancroft Library.

entire region. One, the South Yuba Water Company, was owned locally. The owners of the other, the Eureka Lake and Yuba Canal Company, lived in New York.[48]

By 1860, then, hydraulic mining was strictly big business, with a handful of owners and hundreds of wage laborers. The busiest region was between the middle and the south forks of the Yuba River. Over 684 million yards of gravel were mined in the Yuba watershed, 100 million along the upper Feather, 254 million on the Bear, and 257 million along the American. By 1860, everyone realized that hydraulic mining was destroying the landscape, but little was done to stop it. Twenty years later, it was banned. By then, it had yielded over $100 million in gold, or one-third of the total gold produced.[49]

Meanwhile, in Grass Valley a more capital-intensive form of mining developed. In June 1850, when the town consisted of no more than twenty cabins, several placer miners stumbled upon gold embedded in quartz veins in the hills above Wolf Creek. This find drew the attention of hundreds of prospectors, who with just pick and shovel dislodged some gold. Then, that October, George D. Roberts discovered on Ophir Hill, one mile southeast of Grass Valley, what proved to be an extremely rich vein. He established a claim, thirty by forty feet. In 1851 he sold it for $350 to Woodbury, Park and Company.

The new owners immediately recognized that to mine the quartz and then free the gold from the quartz was a complex, capital-intensive activity. It necessitated copying the methods that had been developed in the hard-rock mines of Cornwall. That meant digging shafts, hoisting rock out of the mine, then crushing it at a stamp mill into sand-sized particles, and then chemically processing the particles. Lacking the necessary capital, Woodbury, Park and Company joined forces with the owners of several nearby claims and formed the Ophir Hill Mine, constructed a six-stamp mill on Wolf Creek, and introduced the Cornish pump to remove water from the shafts.

Unfortunately, the new combination also lacked sufficient capital to cover all the start-up costs. Soon all the partners were in financial trouble, and in 1852 all their holdings were auctioned off. Half went to John P. Rush, half to ten local miners who called themselves the Empire Quartz Mining Company. In 1854, the latter group bought out Rush for $12,000 and formed the Empire Mining Company. By now the main shaft was down 102 feet, and the mine had yielded over $900,000.

By the following year, the Empire Mine had forty employees, thirty-four working belowground.

So began the Empire Mine, one of the more profitable undertakings in the Sierras. With several more changes in ownership, the small thirty-by-forty-foot claim that George Roberts established in 1850 was mined until 1956, producing an estimated 5.8 million ounces of gold from 367 miles of underground tunnels.[50]

The Empire Mine was just one of the major quartz mines that developed in Grass Valley in the early 1850s. The town soon had seven or eight corporations digging deep shafts. Most encountered the same start-up problems as Woodbury, Park and Company. Only a few were major moneymakers from the outset.

Especially lucky were several Irishmen. After spending two years working a placer on Wolf Creek three miles below town, they discovered a quartz lead. Realizing that they knew nothing about hard-rock mining, they tried to sell it for $1,000. They couldn't find a buyer. So

Stamp press, Helvetia quartz mine, Grass Valley. Reprinted from Harper's New Monthly Magazine *20 (April 1860), 608. Used to crush quartz into small particles so that the gold could be removed, stamp presses made an incredible racket. The constant pounding of such presses could be heard miles away.*

they hired a fellow countryman, Con Riley, to run the operation. He proved to be exceptionally able, and they got exceptionally rich. They called the mine Allison Ranch. It remained an Irish operation from top to bottom. The owners were Irish, the top managers were Irish, and nearly all the workers were Irish. Thanks largely to Allison Ranch, about 25 percent of all the miners in Grass Valley by 1860 were Irish.[51]

That did not, however, become the norm in Grass Valley. Most of the other hard-rock mines started looking to the tin, lead, and copper mines of Cornwall for their skilled labor force. Facing hard times at home, many Cornish miners were more than willing to leave England for California. The Cornish were also widely regarded as the most skillful hard-rock miners in the world. They knew how to construct deep shafts. They also knew how to set charges that were effective but didn't endanger the entire mine. They had skills, in short, that few American miners had. As the mines became deeper and more complex, the need for their skills skyrocketed. Mine owners thus increasingly looked to Cornwall, and Cornishmen came, first by the hundreds, then by the thousands, and soon became the dominant ethnic group in Grass Valley, making up about 20 percent of the mine workers by 1860, over 60 percent by 1870. They came with few illusions, usually after higher wages, not dreams of quick fortunes.[52]

As the mines became the workplace of wage workers, mainly Cornish, Irish, and some Chinese, the profits increasingly went to absentee owners. Locals enriched by quartz left town, usually for San Francisco, sometimes New York, occasionally Paris, and soon only a few townsmen owned shares in the mines. On June 11, 1858, the *Sacramento Daily Union* proclaimed that in just ten years a "complete revolution" had taken place "in the methods and means applied to mining." The old order of the independent miner was long dead, said the *Union*. No longer did mine owners mine for themselves. They were now all "men of means who . . . employed others to mine for them."

The big mines also had a worldwide impact. Thanks mainly to their production, the world's gold supply shot up by six or seven times. More gold was extracted between 1848 and 1858, mainly in California and Australia, than the world had produced in the previous 150 years. And because Californians imported nearly everything they needed and paid up to ten times East Coast prices, the gold made its way onto the world market. That, in turn, had enormous consequences for the world economy. It alone may have reversed the global deflation of the previous three decades. It certainly impacted the minting of coins, which also increased by six or seven times. It also allowed gold to replace silver as the standard metal for world currencies.[53]

William Shannon didn't live long enough to see it happen. A month before the convention, he had been elected judge of the Criminal Court of First Instance. So on completing his work in Monterey, he returned to Coloma, sold his store, and moved to Sacramento to take over his judicial duties. There he also practiced law and was active in the formation of the Whig Party. On October 7, 1850, he was elected to the state senate. He never served. That fall, cholera swept through Sacramento, killing 448 people. Shannon tried to help. He tended the sick. On Sunday, November 3, at 9:00 a.m., he experienced cramps and vomiting. Twelve hours later, at 9:00 that night, he died. He died knowing, however, that the constitution he helped write was now the law of the land.[54]

4

---◆---

UPON COMPLETING THE CONSTITUTION, SHANNON AND THE other forty-seven delegates submitted their handiwork to General Riley. Without bothering to get congressional approval, Riley then called for an election, on November 13, 1849, to ratify the document and elect state officials.

The vote was light. Out of an estimated 107,000 people, nearly all of whom were males of voting age, only about 13,000 bothered to vote.[1] The low turnout raised fears among newsmen that Congress would underestimate the population of California—and not admit it into the Union and not let it have two House members. On the plus side, the constitution passed easily, 12,061 in favor, 811 against. The dissenters included 66 voters in Mariposa County, who called for a constitution with no restrictions on slavery, and several hundred voters in southern California, who wanted California to become a territory rather than a state.[2]

On the same day, the voters also elected two members to the House of Representatives. The victors were Edward Gilbert, the editor of the *Alta California*, and George Washington Wright, a onetime Boston merchant. Wright ran as an independent, Gilbert as a Democrat with the backing of David Broderick's emerging machine. Only in San Francisco did party organization matter. Thanks to Broderick and other organizers, the Democrats carried the town easily, winning two seats in the state senate, five in the assembly. They pretended to be neutral, but they didn't fool Mary Jane Megquier, a newcomer from Maine, who noted that they made "very sure not to have a whig nominated to fill any office."[3]

The Whig they most wanted to defeat was T. Butler King, the five-term Georgia congressman whom Zachary Taylor had sent to California to encourage statehood. A Massachusetts native, the forty-nine-year-old King had moved to Georgia when he was twenty-three, married well, and assumed control of a large plantation on St. Simons Island. By the time he was thirty-five, he owned 355 slaves. Politically, he had become a big supporter of cotton interests and commercial expansion. First a Democrat, then a Henry Clay Whig, he had chaired the House Committee on Naval Affairs. He had hoped to become Zachary Taylor's secretary of the navy, but that hope had been dashed by his Georgia rivals—Alexander Stephens and Robert Toombs.[4]

With his political future in Georgia looking dim, King now had his sights on becoming a U.S. senator from the new state of California. To accomplish that, he had to win the support of the newly elected state legislature. Thanks to the Democrats of San Francisco, at least seven legislators were certain to vote against him. King had also been to the diggings hustling for votes. He hadn't done well. By wearing dress clothes and traveling during the heat of the day, he had convinced many a miner that he was a foolhardy aristocrat. To make matters worse, he had an enemy in Edward Gilbert, the editor of California's most influential newspaper. The *Alta California* made much of the poor turnouts at King's rallies, and even belittled him on the grounds that he was a newcomer to California.[5]

In contrast, William Gwin, who arrived in California on the same ship as King, had fared better in the mining districts. Noting that half the legislature would be from the mines, Gwin had campaigned hard in the Sierras. He purposely had toured the mines with a bunch of hard drinkers, including his handpicked candidate for lieutenant governor, John McDougal, who was widely regarded as "the buffoon of the convention," a man who could not speak unless he was drunk.[6] Gwin had also struck a note of rough camaraderie with the miners. According to one observer, on coming into a bar, Gwin said: "I did not come to dig for gold but to represent you in the United States Senate. Come on up to the bar and have a drink." As a result, Gwin had gained the support of many legislators from the Sacramento and San Joaquin districts.[7]

Neither Gwin nor King had corralled enough votes, however, before the newly elected legislature assembled at the state's first capital, Pueblo de San José, on December 15. So both men had their supporters establish an open house, which they called a ranch, to provide the legislators with free drinks. They weren't the only ones to do so. All their rivals did the same thing. The lawmakers made the most of it, earning the appellation "legislature of a thousand drinks" from none other than Thomas Jefferson Green, who after being driven off the Yuba had moved to Sacramento and won a seat in the state senate.[8]

On Thursday, December 20, the key vote was held. The process was for each member of the two houses to voice vote for two candidates. The first choice of many was John C. Frémont. He hadn't campaigned in the mining districts. He didn't have to. No one could match his status as a western hero. Nor could anyone cope with the widespread disdain miners had for his court-martial.[9] Frémont won easily on the first ballot, polling twenty-nine out of a possible forty-one votes. Gwin and King, in contrast, fell short. On the second ballot, Gwin was still short, while King faded. On the third ballot, Gwin polled twenty-four votes and was declared the winner.

Backing Gwin was a coalition of fifteen Southern-born politicians who came to be known as the Chivalry faction in the California Democratic Party. A handful of Chivs, like Gwin, still owned slaves back in their home states. A few, like Thomas Jefferson Green, undoubtedly hoped that California—or at least the southern half of California— might someday be open to slavery. That was not Gwin's position, however. Not only did he verbally endorse the proposal to outlaw slavery in California; he got all the Chiv politicians to stand with him.[10]

Also among those who voted for Gwin was Elisha Crosby. A genuine antislavery man and a fellow delegate at the Monterey convention, Crosby didn't trust Gwin. But he thought that California needed a major slaveholder to get its constitution through Congress. For a while, he had toyed with the idea of supporting King. But he had concluded that King was a lightweight, too much of a "high toned Southern gentleman," incapable of handling the "rough life," and also probably incapable of gaining statehood for California. Gwin, in contrast, was the kind of "extreme southern man" that might get the job done. Not only was he "a most persevering and persistent man"; he was "bound and determined to get into the Senate." He also probably had "a good deal of influence" with the Southerners who dominated Congress. Crosby, however, prayed that Gwin would get the shorter of the two Senate terms so that "he would be there only a few months and we could then send someone else."[11]

To Crosby's dismay, that didn't happen. After the election, the two winning candidates drew straws to see who would get the longer of the two terms. John C. Frémont wound up with the short term that ended in March 1851, and the Mississippi slave owner William McKendree Gwin got the full six-year term. A week later, on January 1, 1850, the newly elected senators and congressmen boarded the steamship *Oregon*, which also carried $3 million in gold, and set off for Washington. With them, they brought the California Constitution.

By the time the California delegation set sail, the Thirty-first Congress had been in session for nearly a month. It had been a miserable month in Washington. On opening day, December 3, the nation's lawmakers had been pelted with sleet and freezing rain as they made their way to the Capitol. Little had gone right since.

The members of the lower house had found that their meeting hall had been redecorated with a new carpet and drapes. It looked splendid. The hall, however, was still an acoustical disaster, with sounds bouncing off the domed ceiling and walls, echoing back and forth, so that no one except the Speaker could hear exactly what a member was saying. In this echo chamber, 229 men from thirty states had been sworn in. Ninety were from the slave states, 139 from the free states. They were a wretched collection of men, according to thirty-nine-year-old Robert Toombs of Georgia, who was beginning his third term in the House. "The present Congress," wrote Toombs, "furnishes the worst specimens of legislators I have ever seen here, especially from the North on both sides. There is a large infusion of successful jobbers, lucky serving-men, parishless parsons and itinerant lecturers among them who are not only without wisdom or knowledge but have bad manners, and therefore we can have little hope of good legislation."[12]

To make matters worse, neither major party had a majority. The membership consisted of 111 Democrats, 105 Whigs, and 13 Free-Soilers. Only the Free-Soilers were united. The major parties, especially the Whigs, were split along North-South lines. Who would be the Speaker? Howell Cobb of Georgia was the choice of most Democrats, Robert C. Winthrop of Massachusetts of most Whigs. Both parties, however, had dissidents who wouldn't support the choice of their party.

After three days of caucusing, Cobb reported that "the slavery question" had "so completely alienated north from south" that it was "utterly impossible" to achieve party unity. The situation had gotten so bad that many of his "warmest friends from the north" had told him they could never vote for him again because "the threats and menaces of southern men" would be reported in their home districts and "destroy their position at home."[13] How, then, was the House to organize itself?

As that battle brewed, so did the issue of California statehood. On December 13, Richard K. Meade, a forty-six-year-old Virginia Democrat, rose to speak. The House members knew what to expect. Not only had they heard from Meade many times before, but he had provided each one of them with a copy of a fiery speech that he had given to his constituents the previous summer.[14]

Meade was a pro-slavery zealot and proud of it. He also typified his peers in one key respect. From his frequent remarks on the California question, no one would have realized that non-slaveholding Southerners were going west by the thousands, that they were clearly welcome in the Sierras, and that a few had even found pound diggings. What concerned Meade, as well as most of his peers, was the slaveholding South, the white minority that owned slaves, and especially the tiny fraction that owned half the South's slave population. They needed room to expand, contended Meade. Cooping up slaves on worn-out land was dangerous. It was certain to generate race war in the long run.

What made matters worse, argued Meade, was that California was ideal for slavery and the owners of the South's black population were being cheated out of it. "But for the fear of robbery under the forms of law, there would be at least 50,000 slaves in California by the first of December. It is the best field for such labor now in America, and it would be invaluable to us as a means of thinning the black population. When people say that the climate and productions are unsuited to slave labor, they are either endeavoring to deceive or are deceived themselves."[15] Not only was exclusion of slaveholders unfair, said Meade. It also endangered the white South. "My race and my country are threatened . . . we are even now engaged in a death struggle. . . . The war against our institutions has been declared. . . . We must retain the power of self-protection, or we must finally yield. What will give us this power? Space-empire. . . . I say, then, to the South, stretch your arm to the Pacific; let no enemy flank or take post in your rear. . . . To effect this you have only to demand half your rights—half justice. To the Pacific, then, I say—to the Pacific. Your future security depends entirely upon your strength; secure to yourselves while you can, an empire."[16]

On December 13, when Meade rose to speak, House members anticipated more of the same, another fiery speech like the ones he had given to his constituents. That didn't happen. Instead, Meade merely asserted that the California question threatened to "destroy this confederacy." His words, however, nearly triggered a donnybrook. First Joseph M. Root, an Ohio Whig, ridiculed Meade. Then others rushed to Meade's defense. Tempers flared. Speeches became hotter. Then William Duer, a New York Whig, called Meade a disunionist. Meade denied it. Duer then called him a liar. Meade charged toward Duer. Colleagues yelled, "Shoot him! Shoot him!" "Where is your bowie knife?" Finally the sergeant at arms, Nathan Sargent, stepped in. Waving a mace over his head, he forced the belligerents back into their seats and restored order.[17]

Robert Toombs, who had made a fortune in Georgia slaves and real estate, then took the floor. Widely regarded as a man of superior intelligence, yet erratic, the tall, broad-shouldered Georgian issued a warning: "I do not . . . hesitate to avow before this house and the country, and in the presence of the living God, that if by your legislation you seek to drive us from the territories of California and New Mexico, purchased by the common blood and treasure of the whole people, and to abolish slavery in this District, thereby attempting to fix a national degradation upon half the States of this Confederacy, *I am for disunion.*"[18]

This outburst even shocked Toombs's closest friend, thirty-seven-year-old Alexander Stephens, who was beginning his fourth full term in the House. Physically, Stephens was everything Toombs was not—small, sickly, and barely eighty pounds. But usually Stephens knew what to anticipate from his burly and overbearing friend. Never, said Stephens, had he "expected to live to see the day, when, upon this floor, he should be called upon to discuss the question of the union of these States."[19]

· · ·

With members threatening disunion, screaming and shouting at one another, and carrying bowie knives and revolvers, organizing the House became a major ordeal. It thus took three weeks and sixty-three ballots to elect Howell Cobb Speaker, twenty-one ballots to elect a clerk, three ballots to elect a chaplain, and eight ballots to elect a sergeant at arms. Among the losers was the mace-wielding Nathan Sargent of Vermont. The members stripped him of his office as sergeant at arms and gave it to Adam J. Glossbrenner of Pennsylvania.

The turmoil amused Joshua Giddings, an antislavery Whig from northern Ohio.[20] Others, however, thought the country was about to fall apart. Among them was seventy-two-year-old Henry Clay, the silver-tongued orator from Kentucky, who had watched the Meade debate with alarm. Clay had first come to Congress in 1806. He had served as Speaker of the House longer than any other man. He had run for president three times, losing twice by substantial margins, once by a whisker. Although a major slaveholder, he looked forward to the day when Kentucky, and perhaps the Deep South, would rid itself of both slavery and free blacks. In the 1844 presidential campaign, he had even referred to slavery as a "temporary institution."[21]

Now, as the senior senator from Kentucky, Clay tried to rally the forces of moderation and restraint. By January 21, he had a package of proposals. That evening he drove to the Washington home of Daniel Webster, his longtime rival as leader of the Whig Party, and got the Massachusetts leader's tentative support. He then scheduled an appearance before the Senate on January 29. On the appointed day, every seat in the Senate gallery was taken long before Clay arrived.

To the packed house, the "Great Pacificator" presented his solution to the nation's crisis. It consisted of eight resolutions. Looked at "together, in combination," said Clay, "they propose an amicable arrangement of all questions in controversy between the free and the slave States, growing out of the subject of slavery." For the North, Clay proposed outlawing the buying and selling of slaves in the District of Columbia. For the South, he would guarantee the right to hold slaves in the District and also enact a stronger law to secure the return of runaway slaves. For the North, he would admit California as a free state. For the South, he would organize the New Mexico and Utah territories without any restrictions on slavery.

The package also dealt with the Texas problem. Already the biggest state, and a slave state, Texas wanted to be a still bigger slave state. It

Henry Clay, the "Great Pacificator," addressing the Senate. From a steel engraving by John M. Butler and Alfred Long, 1854. Library of Congress.

claimed roughly half of present-day New Mexico, all the land east of the Rio Grande. It had done so for years, but had not enforced the claim. For all practical purposes, the land had been in the hands of the federal government and considered free for some time. That the land should now be Texan and slave infuriated Northerners, especially Northern Whigs who regarded the Mexican War as mainly a landgrab in behalf of aggressive slaveholders. The Texans also had another desire, however. They wanted to be rid of the heavy debts that Texas had contracted before becoming part of the United States in 1845. So, as a solution, Clay proposed that Texas relinquish its claim to New Mexico territory in exchange for the federal government's assuming Texas's debts.

In laying out his eight resolutions, Clay dazzled his audience. He began slowly, gained steam, and soon was at his silver-tongued best. He oozed charm. His voice was melodious. He was dramatic. He even held up a fragment from George Washington's coffin that had been given to him a few days before and said he saw it as a "warning voice coming from the grave to the Congress now in session to beware, to pause, to reflect before they lend themselves to any purposes which shall destroy that Union which was cemented by his exertions and example."[22]

Despite Clay's brilliance, his plea for harmony didn't work. Southerners were still furious. They still complained bitterly that the admission of California as a free state would cost the South equal representation in the Senate. And what about New Mexico? Clay's proposal to make it a territory with no restrictions on slavery was meaningless. It could still follow California's example and ask to be admitted as a free state. That clearly was what Zachary Taylor wanted. And that, said one Deep South senator after another, would make a bad situation worse. With California, the fifteen slave states would be outnumbered by sixteen free states, with New Mexico, by seventeen.

Such, then, was the situation when the California delegation arrived in Washington. Could William Gwin, an "extreme southern man," overcome Southern opposition?

Gwin gave it his best effort. He shepherded California's two aspiring House members around the city and systematically courted his old Southern friends. Most were gracious. But his mentor Calhoun, sick and dying, reproached him for his role in writing the California Constitution and told him that the admission of California as a free state would destroy the equilibrium between the North and the South in the Senate. Gwin responded that he had done what was necessary to gain a Senate seat.

What, then, about Elisha Crosby's notion that Gwin, a Mississippi slave owner, might soften the hostility of men like Calhoun to California statehood? Was that just wishful thinking? In all likelihood, yes. Undoubtedly, Calhoun preferred Gwin over Frémont, the onetime South Carolinian who had become not only a free-soiler but also the son-in-law of Thomas Hart Benton, Calhoun's longtime enemy. But the California issue was just too big for one man to make much of a difference. At stake, as Calhoun and his followers saw it, was the social structure of the entire South. If slavery could be excluded from California, it could be excluded from all of the future states that were certain to follow. Gone would be Southern domination of the Senate. Gone, too, would be the chance of slavery to expand. Instead, it would be reduced to a static, confined, and dying institution. To stand by and watch, they thought, was suicidal.

The dying senator, moreover, had spent months preparing his troops for action. In January 1849, a full ten weeks before Gwin had set sail for California in pursuit of a Senate seat, Calhoun had gathered fourteen colleagues into a Southern political caucus to make sure that Congress imposed no bans on slavery within the land taken from Mexico. They soon had the full support of forty-six Southern Democrats and two Southern Whigs. They had been beaten repeatedly in the House, where Northern congressmen made up the vast majority, but in the Senate they had prevailed. That chamber, even though it was equally divided between slave- and free-state men, had been the bastion of Southern power. Would it continue to be so? Yes, if Calhoun and his colleagues had anything to say about it.

Calhoun had also orchestrated a Southern protest movement. At his urging, the South Carolina assembly had called for a Pan-Southern meeting but left it to Mississippi to choose a place and date. Calhoun had then contacted Colonel Collin S. Tarpley of Mississippi, who in turn circulated Calhoun's sentiments about the state, and in May 1849 a public meeting at Jackson recommended a statewide convention. To that meeting, Calhoun urged South Carolina governor Whitemarsh Seabrook to send a representative to get the support of Mississippi's governor. For that task, Seabrook dispatched South Carolina representative Daniel Wallace.

The meeting took place in October 1849, just as Gwin and the other delegates at the Monterey convention were putting the finishing touches on the California Constitution. Calling themselves the Mississippi States' Rights Convention, Tarpley and his associates endorsed Calhoun's common-property doctrine and threatened secession if slaveholders were barred from any of the territories taken from Mexico. They also called for a larger gathering, one of all the slave states, in Nashville the following June. Seven other Southern states soon began making arrangements to send delegates.[23]

Wallace, meanwhile, sought the support of Mississippi's governor. He worried about the outcome, but he actually had little to worry about. The incoming governor was John A. Quitman, who in many ways was even more radical than Calhoun. A New York native, the fifty-year-old Quitman had moved to Natchez, Mississippi, when he was twenty-two. He had arrived "penniless" but had risen quickly in Mississippi thanks to his athletic prowess, his flamboyance, and a favorable marriage, which provided him with both land and slaves. He eventually owned a mansion in Natchez, four plantations in Mississippi and Louisiana, and more than four hundred slaves.

Politically, Quitman was a warrior. Not only was he pro-slavery; he was belligerently so. And having won the governorship with 70 percent of the vote, he construed his election as a mandate to be even more aggressive. Within just a few months, he threw his support behind a plan to seize Cuba with a privately armed military force.[24]

On January 10, 1850, the new governor gave his inaugural address. Privately, he had toyed with the idea of relocating some of his own slaves to the Far West. He also claimed that some of his Natchez neighbors had the same inclinations. In his speech, he avoided such personal remarks but made it clear that California's stand on slavery, as well as Zachary Taylor's actions, had infuriated him. He accused Northerners of waging "war upon slavery," a "war of extermination" against the South's "most valued rights."

What, then, should the South's elected representatives do? "The South," said Quitman, "has long submitted to grievous wrongs. Dishonor, degradation, and ruin awaits her if she submits further. The people of Mississippi have taken their stand, and, I doubt not, their representatives will maintain it."[25]

News of California's stand on slavery, as well as Zachary Taylor's actions, had also enraged Mississippi's congressional delegation. All six had gone to Washington primed for battle when Congress convened in December. They were not about to help their former colleague William Gwin gain statehood for California.

On January 21, they contacted Quitman. They told him that they regarded "the proposition to admit California as a state . . . as an attempt to adopt the Wilmot proviso in another form." They asked Quitman for advice—and through him for advice from the state legislature. They obviously wanted the Mississippi legislature to endorse their position.[26] They expected no resistance from either Quitman or the legislature. The Democrats controlled both houses of the legislature by whopping majorities, and Democrats statewide had vociferously opposed Zachary Taylor's plan to admit California as a free state.

In a minority report, five prominent Whigs came out foursquare behind Zachary Taylor. They made it clear that they didn't regard the admission of California with its free-state constitution as the Wilmot

Proviso under another form. They also claimed to have the support of Whigs around the state. But the Whigs were a minority, a hopeless minority, and thus no help to Gwin.[27]

The Mississippi congressional delegation, meanwhile, continued to treat California statehood as just another version of the Wilmot Proviso. In doing so, they weren't alone. Several dozen Southern congressmen made the same claim. Especially forceful was Thomas Clingman, a thirty-seven-year-old non-slaveholding Whig from the hill country of North Carolina. Northerners, said Clingman, were obviously imposing the Wilmot Proviso by indirection. Indeed, had it not been for antislavery agitation, "southern slaveholders would have carried their negroes into the mines of California in such numbers . . . that the majority there would have made it a slaveholding State." The free-state alternative was so outrageous, said Clingman, that Southerners who would now "consent to be thus degraded and enslaved ought to be whipped through their fields by their own negroes."[28]

In echoing this argument, the Mississippi delegation was led by a man whom Gwin knew well. Four years earlier, he had been preferred over Gwin for a seat in the House of Representatives. He now held the position that Gwin had long coveted. That was Jefferson Davis, now a U.S. senator.

A native of Kentucky, the forty-one-year-old Davis had moved to Mississippi as a young child. The youngest of ten children, he had been greatly influenced by his oldest brother, Joseph, who established a flourishing plantation on bottomland next to the Mississippi River and had arranged young Jefferson's appointment to West Point. Tall and striking, with deep-set eyes and high cheekbones, Davis was outgoing but also haughty. He had been court-martialed twice, once at West Point for visiting an off-limits tavern, once later for insubordination. He had also been involved in a half-dozen near duels.[29]

In 1849–50, Davis was in an odd position, as he had once been the son-in-law of Zachary Taylor. He had married Taylor's daughter in 1835. She had died within months of their marriage of either malaria or yellow fever. He had married again in 1845. Socially, Davis and his former father-in-law maintained a cordial relationship. Politically, however, the two men rarely saw eye to eye. Unlike Taylor, Davis was a zealous expansionist and defender of slavery and Southern interests. Following Calhoun's common-property doctrine, Davis asserted that the territories belonged to all the states and that no decision could be made to exclude slavery from a territory. He also insisted that slave-holders must have an opportunity to see if slavery was suited to any new territory. As for California, he contended that slaves would do better in the mines than "any other species of labor."[30]

But Davis was also a realist. He expected California to gain state-hood even though he regarded its constitution as worthless. In his mind, the document had been written by "a few adventurers uniting with a herd as various in color and nearly as ignorant of our govern-ment, as Jacob's cattle." That such lowlifes might be allowed to "deprive the people of the South of equal participation in the common property of the States" irritated him even more than the Wilmot Proviso. Nonetheless, he expected the "plan of concealing the Wilmot Pro-viso under a so called state constitution" to succeed. The South simply lacked the votes to stop it. Not even the two Northern senators who could be counted on to support the South on other matters, Daniel S. Dickinson of New York and Daniel Sturgeon of Pennsylvania, would "vote against California as a state."[31]

Yet despite his pessimism, Davis led the battle against Clay's com-promise proposal. It enraged him. He wanted to destroy the eight reso-lutions the moment he heard them. He had trouble restraining himself. He insisted that Clay immediately defend his proposals. Clay refused. So on January 29, the day Clay presented his resolutions, Davis had to limit his protest to a few remarks. Nonetheless, he ripped into Clay's contention that the mines were unsuited for slave labor. "I do not accord," said Davis. "It was to work the gold mines on this continent that the Spaniards first brought Africans to the country. The European races now engaged in working the mines of California sink under the burning heat and sudden changes of the climate, to which the African race are altogether better adapted. The production of rice, sugar, and cotton is no better adapted to slave labor than the digging, washing, and quarrying of the gold mines."

He also took the opportunity to counter Clay's compromise with one of his own. He essentially called for splitting California in two. "I here assert," said Davis, "that never will I take less than the Missouri compromise line extended to the Pacific ocean, with the specific recog-nition of the right to hold slaves in the territory below that line; and that, before such territories are admitted into the Union as States, slaves may be taken there from any of the United States at the option of their owners." That, he added, was the only fair and peaceful way to make a division of "the common property of the States."[32]

This proposal wasn't new, either. For some time it had been the fall-back position of many Southern Democrats, including men like Davis who had repeatedly embraced Calhoun's common-property argument. Obviously, it was just an expedient. The southern border of Missouri, the famous 36°30′ line, was intrinsically no better than any other line. It just had the advantage of being well known, of having been bandied about many times before, of having the backing of such luminaries as former president Polk. It also had wide support in the South. To most Southerners, extending the 36°30′ line to the Pacific seemed the best way to restore lost equilibrium. Neither section would have to surrender basic principles.[33]

Two weeks later, on February 13, Davis got his opportunity to lambaste Clay's compromise. He spent two days doing so, calling Clay's resolutions "dangerous doctrines" and accusing Clay of throwing his support to the "aggressive" Northerners who had "declared war against the institution of slavery," rather than to "the cause of the weak against the strong, the cause of the Constitution against its aggressors." He also declared that the South needed room to expand. Not only did plantation slavery rapidly wear out the soil, but the South needed fresh land for an expanding population of both whites and blacks. Take away the North's gains from foreign immigration, said Davis, and the increase in population of the two sections was roughly the same. To coop up the slave population on declining soil, moreover, would be to invite trouble.

Davis's main argument, as before, was constitutional. He contended that since slaves were property "and so recognized by the Constitution," a slaveholder had "the right to go with that property into any part of the United States where some sovereign power has not forbidden it." Didn't the federal government, then, have the right to prohibit it? No, said Davis. "I deny, sir, that this Government has the sovereign power to prohibit it from the Territories. I deny that any territorial community, being a dependence of the United States, has that power, or can prohibit it."

As for California, he repeated his earlier argument. Nothing, he insisted, could be more outrageous than allowing a bunch of "first-comers, a conglomerated mass of gold hunters, foreign and native," to exclude slaveholders from the diggings. That was even worse than applying the Wilmot Proviso. However, for the sake of peace and harmony, he was still willing to allow California to be split in two.³⁴

So spoke the man who hoped to be Calhoun's replacement as the voice of the South. The real article, the sixty-seven-year-old Calhoun, missed most of the fireworks. He didn't hear Clay present his proposals. Nor did he hear most of the subsequent debate. He was confined to his quarters at Hill's boardinghouse across from the Capitol.

Like Clay, Calhoun had long had star status. He had first come to Congress in 1811, been secretary of war under James Monroe, and vice president under both John Quincy Adams and Andrew Jackson. Yet for the past twenty years, he had not been seen as a national leader. He had been hailed instead as the voice of the Deep South, the voice of true Southerners in the eyes of his friends, the voice of extremism in the eyes of his critics. Frail and feeble, he was now fighting a losing battle against tuberculosis and bronchitis.

In early March, having mended slightly, the dying senator obtained permission to have someone read a speech he had prepared. The task, after some confusion, went to Senator James M. Mason of Virginia. In a very defiant tone, Mason then read what everyone knew would be Calhoun's last words. It would later be described as a last-ditch heroic effort on Calhoun's part to save the Union. That, however, is sheer nonsense. To Calhoun the admission of California was "worse than the Wilmot Proviso." It left the South with only two choices: "submission or resistance." And Calhoun left no doubt where he stood. He clearly championed resistance.

The South, contended Calhoun, was in a state of "almost universal discontent . . . wide and deep." The North's "long-continued" agitation of the slave question and its "many aggressions" against the South had destroyed the equilibrium between the two sections. Especially egregious had been the North's usurpations of public lands—first through the Northwest Ordinance, then through the Missouri Compromise, and most recently in the prohibition of slavery in the Oregon Territory. And if the present trend continued, the Senate, the last bastion of balance, would be stacked against the South by the end of the decade, with forty Northern senators to twenty-four Southern senators.

None of this was new. Nor were the paragraphs that followed. But then Calhoun went a step further. He called for a constitutional amend-

John C. Calhoun's last Senate appearance. Reprinted from Ben: Perley Poore, Perley's
Reminiscences, *2 vols. (Philadelphia, 1886), 1:366. Unlike most commentators, Perley
took note of the fact that Calhoun was accompanied by one of his slaves.*

ment guaranteeing equilibrium. There should be a dual executive, representing the two great sections, each with a veto power over acts of
Congress. Unknown to most of his fellow senators, across the street in
Calhoun's quarters were notes detailing this arrangement. The dying
senator had been working on it for months.[35]

California, concluded Calhoun, was to be the "test." If it were
admitted under the conditions that had been proposed, then the South
would infer that the North meant to exclude the South from all of the
acquired territories "with the intention of destroying, irretrievably, the
equilibrium between the two sections." The message was clear. For
the South to remain in the Union, the North had to rectify the growing
imbalance, both by the rejection of California and by an amendment to
the Constitution.[36]

Three weeks later, on March 31, Calhoun died. Many eulogized
him. Thomas Hart Benton did not. Instead, he told Daniel Webster:
"He is not dead, sir—he is not dead. There may be no vitality in his
body, but there is in his doctrines. . . . Calhoun died with treason in his

heart and on his lips. . . . Whilst I am discharging my duty here, his dis-
ciples are disseminating his poison all over my State."[37]

Benton wasn't the only one who worried about the dead senator's
impact. So, too, did Mississippi's other senator, Henry Foote, who
almost jumped out of his seat when Calhoun called for a constitutional
amendment. To Foote, it was "most alarming," certain to make a bad
situation even worse.[38]

If the Senate had a gadfly, the forty-six-year-old Foote was it. Every
day he was on his feet, interrupting a fellow senator, quoting Greek,
Latin, Shakespeare, the Bible, and whatever else came to his mind. A
short, slight, bald man, Foote had the bad habit of picking on men twice
his size. He had grown up in Virginia, attended Washington College,
and practiced law in Richmond, then moved west, first to Alabama and
then to Mississippi, where he had become the state's leading criminal
lawyer and famous for his flamboyant and vituperative rhetoric. Over
the years, he had fought four duels with political rivals, one in Alabama,
three in Mississippi. He had been shot three times, twice by the same
opponent. He had also been involved in numerous brawls, including
one with his fellow Mississippi senator, Jefferson Davis, on Christmas
Day 1847.[39]

Oddly, Foote saw himself as a peacemaker, "a lover of concord."
Others saw him as meddlesome, ornery, and contentious. In any event,
Foote could usually be counted on to take issue with whatever was
said—and to advocate a different approach. Elected senator in 1846,
Foote showed little interest in Calhoun's call for a Nashville conven-
tion. He also refused to support Davis's proposal that California be
divided at 36°30'. Instead, he moved that it be divided at 35°30',
approximately sixty miles farther south (roughly on line with today's
Bakersfield), and that the new territory be called Colorado. Other Deep
South senators backed his proposal and kept his maneuver alive. But
Clay opposed slicing off the bottom third of California, and half of the
upper South senators followed Clay's lead.[40]

Foote's main fear was that Clay's proposals, voted on separately,
would leave the South with nothing. Clay's strategy, said Foote, was
dead wrong. It left the North with "all the *trump cards*." Once Northerners "smuggled" California into the Union, that would be the end of
it. Nothing for the South would be done. The territorial bill would
soon die. So, too, would the fugitive slave bill. Either Northerners in

the House would refuse to vote for these measures, or Zachary Taylor would veto them. The only way around this problem, said Foote, was to tie California to all the other proposals, to bind all of Clay's resolutions together, to stuff them all into a single omnibus bill.[41]

Once Foote decided on this course of action, he was persistent. He badgered Clay constantly, and after Calhoun's death he stepped up the pressure. He called for the formation of a Senate committee to put all Clay's proposals into a single bill. Several Northern senators, including Daniel Webster, objected. They pointed out that the Senate had been talking about these matters for four months and hadn't yet done anything. They wanted to get on with it, to deal with California immediately, and then move on to the territorial bills and all the rest. Southern senators, including Virginia's James Mason and South Carolina's Andrew Butler, made it clear that they wanted to deal with the territories first. So it went, back and forth, back and forth.

Finally Clay relented. Rather than admit California immediately and then move on to the other resolutions, he decided that California statehood would not happen unless it was combined with the territorial bills. He thus embraced Foote's bundling approach. That decision, in turn, created even more turmoil. Thomas Hart Benton, among others, was furious. He deemed the omnibus bill a "monster" and tried to cripple Foote's proposed Senate committee with amendments.

Then, on April 17, after many days of wrangling, Foote, who was about half Benton's size, launched a personal attack. He had done it many times before. At first Benton just fumed. Then suddenly he rose from his desk, threw aside his chair, and went after Foote. The diminutive Mississippian pulled out a revolver, pointed it at Benton, and cocked it. Other senators tried to intervene. Benton threw them out of his way, repeatedly called Foote an "assassin," and dared him to shoot. Finally, Foote turned his weapon over to Daniel Dickinson, a New York Democrat.[42]

Nothing was done to punish Foote. He wasn't expelled. Nor was he contrite. In fact, he eventually got his way. All of Benton's amendments were voted down, the committee was established, and the omnibus bill became "the" bill. Getting it passed, however, proved impossible. Only a handful of Southerners were willing to vote for California as a free state, and only a handful of Northerners were willing to accept a new, tougher Fugitive Slave Law. With men from both camps casting "no" votes, the "ayes" didn't have a chance. Henry Clay addressed the Senate

Henry Foote attacking Thomas Hart Benton.
Scene in Uncle Sam's Senate, 17th April, 1850. Library of Congress.

seventy times in support of the proposal. But finally, after suffering a major defeat on July 31, he gave up.

Foote then reintroduced his proposal to split California at 35°30′. That, too, was voted down, 33 to 23, with Clay, Benton, and two Delaware Whigs voting with the solid Northern bloc. Clay, physically and emotionally exhausted, then left for Newport, Rhode Island, to recover.

Stephen A. Douglas, "the Little Giant" of Illinois, now stepped into the breach. To Douglas the essence of the situation had long been clear. No more than four or five senators would ever vote in favor of the entire compromise package. Thus trying to get the omnibus bill through the Senate was impossible.

But the package, thought Douglas, could be put through piece by piece. On the California question, Northern support was a sure thing; so all that was needed was the backing of one or two slave-state senators. The same was true on the abolition of the slave trade in the District of Columbia. More daunting was putting together a majority in behalf of the other measures, especially the Fugitive Slave Law. That necessitated getting a sizable number of Northerners in the House to either vote with the South or miss the crucial vote. Who might that be? Northern Whigs? Not a chance. Northern Democrats? That, Douglas knew, was more than likely.

By the time Clay left for Newport, moreover, one major obstacle to compromise was gone. For months Zachary Taylor had made it clear that he opposed the compromise package. He said it was unnecessary, that California should simply be admitted as a free state. What, then, would "Old Rough and Ready" have done if Clay's package had some-how got through Congress? Would he have vetoed it? Many thought he would. And then what? Clay certainly couldn't have found the two-thirds majorities in both houses necessary to override the veto.

Then, to everyone's surprise, the sixty-five-year-old president sud-denly became ill. On July 4, after spending hours listening to Henry Foote and other speakers wax eloquent in the hot Washington sun, he returned to the White House and feasted on fruits and vegetables and drank glass after glass of ice-cold water and milk. The next day he was sick. His doctor said he had "cholera morbus" or acute gastroenteritis. Four days later, on the night of July 9, he died.

Was Taylor's death decisive? It certainly changed the odds dramati-cally. For the new president, Millard Fillmore of New York, was a com-promiser by nature. He saw himself as a peacemaker. He supported the compromise as vigorously as Taylor had opposed it. He was more than willing to use the power and influence of his office to round up votes in its behalf. With Fillmore's backing, Douglas knew he had a winning formula. He wasted no time. In less than six weeks, he maneuvered every part of Clay's original proposals through the Senate and House.

In doing so, Douglas never got the two warring sides to actually "compromise." In the end, most Northerners still voted one way, most Southerners the opposite way. Only four of the sixty senators, for exam-ple, voted for all the compromise proposals, whereas forty-eight voted against at least one of the proposals. Among Deep South senators, only Sam Houston of Texas voted for California.[43] But Douglas, by getting some men to miss a crucial vote and others to vote with the other side, cobbled together majorities in both houses, and Fillmore signed the measures into law as fast as they were adopted.

Thus on September 9, 1850, California became the thirty-first state in the Union. The next day William Gwin and John C. Frémont were sworn in as senators. And the following day Edward Gilbert and George W. Wright took their seats in the House.

The outcome created storms of protest across the Deep South. From Charleston to New Orleans, fiery speeches and angry letters dominated the news.[44] All deplored the admission of California as a free state. Many insisted that California should have been split in two, either at the $36°30'$ line or at the $35°30'$ line, and two states admitted to the Union, one slave and one free. Many also objected to Californians taking matters into their own hands and framing a state constitution without congressional permission to do so. Whose fault was that? Some blamed it on Zachary Taylor, many on General Riley.

In South Carolina, Calhoun's replacement in the U.S. Senate, Robert Barnwell Rhett, led the protest. That was as expected. For nearly twenty years, the forty-nine-year-old South Carolina native had been fanning the flames of Southern secession, as well as lambasting Northern abolitionists, the federal tariff, and anyone who disagreed with him. That June he had tried to get the 175 delegates at the Nashville Convention to lead the South out of the Union. Failing there, he now insisted that South Carolina lead the way. He had a wide audience, thanks to his son's newspaper, *The Charleston Mercury*.[45]

In neighboring Georgia, the *Columbus Sentinel* joined Rhett and the *Mercury* in calling for secession. "We have all along contended that the admission of California would fill to overflowing the poisoned cup of degradation which the North has for years been preparing for the South. . . . We are for secession, open unqualified secession. Henceforth we are for war upon the government; it has existed but for our ruin and to the extent of our ability to destroy it, it shall exist no longer."[46]

Farther west, in the Mississippi Delta, the call for secession was also strident. Leading the pack was Louisiana's flamboyant senator, Pierre Soulé. The son of a Napoleonic officer and magistrate, the forty-nine-year-old Frenchman had been a fiery militant most of his adult life. Arrested for revolutionary activity in France in the 1820s, he had broken out of jail, sought refuge in England, then Port-au-Prince, Baltimore, and New York, before settling in New Orleans, where he had become a prominent defense lawyer and Jacksonian Democrat. Elected to the U.S. Senate first in 1847, then again in 1849, he had aggressively championed the expansion of slavery and vehemently opposed free soil.

On the floor of the Senate, Soulé had repeatedly denounced Clay's compromise. "Will honorable Senators," he asked, "point out to me a single concession from the North to the South which these bills contain? Sir, there is none; no, not ONE." The compromise, thundered Soulé, was a swindle. It covertly and deceitfully gave the Wilmot Proviso's sponsors what they had failed to achieve in the previous Congress. And now that its provisions had become the law of the land, he called for secession. He was adamant. The South, he said, had no other choice. He also joined forces with other ardent secessionists in and around New Orleans in seeking "a redress of the balance" by forcibly taking Cuba.[47]

Marching to the same drummer was Governor John A. Quitman of Mississippi. No one, it seemed, was angrier about the outcome in Washington than the Mississippi governor. The "so-called Compromise," he fumed, was a defeat for the South and a victory for the supporters of the Wilmot Proviso. Not even the fugitive-slave clause was a Southern gain. Not only would Northerners not enforce it, but slaves now had much more free land to escape to. The clauses allowing the possibility of slavery in New Mexico and Utah, moreover, were meaningless. The land was certain to become free soil. Also, the Texas border settlement with New Mexico cost the slave states 100,000 square miles of slave territory. In essence, the so-called compromise established free soil everywhere west of Texas. It left slaveholders with nowhere to expand in the present United States. The only hope, contended Quitman, was the annexation of Cuba.

In the meantime, thought Quitman, he had to do something to stop "Yankee fanatics" from securing the Wilmot Proviso through this "stupendous plot." Submission amounted to Southern treason. Not only was California fit for slavery, but Southern slaves would make California mines hum, its ports boom, its fields yield cotton. The value of Southern slaves, moreover, would increase by "at least" 50 percent. In exchange for giving up California, then, the South had to get something substantial—at least half of the territories and massive constitutional guarantees. Let the North have California, but only if the South received all land east of the Sierras up to the 40th parallel. With such thoughts, Quitman called the Mississippi legislature into a special session on November 18 to combat "deep political intrigue" and to assert Mississippi's "sovereignty."[48]

Quitman's summons rang like a fire bell through the Deep South. As soon as Robert Barnwell Rhett heard about it, he fired off a letter of

John A. Quitman. Library of Congress. Quitman always wanted to be seen as a commanding general on horseback. In this portrait, he got his wish.

approval. The people of Charleston, said Rhett, were delighted. They all saw it as the first step toward Southern independence. Governor Seabrook of South Carolina agreed. Secession, said Seabrook, was popular throughout South Carolina, even in districts "where a large portion of the population" were "non-slaveholders." He had just toured the state and had not met "with one man who was not favorable to the only certain remedy—secession." He also promised that South Carolina would be quick to follow Mississippi's lead.[49]

On November 18, Quitman addressed the Mississippi legislature.

After condemning at length California statehood and Northern "aggression," he spoke of the future of slavery. The "institution," he contended, was obviously "doomed" if "left to the tender mercies of the federal government." For there was no doubt that the national government was "now hostile to slavery." And while last-ditch efforts might be made to get the non-slaveholding states "to remedy the wrong" by splitting California in two and by granting amendments to the Constitution, it was his "decided opinion that the only effectual remedy" was "peaceable secession of the aggrieved states." He thus called for a convention to consider all the state's options, especially secession.[50]

In response, the legislature scheduled an election of delegates for early September 1851. That election, in turn, quickly became part of a larger contest between unionists and states' righters for control of the state. The states' righters backed Quitman, the arch secessionist, for another term as governor. The unionists chose Henry Foote as their gubernatorial candidate. The two candidates then set out on a joint speaking tour. Foote, who was widely regarded as "the best stump speaker then living," generally got the better of Quitman, who was a man of action, not of words. Meanwhile, their followers literally got into hundreds of fistfights and dozens of duels. Then, at Sledgeville, the two candidates themselves got into a brawl. That ended the speaking tour.[51]

In September, the unionists prevailed, winning forty-one out of fifty-nine counties. Quitman viewed the outcome as a personal defeat and promptly resigned his candidacy. The states' righters then turned to Jefferson Davis, who toned down the party's secessionist rhetoric and came within 999 votes of beating Foote for governor. The unionists, however, had prevailed, not only in Foote's election, but in state legislative elections, winning sixty-three of ninety-eight assembly seats, and seven of sixteen senate races.[52]

With that, any hope of secession in the Deep South came to an end. The South Carolina legislature, rather than actually secede, merely declared the state's right to secede. It was all over, noted one South Carolinian. Rhett, Seabrook, and every other secessionist now "may hang up their fiddles."[53] In disgust, Rhett resigned his U.S. Senate seat.

Southern Whigs and moderate Southern Democrats thus succeeded in keeping the secessionists at bay. But did a free California really matter?

Were the two California senators sitting on the doorstep really a threat to Southern dominance of the Senate?

John C. Frémont, had he received the full six-year term, might have been a serious threat. Although born and raised in the Deep South, and the son-in-law of a Missouri slaveholder, Frémont was a free-soiler. He supported the abolition of the slave trade in the District of Columbia and voted against harsh penalties for those who assisted runaway slaves. He showed strong signs of opposing the Deep South. But having drawn the lot for the short term that ended in March 1851, he had just twenty-one working days to serve before he had to stand for reelection.

Would he be reelected? Within the California legislature, there were now sixteen men who were determined to make sure that the South retained the upper hand in the U.S. Senate. The nucleus of the Chivalry faction of the California Democratic Party, they supported Solomon Heydenfeldt, a dapper little man with noticeably small hands and feet. Like Frémont, the thirty-five-year-old Heydenfeldt hailed from the Deep South, having grown up in Charleston, South Carolina, and having practiced law in Alabama. Unlike Frémont, however, Heydenfeldt could be counted on to support the Deep South in the national legislature.[54]

To thwart the Chivs' attempt to unseat him, Frémont rushed back to California via the isthmus. Making his headquarters near the state capitol, he established a newspaper, the *San Jose Daily Argus*, to push his candidacy. Still, he managed to win only eight votes on the first ballot, well short of the twenty-nine votes he had won the year before. Outpolling him was the Chiv candidate, Heydenfeldt, with sixteen votes. Also, a handful of votes went to the Whig candidate, T. Butler King, who still had hopes of becoming a U.S. senator. Frémont also had trouble with several legislators who wanted to move the state capital to Vallejo. Their votes were for sale. They would vote for any candidate who backed their proposal.

As the balloting continued, the sixteen Chivs were relentless. Determined to block Frémont's reelection, they launched a full-scale attack of his twenty-one-day Senate record, making much of his sponsorship of two bills that benefited him personally. One, which he had co-sponsored with his father-in-law, essentially called for rubber-stamping Mexican land grants. Since he himself owned a gold-rich Mexican land grant, Las Mariposas, this appeared to be a blatant conflict of interest. The Chivs thus made the most of it, although it clearly didn't bother the chief spokesman for the settlers on the Mexican grants, Dr. Charles Robinson, who supported Frémont's candidacy. The other bill prohibited foreigners in the gold diggings from working for themselves. In the U.S. Senate, Henry Foote had claimed that this piece of legislation would enable rich mine owners like Frémont to hire thousands of foreign workers for peon wages. His Chiv opponents called it "Frémont's Gold Bill."[55]

Thanks to their politicking, Frémont couldn't get a majority. Nor could Heydenfeldt, King, or any other candidate. One ballot thus followed another. Finally, after 142 ballots, the legislature decided to wait a year, until January 1852. Meanwhile, the state would have only one U.S. senator, William Gwin.

During the interlude, Gwin succeeded in getting complete control of federal patronage. It took little effort on his part. The Fillmore administration was desperate. It had to staff the entire federal apparatus in California—the postal service, the courts, the San Francisco Custom House, the Indian office, and the land office, as well as a host of lesser offices. And it needed Gwin's help. For without his backing, it would not be able to get its California nominees approved by the Senate.

The rules were well established. Although the president had the power to appoint, many of his appointments needed Senate approval. By 1850 there were over nine hundred such offices. Some had required confirmation since Washington's day, others since the Tenure of Office Act in 1820. In the Senate, it had become custom, if not a hard-and-fast rule, that if a senator objected to a nominee to any post in his home state, the other members of the Senate out of "senatorial courtesy" would support him regardless of his reasons. Gwin, in short, essentially had a veto over nearly all federal appointments in California.

As a result, President Fillmore and the members of his administration never tried to buck Gwin. And for a full year, only Gwin had the president's ear. No longer did he have to worry about Frémont—or someone like him—giving the president contrary advice. Gwin made the most of it. He recommended only his own followers for the more powerful federal posts, such as head of the San Francisco Custom House or U.S. marshal. By year's end, he fully controlled federal patronage in California, and he retained control for most of the decade. Nearly all his choices were Southerners. Indeed, he was so blatant in favoring men from the South that the San Francisco Custom House came to be known as the "Virginia Poorhouse."[56]

When the California legislature met again, Frémont didn't contest the election, and on the eighth ballot the Gwin forces triumphed. Their choice was now John B. Weller of Ohio, who had served with Gwin in Congress.

The forty-year-old Weller had been a three-term Ohio congressman, a colonel in the Mexican War, and an appointee of James K. Polk to head the Mexican Boundary Commission. He also had always been a doughface, a Northern man with Southern principles. In Ohio he had not only opposed the Wilmot Proviso. He had also spoken openly in favor of the expansion of slavery. At the time he was married to Susan P. McDowell Taylor, the daughter of a slave-owning Virginia congressman. She died during the cholera epidemic of 1848. Shortly thereafter, Weller left Ohio for California. Arriving in San Francisco on the same ship as Gwin, the steamer *Panama*, he had become a staunch Gwin supporter and stalwart Chiv.[57]

With Weller's election, California was no longer any threat to Southern dominance of the U.S. Senate. In North-South struggles, Weller and Gwin might as well have been representing Mississippi. Both supported the Kansas-Nebraska Act of 1854, the bill that repealed the ban on slavery above the 36°30′ line in the Louisiana Purchase. Both endorsed Chief Justice Roger B. Taney's dicta in the famous Dred Scott case of 1857, the contention that the Missouri Compromise's prohibition of slavery in the northern half of the Louisiana Purchase was unconstitutional. Both backed to the hilt President James Buchanan's attempt in 1858 to bring Kansas into the Union as a slave state, even though its pro-slavery constitution had been drafted by a notoriously unrepresentative convention. Both actively campaigned for John C. Breckinridge, the Southern pro-slavery candidate, in the 1860 presidential election. And both supported Southern independence during the Civil War.[58]

In a nutshell, then, the two men who represented California for most of the 1850s never threatened the South's hold on the Senate. If anything, they enhanced it. In the case of Gwin, Jefferson Davis and other Deep South senators who ranted and raved about a free California undoubtedly knew all along that they could count on his vote. He told them as much when he arrived in Washington bearing California's request for statehood. And, as they well knew, he still owned two hundred slaves in Mississippi. Did any of them seriously believe that he might intentionally jeopardize his own wealth and well-being?

In any event, they got Gwin's vote time and again. And, thanks to his efforts, they also got a dependable ally in John B. Weller. For several years, Gwin made sure that California as the thirty-first star was never a threat to his beloved South. Would it last? That question haunted not only men like Davis, Quitman, and Soulé. It also haunted Gwin.

5

━━━━◆◆◆━━━━

THANKS TO GWIN AND HIS CHIV FOLLOWERS, THEN, THE ADMISSION of California as a free state was no immediate threat to Southern domination of the Senate. But that did not mean that Southern hotspurs like John Quitman and Pierre Soulé were willing to let the matter rest. As soon as it became clear that California and the Far West were a lost cause, the Mississippi governor and the Louisiana senator sought a counterweight. Their first choice was Cuba, "the pearl of the Antilles."

Prior to the California issue, Quitman's interest in Cuba was minimal. Other than a fondness for Havana cigars, he paid scant attention to the Caribbean island, even though it lay just ninety miles off the Florida coast, had over 300,000 slaves, and was a major sugar producer.[1] In 1848, President James K. Polk and his secretary of state, James Buchanan, had tried to buy Cuba from Spain for $100 million. Both saw it as a valuable addition of slave territory, and both apparently had been willing to run roughshod over the antislavery principle of the Wilmot Proviso to get it. To their dismay, however, they found that the Spanish regarded "Cuba as their most precious gem and nothing short of extreme necessity" would "ever induce them to part with it."[2]

None of this had interested Quitman. Nor had it stirred much interest among pro-slavery expansionists in the Mississippi Delta.[3] But once it appeared that the entire West might be lost to slavery, interest soared. Ardent pro-slavery men in and around New Orleans seriously began looking for a counterweight. Where was it to be? Then, with admission of California as the thirty-first state, one New Orleans newspaper after another pointed to Cuba. Leading the charge was *The Daily Delta*, a Democratic paper owned by a former state senator, Laurent J. Sigur. Not only did the *Delta* call for annexation to "restore" the balance of power. It envisioned "at least" two more slave states being carved out of Cuba.[4]

The idea also came in the person of Narciso López, a muscular and strikingly handsome fifty-two-year-old Venezuelan.[5] López had once been a field marshal in the Spanish cavalry. But following several reversals of fortune, he had turned against Spain and now sought to overthrow Spanish authority in Cuba. In September 1849, he had attempted to launch an invasion of Cuba from Round Island, off Mississippi's eastern coast. That operation had never set sail. It had been stifled when the U.S. government, upon orders from Zachary Taylor, seized López's transport ships, blockaded the island, and forced his men to flee. López had no interest in the California question, but in claiming that Cuba was ripe for rebellion, he quickly gained the backing of Sigur's newspaper and soon had a wide following in the Mississippi Delta.[6]

In March 1850, López called on Quitman at the Governor's Mansion in Jackson. He told Quitman that the Cuban people were ready for rebellion and offered him the command of a four-thousand-man "Liberation" army that would set sail on May 1 and the opportunity to become the first ruler of independent Cuba. Although tempted, Quitman turned down the offer. At the same time, he put López in touch with some of his powerful friends in New Orleans and tentatively agreed to command a reinforcement expedition that would leave New Orleans sometime

Narciso López. Library of Congress.

between June 1 and June 15. All of this was supposed to be hush-hush. But the news of Quitman's involvement became so widespread that even his sister in Philadelphia heard about it.[7]

López's second invasion attempt, unlike the first, actually set sail. Three ships left New Orleans in May 1850. On board were five Cubans and some five hundred Americans, mainly hired guns from Kentucky and Louisiana. Rendezvousing off the Yucatán peninsula, they switched to one ship and attacked Cárdenas, on the north coast of Cuba. Running into stiff resistance from a small Spanish garrison, they suffered some sixty casualties and were chased back to Key West by a Spanish warship. A month later the U.S. government arrested López in New Orleans for violating American neutrality laws, and a few weeks later a New Orleans grand jury indicted many of López's co-conspirators, including Governor Quitman.

Rather than allow himself to be arrested as a sitting governor, Quitman first wheedled enough time from a pliant U.S. marshal to establish procedures for Mississippi to secede from the Union, and then resigned the governorship and stood trial in New Orleans as a private citizen. Hailed as a hero in New Orleans, he had nothing to fear. The federal government had no chance of convicting him. It couldn't convict López, either. It tried three times to get a conviction, wound up with hung juries on each occasion, and finally dropped the charges against all the accused in March 1851.

In August 1851, López with 435 men tried again. Sailing from New Orleans, the invasion force landed at Bahía Honda, about fifty miles from Havana. Instead of being welcomed as "liberators," they were met by Spanish troops. After two weeks of skirmishing, the Spanish prevailed and captured many of the fleeing invaders. The Spanish then executed fifty-one captives by firing squad, including Colonel William L. Crittenden of Louisiana, the twenty-eight-year-old nephew of the U.S. attorney general. Sixteen days later, before some twenty thousand cheering soldiers and civilians in Havana, a black executioner strapped López into an iron garroting chair and cut off his head.

News of the executions led to anti-Spanish riots and the wrecking of the Spanish consulate in New Orleans. Among the suspected instigators was Senator Pierre Soulé, one of the most outspoken champions of López and his men. The Spanish government then sent 162 of López's followers, half of them Americans, to work in the quicksilver mines of Spain. To get their release, the State Department had to apologize effusively, and Congress had to approve a $25,000 indemnity for damages to the New Orleans consulate.

The same month that López was garroted, his former associates in New Orleans formed a secret society, the Order of the Lone Star. Soon expanding to fifty chapters in eight Southern states and an estimated membership of fifteen to twenty thousand, the order made plans to invade Cuba in the summer of 1852, in support of a Cuban insurrection that was to be fomented by Francisco de Frías, López's wealthy brother-in-law. The planned upheaval never got off the ground.

A year later another organization, the Junta Cubana of New York, contacted Quitman. They wanted him to lead an invasion of Cuba and proposed to make him "exclusive chief of our revolution, not only in its military, but also in its civil sense." In April 1853, Quitman signed a formal agreement with the Junta Cubana in which he was appointed "civil and military chief of the revolution, with all the powers and attributes of dictatorship as recognized by civilized nations," and in which he promised to preserve slavery in Cuba. He was also to receive $1 million when Cuba became "free."[8]

Meanwhile, in the U.S. Senate, Pierre Soulé distinguished himself as the chief proponent of taking Cuba by force. In late January 1853, he lambasted his fellow senators for referring to López and his men as marauders:

> Why talk you of marauders? Lafayette and Kosciusko were just such marauders. The one has his picture hung up in the other House of this our National Legislature, and the other his impress wherever beats an American heart! What are the late conquests of England in Eastern India, of the French in Africa, but marauding upon a large scale? What has been the course of Britain within the last century, on the coast of Central America, but a continuous marauding? . . . Why should Senators show themselves so supremely fastidious about marauding, when they admit themselves, while speaking of the vexed acquisition [of Cuba], that they but await for the ripening of the fruit? Will the plucking of it when ripe be less "marauding" than the plucking of it while still green?[9]

Shortly thereafter, Soulé resigned his Senate seat to become the American minister to Spain. Appointed by President Franklin Pierce,

Soulé was to secure Cuba from Spain. The night before he sailed to Spain, the Cuban junta conducted a going-away ceremony for him in New York. While he stood on the balcony outside his hotel room, they serenaded him and urged him to bring back "a new star." In response, he promised that as an envoy of the United States he would speak "tremendous truths to the tyrants of the old continent."[10]

Upon arriving in Madrid, Soulé immediately alienated the Spanish government. He denounced the monarchy and cavorted openly with revolutionaries. He got into a duel with the French ambassador after one of

Pierre Soulé. Library of Congress.

the ambassador's guests made a disparaging remark about Mrs. Soulé's plunging neckline. For this affront the ambassador suffered a debilitating leg wound. From the outset, Soulé also made it clear that his mission was to acquire Cuba by hook or by crook. By this time, moreover, the Spanish, as well as every other European power, had heard that Quitman was raising troops to invade Cuba.

In September 1853, the Spanish government responded. It appointed the Marqués de la Pezuela captain general of Cuba, a post that put him in command of both the military and the government, with orders to take steps to defend Cuba. In December he issued decrees that among other things cracked down on those illegally engaged in the slave trade and gave citizenship rights to blacks illegally imported before 1835. At the same time, he recruited free blacks into the militia. Coming from a government that had no interest in abolishing either slavery or the African slave trade, Pezuela's policy of "Africanization" made it clear that he was willing, if necessary, to use black troops against Quitman's invaders and against any Cuban planter who sympathized with them.

Pezuela's policy was also risky. It sparked fears of slave rebellion throughout the white South and calls for reprisals. It also aroused militants in the Mississippi Delta. They wanted action quickly. In response, the Louisiana legislature demanded "decisive and energetic measures." Quitman, however, was unwilling to move until he had three thousand men, one armed steamer, and $220,000 at his disposal.[11]

Meanwhile, the Pierce administration decided that it might be possible to purchase Cuba if firebrands like Quitman were temporarily restrained. On April 3, Secretary of State William L. Marcy sent new instructions to Soulé, authorizing him to purchase Cuba for up to $130 million. If Spain refused, Soulé was then to concern himself with the problem of how to "detach" Cuba from Spain.[12] Eight weeks later, the administration announced that it would prosecute all men who violated U.S. neutrality laws. The New Orleans grand jury then required Quitman to post a $3,000 bond guaranteeing his adherence to the neutrality laws for the next nine months. In the interim, in Cuba, Pezuela arrested more than a hundred pro-American planters and put some to death. Later that same year, Pierce called Quitman to Washington and showed him evidence that Cuba was strongly defended.[13]

Meanwhile, in Madrid, Soulé had no luck trying to buy Cuba. So the Pierce administration decided to let him confer privately with the other ministers in Europe—James Buchanan at London and John Y. Mason at Paris—and decide if it was feasible to persuade Spain to sell Cuba to the United States. Meeting in Ostend in October 1854, the three diplomats put their names to a dispatch that came to be known as the Ostend Manifesto.

The dispatch was a bombshell. Written mainly by Soulé, it urged the United States to immediately buy Cuba at any price up to $120 million. It also proclaimed that if Spain refused to sell and if its possession of Cuba seriously endangered the "internal peace" of the slave states, then the United States would be justified in seizing Cuba "upon the very same principle that would justify an individual in tearing down the burning house of his neighbor if there were no other means of preventing the flames from destroying his own home."[14]

News of this saber-rattling manifesto sent shock waves through the Northern wing of the Democratic Party. They had just suffered huge election losses that fall. They had entered the election holding ninety-three seats in the House. They now had only twenty-two.[15] What, many asked, was the Pierce administration up to? Didn't they realize that the "burning house" rhetoric would provide Horace Greeley's *New-York Tribune* with even more ammunition to attack the party faithful? One Democratic newspaper after another thus distanced itself from the manifesto, even branding its authors "brigands" and "highwaymen." The Pierce administration also ran for cover, disavowing the proposal and letting "the three wise men of Ostend" fend for themselves.[16]

That December, enraged by the reaction, Soulé resigned as minister to Spain. Several months later, in April 1855, Quitman gave back to the Cuban junta the powers it had bestowed upon him. No longer did either warrior have much hope of acquiring "the pearl of the Antilles" to offset the addition of California as a free state.

Meanwhile, other Southern leaders still hoped to find some way to split California in two. Leading the pack was a sixty-three-year-old Charleston railroad man, James Gadsden.

In 1850, Gadsden had been one of the leaders of the secession movement in South Carolina.[17] In his youth, however, he had marched to a different drummer. A native of South Carolina, he had gone north to college, to Yale, and soldiered under Andrew Jackson, rising to the rank of colonel. During those years he had been a zealous nationalist and an outspoken critic of any form of sectionalism. But in 1821 the Senate had rejected his nomination to adjutant general of the army because of his close ties to Jackson and Calhoun. This affront so soured Gadsden that he became a bitter opponent of everything the Senate did.

In 1823, at the behest of President James Monroe, Gadsden went to Florida to build the first government roads and to move the Seminoles to reservations. He remained there for the next sixteen years, spending half his time building a rice plantation, which bored him, and half running for one public office after another, which excited him. He never won, but he became well known for his hostility to the federal government. He talked frequently about territorial rights and in 1831 called on Floridians to nullify federal law and become truly "independent." That, in turn, cost him the patronage of Jackson.

At the same time, Gadsden became more ardent in behalf of slavery. He deemed it "a social blessing" and denounced Northern abolitionists as "the greatest curse of the nation." By 1840, he had exceeded even Calhoun in his pro-slavery zeal.

To expand slavery and secure it against Northern opposition, Gadsden looked to the West. He hoped to unite it with the South, partly by taking slaves west and partly through an imaginative railroad system. Long interested in railroads, he said good-bye to his boring Florida plantation in 1839 and became the president of the South Carolina Railroad Company, a rather shaky enterprise that had only 136 miles of track and $3 million in debt. With Charleston as the base, his dream was to knit all southern railroads into one system and then connect it to a southern transcontinental railroad to the Pacific. That, in turn, would make the West an appendage of the South rather than of the North. It would also give the South access to Asia and weaken Northern commercial power, which, in his judgment, rested largely on the North's control of ocean trade.

In July 1845, Gadsden tried to sell this idea to delegates at a commercial convention in Memphis. He proposed building a transcontinental railroad from Memphis through Arkansas and Texas to the Pacific. A few months later, in February 1846, he made the same pitch in his annual report to stockholders of the South Carolina Railroad. To his dismay, they didn't share his enthusiasm about tying all the southern railroads together, much less about laying track all the way to the Pacific. Instead, they demanded dividends.[18]

Even harder for Gadsden to stomach was California's decision to become a free state. He was furious. He first called on his fellow South Carolinians to secede from the Union. When that effort failed, he conspired to split California in two. Among his collaborators was his fifty-five-year-old cousin, Isaac Edward Holmes, who had represented South Carolina in Congress for six terms. Holmes left Charleston for California in 1851 and established a law practice in San Francisco. Also working with Gadsden was none other than Thomas Jefferson Green, who had once lived in Florida and was now a sitting California state senator.

Gadsden and his fellow conspirators had several goals. First, they wanted to establish a slaveholding colony in southern California that would produce rice, cotton, and sugar. Long term, they also wanted to build a southern railroad to the gold country, starting either from the Red River or from San Antonio. In the meantime, they envisioned building a "high way" in stages by "an organized Corps of Pioneers & Axe men & reach California with both Negroes & animals in full vigor to go to work."

Gadsden himself planned to become the leader of the proposed slaveholding colony. But first some preliminary work had to be done. On December 31, 1851, he contacted Green with instructions. He wanted Green and Holmes to obtain a land grant at the "Sources of the Joachin." They were to petition the legislature for a large land concession, somewhere between the 34th and the 36th parallels, which he perceived to be a natural point to divide the state. Once they got the grant, he would bring in slaves to produce "rice and cotton and sugar."[19]

A few months later, Gadsden and some twelve hundred citizens of

South Carolina and Florida petitioned the California legislature for permission to become permanent citizens. In their memorial, they deplored free labor and described California's agricultural potential in glowing terms. They said that to make California agriculture flourish, the legislature only had to grant them "permission to colonize a rural district" with "not less than Two Thousand of their African Domestics" who had skill and experience "in the cultivation of Cotton, Rice, & Sugar." Only "by this peculiar labor" could California's "valuable soils" be "rendered productive."[20]

The job of presenting this petition fell to Archibald C. Peachy, a young Virginia lawyer who now represented San Francisco in the California assembly. As Peachy read the document, many of his fellow legislators couldn't believe their ears. Didn't Gadsden and the twelve hundred co-signers realize that California was a free state? What did they expect the legislature to do? To simply ignore the state constitution? The petition thus generated a "highly exciting discussion" and a "multitude of motions." Finally the members decided to send the memorial to the Committee on Federal Relations. There it quietly died.[21]

Meanwhile, news circulated in San Francisco about additional slaves being brought into the state. Much quoted was an article in the *Charleston Courier*, which boasted that a steamer out of Charleston had taken seventy-four slaves to the diggings that winter. Then, on April 15, the steamer *Isthmus* arrived in San Francisco. The passenger list included "several gentlemen with a number of servants—one with twelve, another eight, another seven, another five, and so on." What did they think? That California might soon become a slave state?[22]

The timing of the petition and the strange new arrivals coincided with an all-out effort by Chivs in the state legislature to make California more friendly to the nation's slave owners. Leading that effort was Henry A. Crabb, the twenty-four-year-old son of a Tennessee aristocrat with "heavy investments in slaves."[23]

Now a San Joaquin assemblyman, Crabb had briefly practiced law in Vicksburg, Mississippi. Even though he was barely old enough to vote, he had been a Whig in politics and had killed a rival in a duel, one of the bloodiest in Vicksburg memory, following the 1848 election. Shortly thereafter, he had come overland to California and established a law practice in Stockton. Despite his Whig past, he had teamed up with

Henry Crabb. Courtesy Arizona Historical Society, Tucson.

the followers of Gwin, whom he had known in Mississippi.

In January 1852, Crabb introduced two bills in the assembly. The first placed California four-square behind the national Fugitive Slave Law of 1850 and also supplemented that act. In the heat of the sectional battle over the Wilmot Proviso, Southerners had demanded a tougher Fugitive Slave Law. The original law of 1793, they contended, didn't work. Northerners had failed to faithfully perform their duties. And the Supreme Court, in the case of *Prigg v. Pennsylvania* in 1842, had relieved Northern states of their enforcement obligations and placed them entirely on the shoulders of the federal government.

In 1850, Henry Clay had included a stricter law among his compromise proposals, but Southern senators led by James M. Mason of Virginia had rejected it, partly because it provided the accused fugitive with the right of habeas corpus and a jury trial in his home state. They made it clear that slaves were property and, just like horses and cows and other forms of property, had no right to trial by jury and habeas corpus. They demanded a more stringent law to protect their property, and they got it.

The final bill gave federal commissioners the authority to summarily decide the fate of the accused and provided an extra $5 fee if they decided in favor of the claimant slave owner. It left Northern blacks at the mercy of venal tribunals, with no legal protections whatsoever. It also imposed heavy fines on Northern whites who hid fugitives and helped them in any way. All in all, it was a tough measure for Northern legislators to support, and in the end only one in five—almost all Democrats—voted for the bill.[24]

The new law sparked several spectacular acts of resistance, including the Christiana Riot in southeastern Pennsylvania, the "Jerry" rescue in Syracuse, and the Anthony Burns trial in Boston. It also inspired Harriet Beecher Stowe to write *Uncle Tom's Cabin*, a melodrama that sold some 300,000 copies the first year and eventually 7 million worldwide. But despite the headline events, most Northern communities complied with the new law.[25] In San Francisco, however, a judge had ruled in 1851 that the new federal law didn't apply to "Frank," a Missouri slave who had been brought to California to mine gold and had fled in 1849, because California was not a state at the time and Frank had not crossed state lines. That decision had infuriated pro-slavery men.

To nullify it, Crabb's bill deemed any slave who had come to California before its admission to statehood a fugitive under the new federal law. The bill also levied heavy fines on anyone who aided a runaway, and enabled a slave owner to reside in California for an indefinite time with an alleged slave. And since black testimony was forbidden under California law, it essentially forced free blacks to carry freedom papers or be victimized by any white looking for human chattel.

Titled "An Act Respecting Fugitives from Labor, and Slaves Brought into This State Prior to Her Admission into the Union," the measure got through the assembly but ran into trouble in the senate, thanks to the opposition of David Broderick. On April 15, however, the Chivs mustered enough votes to get the measure passed, 14 to 9. The new law was then upheld that summer when a Mississippian named Perkins, through his agents, claimed that three black men working in Placer County, two of them also named Perkins, were his fugitive property. A battery of legal talent tried to keep the black men from being sent back to slavery. But two judges on the California Supreme Court, one from Missouri, the other from Tennessee, ruled in the master's favor. The law was renewed in 1853, and then again in 1854. Finally, in 1855, antislavery forces in the legislature made sure that it lapsed.[26]

The California Fugitive Slave Act was largely symbolic. The state's total black population was minute, about two thousand, and very few had fled the cotton fields of the Deep South. More ominous was the second bill that Crabb introduced. For one thing, it had a powerful co-sponsor, Richard P. Hammond, the Speaker of the assembly. It also called for another constitutional convention. For what purpose? The state had just written a constitution three years earlier. Why did it need another—and so soon? What were Crabb and Hammond up to?

The two legislators never tipped their hand. Nearly every observer, however, thought they had a hidden agenda. And many saw their bill as just the first step in an all-out effort to split the state in two and open the southern half to slavery. Talk of division had been brewing for months. The previous summer, at a convention in Santa Barbara, some disgruntled southern Californians had lambasted the new state government for costing them too much in taxes and leaving them out of patronage spoils. They wanted out. They wanted to become a separate territory.[27]

Crabb and Hammond's motives in embracing this proposal were suspect. No one believed that they were truly concerned about the plight of southern Californians. Many, however, thought they wanted to split the state in two and establish slavery in the southern half. Wrote Antonio Maria de la Guerra, the assemblyman from Santa Barbara: "There is a suspicion here that all these questions are only a pretext to put in time awaiting division." Noted one pioneer in his diary: "The proposition now before the legislature, to submit the question of a constitutional convention to the people, has for its secret purpose the introduction of slavery." Echoed the San Francisco *Pacific*: "It is now too well known to need repeating that the principal objection in view by those who advocate the proposed convention is that our Constitution may be so amended as to permit slavery." Reported the *Alta California*: "It is evidently the design of a clique in the Legislature to divide the state at all hazards." In the same editorial: "Those who don't want the dark cloud of slavery spread over the sunny hills and valleys of California have little to look for from the present Legislature of California."[28]

The *Alta* spoke too soon. With Speaker Hammond's backing, Crabb successfully maneuvered the proposal through the assembly. In the senate, however, was David Broderick. Determined to kill the bill, Broderick made full use of his parliamentary expertise. He first rounded up enough votes to postpone the measure indefinitely. He then filed a motion to reconsider the bill and got enough votes to defeat his own motion. Under the rules, the second vote barred further consideration of the bill for the rest of that legislative session.

The next year Crabb wrote a "Whig Secret Circular" that called for a state convention to frame a new constitution and to divide the state. He also ran for the state senate and got elected. With him in the upper house, the Chivs and their Whig allies tried again. This time Broderick wasn't in the senate, and they succeeded in getting the measure through both houses. Nonetheless, they still had to deal with Broderick. In their bill, they had not provided for voter ratification of whatever the constitutional convention decided. Why the omission? asked Broderick. Did they plan to sneak the new constitution by the electorate? Broderick demanded that this "oversight" be rectified, and at the state Democratic convention he got an overwhelming majority to agree with him. That effectively killed the bill.[29] The next year the voters turned Crabb out of office.

Upon losing political office, Crabb shifted his attention to Mexico. He had recently married Filomená Ainsa, the daughter of a rich Spanish merchant, Manuel Ainsa. Her family had migrated to California from Sonora thirty years earlier, right after Mexico had gained independence from Spain. They had left behind considerable wealth in Sonora. With the help of their new son-in-law, they hoped to get some of it back and take over Sonora in the process. Did such a takeover also provide a chance to establish a slave state in northern Mexico? Crabb thought it did and jumped at the opportunity.[30]

In 1856, Crabb and his in-laws decided that the time was ripe. One of Sonora's frequent revolutions had led to the ouster of the faction headed by Ignacio Pesquera. The ousted leader now wanted help. They went to see him. Pesquera, in turn, begged Crabb to rally Americans to the cause and told Crabb that his men desired to be annexed to the United States. Crabb then formed the Arizona Colonization Company, a motley collection that included one sitting California state senator, eight former state legislators, and several former soldiers.[31]

Crabb also received help from Senator Gwin. The Chiv senator called upon General Ethan Allen Hitchcock, who was in charge of troops in San Francisco, to provide "safe conduct" for Crabb so that he could successfully make an "independent move on Sonora." Noted the general: "A pretty thing indeed, that I should be dragooned into giving such a protection to a leading man of a hostile force against Sonora!—and at the solicitation of a senator of the United States!"[32]

By the time Crabb and his men invaded Sonora, the situation had changed for the worse. First, some of his followers got drunk and boasted that Sonora would soon be theirs. Their boasts traveled faster than they did and alienated all who might have welcomed them. To smooth things over, Crabb had to explain how he had been invited into Sonora by "some of the most influential citizens." He also warned, "If blood is to flow, with all its horrors, on your head be it, and not on mine." Second, and more important, the Pesquera group had made peace with their rivals and were eager to make up for their traitorous past. Pesquera now called on his supporters to kill the invaders.[33]

Ignorant of all this, Crabb led his men into Sonora in March 1857. On the morning of April 1, they ran into trouble. Ambushed just outside Caborca, they fought their way into town and in the process lost twenty-one men, wounded or dead. They sought refuge in some adobe houses. They then decided that a nearby church offered more protection and tried to blow the doors open with a keg of gunpowder. They botched the attack. Several more men were killed, and Crabb was wounded. They then holed up in a row of houses. On April 6, Mexican authorities set fire to the roofs with flaming arrows. Crabb's men then attempted to blow the roof off one of the houses with a keg of gunpowder, only to choke themselves and further expose themselves to the enemy.

Many of Crabb's men wanted to fight their way out, but Crabb thought this would be foolhardy. He asked instead for terms of surrender. Shortly after midnight, upon getting a promise of medical attention and a fair trial, Crabb and his men put down their weapons and walked single file to the church, where they were hog-tied. The next morning, at dawn, fifty-nine men were executed by firing squad, in groups of five to ten. The last to be executed was Crabb. Tied with his face to the pole and hands above his head, he had some one hundred rounds fired into him. His head was then chopped off and put on display in a large jar of mescal.[34] Only one invader, fourteen-year-old Charles Edward Evans, survived the assault.

Meanwhile, frustrated in his effort to establish a slave colony at the "Sources of the Joachin," James Gadsden turned his attention to a southern transcontinental railroad. Here, too, he faced an uphill struggle. For other entrepreneurs had already taken steps to gain control of the gold trade.

No sooner had gold been discovered in California than the question arose over how to get there. Equally important was how to get the gold back east. The value of gold coming out of the Sierras skyrocketed—from $5.69 million in 1848, to $12.48 million in 1849, to $53.02 million in 1850, to $64.68 million in 1851, to $66.64 million in 1852.[35] Overnight, California gold became the nation's most valuable mineral. What was the best way to move it? The safest way? Going around the Horn was long and treacherous. So, too, was going overland by wagon train, while going through Panama meant going through a foreign country. In the long run, contended Gadsden, the only solution was a transcontinental railroad.

But that solution, to Gadsden's dismay, was jeopardized by bold and cunning men who moved faster than he did. Among them was William Aspinwall. As soon as the gold rush began, the astute New Yorker realized that he needed more ships. Three wouldn't do. By 1851 he had expanded his gold fleet to nine ships. Simultaneously, Aspinwall and his partners lobbied Congress and the government of New Granada for a railroad across the Isthmus of Panama. They moved fast and worked out a deal with New Granada on December 21, 1848, months before California became a state.

The contract gave Aspinwall and his partners eight years to build a road, a large grant of land, a right-of-way, and permission to select their own route. After completion, they were to have the exclusive right to operate a railroad, turnpike, or canal for forty-nine years. They could fix their own tolls, provided that the tolls were uniform and treated the citizens of all nations alike. The ports were to be free ports. After twenty years, New Granada had the right to purchase the property, and it was to receive 3 percent of all dividends.

Upon ratification of this deal, Aspinwall and his partners tried to improve upon the U.S. mail contract that they already had. It paid them $500,000 a year to carry the mail to California. In addition, they sought from Congress a twenty-year contract for transporting government officials, troops, munitions, and army and navy supplies. The House Committee on Naval Affairs responded favorably, citing the advantage it would give the United States over Great Britain in the Pacific and the great traffic between the East Coast and California. There was one snag, however. The committee wanted limitations on the rates that the company might charge, and Aspinwall and his partners rejected such restrictions.[36]

In the Senate, Thomas Hart Benton, chair of the Committee on Military Affairs, tried to find middle ground. Benton and his fellow committee members introduced a bill that authorized the secretary of the navy to make such a contract for twenty years with compensation of $300,000 per annum, the contractors to begin their railroad within one year from June 1, 1849, and complete it within three years. Getting the bill passed, however, proved impossible. Among those in opposition were Jefferson Davis, who argued that such a bill would delay building a railroad on American soil, and Henry Foote, who supported a rival railroad project across the Tehuantepec isthmus.[37]

Nonetheless, with their $500,000-a-year federal mail contract and the backing of New Granada, Aspinwall and his partners plunged

JOHN L. STEPHENS   WILLIAM H. ASPINWALL   HENRY CHAUNCEY

William Aspinwall and associates. Reprinted from Harper's New
Monthly Magazine *18 (January 1859), 147.*

ahead. Work began in May 1850. Two engineers, J. C. Trautwine and
George M. Totten, headed the project. They expected to finish the job
in two years at $2 million. Both men had tropical experience, but find-
ing and keeping a labor force was beyond them. They tried local labor.
They then brought in Irish workers, then Jamaicans and other West
Indians, then Chinese and Hindu coolies. One group after another,
however, succumbed to fever, malaria, cholera, dysentery, and smallpox.
The death rate was staggering. In 1852, of some fifty American engineers, draftsmen, and officials, all but two died. Wags later said that one

man died for each of the seventy-four thousand ties that was laid. That was a wild exaggeration, but many thousands died, maybe one for every twelve ties laid. The project thus took five years to complete and cost $8 million.

On January 18, 1855, the last track was laid. A few hours later, the first locomotive made the 47.5-mile trip across the isthmus and rolled into Panama City. It took three hours. Thereafter, one train crossed per day in a six-day workweek. The cost for a one-way ticket was $25 in gold. By Christmas 1859, the railroad had carried 196,000 passengers, $300 million in gold bullion, and 100,000 bags of mail. In its first seven years, it netted about $6 million in profits and regularly paid dividends of 15 percent and once a whopping 44 percent. At one point, it was the highest-priced stock on the New York Exchange at $295 a share.[38]

William Aspinwall was not the only wily New Yorker who got a jump on James Gadsden. So, too, did Cornelius Vanderbilt.

The fifty-five-year-old Vanderbilt, in 1849, was already a New York legend. Big, bumptious, loud, and coarse, he had dropped out of school when he was eleven or twelve and gone to work full-time for his father, a poor Staten Island farmer, transferring farm produce to Manhattan. When he was sixteen, his parents had lent him $100 to purchase a small sailboat. With it he set up a freight business and ferried passengers, 18 cents one way, 25 cents round-trip, and earned over $1,000 the first year. From sailing he got into steamboats and railroads and was probably worth $1 million by the time he was forty-five.

Generally known as the Commodore, a title bestowed on him by *The New York Journal of Commerce*, Vanderbilt had earned a reputation

Cornelius Vanderbilt. Library of Congress.

for being both a man of his word and a hardheaded businessman. He had little concern for the people around him, including his wife (a first cousin whom he married against his parents' wishes) and his thirteen children, whom he generally ignored or treated as worthless. In his judgment, only one of his sons, William Henry, amounted to much.[39]

With the California gold rush in 1849, Vanderbilt immediately took stock of the situation. He knew that Aspinwall initially had an edge. Was there any way to get the better of him? After studying maps of Central America for many hours, Vanderbilt saw an opening. North of Panama, the San Juan River runs along the Nicaragua border with Costa Rica for 119 miles and then empties into Lake Nicaragua. The western shore of the lake, which is one hundred miles long and fifty miles wide, is only twelve miles from the Pacific Ocean. If Vanderbilt could make use of the San Juan River and Lake Nicaragua, all but twelve miles of Nicaragua could be crossed by boat, and the route to California could be shortened by at least five hundred nautical miles.

To take advantage of this situation, Vanderbilt invested in the

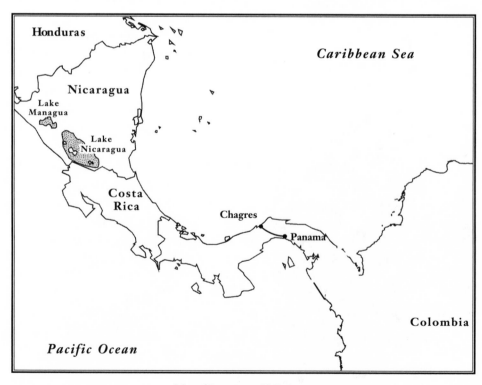

Map of Panama and Nicaragua

American Atlantic and Pacific Ship Canal Company and sought a monopoly from the Nicaraguan government. In late August 1849, he had his agent, Joseph L. White, with the connivance of the American minister to Nicaragua, E. George Squier, strike a deal with Nicaraguan authorities. It gave Vanderbilt and his associates the exclusive right to operate a transit system across Nicaragua. In twelve years, Vanderbilt was to construct a canal (or railroad, if more feasible) to link the final few miles to the Pacific.

The Nicaraguan government was to provide construction materials, convict labor to do the work, customs exemptions, and eight sections of land. In return, Vanderbilt had to pay the government $10,000 up front, $10,000 a year during canal construction, $200,000 in canal stock when the stock was issued, 10 percent of the annual profits until the canal was completed, 20 percent of the profits for the first twenty years thereafter, then 25 percent, and finally ownership of all the assets after eighty-five years.[40]

To test the route, which many locals said wasn't navigable, Vanderbilt personally piloted a small steamboat up the San Juan River. He then had the river cleared of obstacles, placed a steamboat on Lake Nicaragua, and built a road from the western shore of the lake to San Juan del Sur—a port he constructed on the Pacific coast. Vanderbilt then organized the Accessory Transit Company and in 1851 secured a modification of his original contract that gave him a monopoly of transit from the Atlantic to the Pacific. He began with two steamships on the New York run, three on the Pacific, and quickly expanded to four and five.

The completed project cut six hundred miles and two days off the trip to and from California. Between 1851 and 1856, about twenty-four thousand Americans per year took this route. Since Vanderbilt's costs were less than Aspinwall's, he immediately put pressure on his business rival, slashing the prevailing fare of $600 to $400. He also offered to carry the mail for free. Eventually he dropped the fare to $150 and still made money.

By 1853, Vanderbilt was worth $11 million. To impress New York society, which had always shunned him because of his poor roots and boorish behavior, he built the *North Star,* a twenty-five-hundred-ton and 170-foot steam yacht, for a fifteen-thousand-mile trip to Europe and the Mediterranean. Since he was to be gone for six months, he decided to temporarily turn over control of his companies to other men. To run the New York branch of the Accessory Transit Company, he chose Charles Morgan, a fellow shipowner and friend who had been born and raised in Connecticut but had a long interest in the Gulf trade and used slave labor on his steamers.[41]

Morgan then suggested that Vanderbilt hire Cornelius Garrison to be his San Francisco agent. A New Yorker by birth, Garrison had moved to Panama City at the time of the gold rush. There, he had become famous as an extremely aggressive banker and shipper who also owned and operated three-card monte tables. To get him, Vanderbilt had to offer him a salary of $60,000 per year and letters of credit to transport $1 million per month in gold to eastern firms. Garrison then moved to San Francisco and within six months became the city's mayor. He was known for his slippery ways, and an admirer said that it took "twenty men to watch him."[42]

While Vanderbilt was away, Garrison and Morgan tried to take over his company. First they manipulated stock prices in Accessory Transit in such a way that they profited while Vanderbilt lost heavily. Then they tried to get control of the Nicaraguan government and have a new government transfer the Transit concession to themselves. For that task, they turned to William Walker.

The twenty-nine-year-old Walker was an enigma. At first glance no one thought much of him. All agreed that he was short, probably about five feet six, thin, freckled, extremely shy, unpretentious, seldom spoke, and always kept his hands in his pockets. Upon meeting him, one man wrote: "There he sat!— a little, white-haired, white-eyebrowed, boyish-looking man, with cold, icy-gray eyes, a quiet, passionless manner, which renders him exceedingly mysterious and enigmatical, even to his most intimate friends."[43]

William Walker. Reprinted from Ben: Perley Poore,
Perley's Reminiscences, *2 vols. (Philadelphia, 1886),*
1:402.

Yet somehow Walker was able to command men and inspire loyalty. Indeed, he had an uncanny ability to get hundreds of men to follow him to their death. Why? Few could explain it.

A native of Nashville, Walker had attended the University of Nashville, and then earned a medical degree from the University of Pennsylvania. Then, after traveling through Europe, he returned to Nashville, practiced medicine for a short while, and then moved to New Orleans, where he became first a lawyer and then the editor and co-owner of the New Orleans *Crescent*. He also fell in love with Ellen Martin, a deafmute, and learned sign language to communicate with her. In April 1849, she died of cholera. Her death, all agreed, left a permanent mark on Walker, and some thought it explained everything about him—his daring, his reckless disregard of life, his ability to burn whole towns and execute rivals and deserters with few regrets.[44]

Shortly after Ellen Martin's death, Walker took off for California. Arriving in San Francisco in 1850, he became the associate editor of *The San Francisco Daily Herald*. He soon ridiculed the judicial system, particularly Judge Levi Parsons, who had him arrested. Released as a result of public outrage, Walker then fought a duel with one of the judge's backers. Slightly wounded, he moved to Marysville in 1851, where he again practiced law. In his spare time, he followed the exploits of two French filibusters, Raousset-Boulbon and Charles de Pindray, who had led private armies onto foreign soil. Influenced by their example, Walker decided to establish American colonies in Sonora and Baja California.

Walker, in 1853, first sought permission from Mexican authorities, who turned him down. He and his law associate, Henry P. Watkins, then planned an invasion, with Walker leading the first batch of troops, Watkins bringing reinforcements. Helping them plan the assault were members of the California state legislature and their clerks. They also had the backing of both California senators, William Gwin and John Weller.[45]

With forty-five men and a brig, Walker landed at La Paz in November 1853 and proclaimed the Republic of Lower California with himself as president. Watkins and the planned reinforcements, however, were detained by the U.S. government and never arrived. Mexican troops then drove Walker and his men out of La Paz, into Sonora, and blocked their path at the border. Charging the Mexican line, Walker and his men broke through and crossed the border, only to be arrested by the U.S. Army and brought to trial in San Francisco for violating U.S. neutrality laws. The trial was futile. The jury acquitted Walker after just eight minutes of deliberation.

Settling again in San Francisco, Walker now turned his attention to Nicaragua. It was easy pickings. The country was plagued by constant civil war, and one of Nicaragua's warring factions—the Liberals—desperately needed troops. In 1854, they offered Byron Cole, a Walker associate from San Francisco, a large land grant in return for help in ousting their Conservative rivals. After persuading Walker and Cornelius Garrison to support the Liberal cause, Cole signed two contracts with the Liberals in which Walker was to bring in three hundred men, and the men were to be guaranteed five hundred acres after their service, and the Accessory Transit Company was to provide some three hundred company men.

In 1855, Walker marched into Nicaragua, took the enemy capital of Granada by surprise, and had a cabinet minister of the opposing government shot. Soon the opposition, fearful for their lives, came to terms. Walker named himself head of the army but allowed Patricio Rivas to become provisional president, and then ousted him and took over the presidency himself. In 1856 the U.S. government recognized his regime.

Walker's success attracted followers by the hundreds. So, too, did his offer of 250 acres of Nicaraguan public land for free to any American who immigrated to "his" country. Between 1855 and 1857, according to one observer, some seven thousand men from the Atlantic states arrived via the San Juan River and another thirty-five hundred from California.[46]

Among the recruits was a young Missourian, James Carson Jamison, who had tried his luck at mining gold in El Dorado County. Once he heard about Walker, his "blood grew hot at the thought of the stirring adventures" that awaited him if he could "attach himself" to Walker's army. So Jamison joined one of the California companies that was being formed and in the election of officers was chosen a first lieutenant. Upon receiving his commission from Walker in Granada, he could barely believe his ears: "A woman's voice was scarcely softer than Walker's, and so imperturbable was he that his praise of a valorous deed or his announcement of a death penalty were equally calm in tone and deliberate in enunciation."[47]

Walker's glory days, however, were short-lived. In December 1855, Cornelius Garrison's son arrived in Granada. He had a proposal. Garrison and Morgan would furnish Walker with reinforcements and cover the costs of transporting them to Nicaragua. In return, they wanted Walker to annul Vanderbilt's contract on the grounds that the Commodore had not kept up his payments to the Nicaraguan government. Walker would then issue a new charter giving Garrison and Morgan exclusive transit rights. He would also turn over to them all Accessory Transit Company property in Nicaragua. Walker accepted the deal and in February 1856 had President Rivas sign the necessary paperwork.

It proved to be a colossal mistake. On returning from six months abroad, Vanderbilt sought revenge against all who had wronged him. He had no time for legal action, he said; the law was too slow. He intended instead to destroy his adversaries. With capital at his command, he formed a new shipping company, the Independent Line, with Edward Mills, a California shipping magnate. Then, to drive Morgan and Garrison into bankruptcy, he operated his steamboats below costs. By the end of the year, he had the two "interlopers" in deep financial trouble, hanging on, but barely.

To bring down Walker, Vanderbilt began working closely with Walker's Central American enemies. They had far more men than Walker, but their armies were rife with corruption and reluctant to fight. Vanderbilt used his money to prod them into forming an alliance to invade Nicaragua and expel Walker. He also sent in men to lead and plan the attack. One was William Webster, an English adventurer with a criminal record, who mapped out a plan for Costa Rican troops to seize the transit route and cut off Walker's supply lines. Another was a New Yorker, Sylvanus M. Spencer, who ended up commanding the Costa Rican operation.[48]

As Walker's troubles mounted, he received help from Pierre Soulé, whom he probably knew from having lived in New Orleans. In April 1856, at a New Orleans fund-raiser, Soulé sang Walker's praises and pledged $25,000. In August, Soulé went to Nicaragua, the first and only Southerner of his standing to do so. He helped Walker establish procedures for issuing bonds redeemable at the end of twenty years in gold and silver at the Bank of Louisiana.[49]

Soulé also probably had a hand in getting Walker to reinstitute slavery in Nicaragua. Realizing that men like Soulé represented his only hope, Walker decided "to bind the Southern States to Nicaragua as if she were one of themselves."[50] On September 22, 1856, he revoked Nicaragua's 1824 emancipation decree. That decision sparked an enthusiastic response throughout the Deep South. Gulf States journals now portrayed Walker as the "grey-eyed man of destiny." Several boatloads of troops soon left New Orleans to bolster Walker's cause.

But neither fresh troops nor Southern support saved him from Vanderbilt's revenge. By late 1856, the Commodore had gained a stranglehold over the Accessory Transit Company, and Costa Rican battalions were wreaking havoc on Walker's army. Always outnumbered, his troops suffered casualty rates approaching 20 percent. Then, to make matters worse, cholera ravaged one company after another. Forced to abandon Granada, Walker ordered the ancient capital city burned to the ground. In May 1857, having suffered heavy losses, he surrendered to the U.S. Navy. Brought to New Orleans, he was hailed as a hero. Tried there in June 1858 for violating neutrality laws, he again was quickly acquitted.

Walker then toured the South seeking men and financial support for another invasion. Soulé and other leading New Orleans enthusiasts formed a Nicaraguan committee to sell bonds and rally public support for the cause. The plan now was to invade Nicaragua via Honduras. The first attempt barely got off the ground. In November 1857 Walker sailed from Mobile. The U.S. Navy ran him down and hauled him and his invading army back to the states. The naval action, in turn, enraged several dozen Southern congressmen. Led by Representative Alexander Stephens of Georgia, they demanded that the Commodore who had detained Walker be court-martialed.

Still treated as a hero in the Deep South, Walker easily raised support for yet another invasion. Sailing from Mobile in December 1858, he and his troops got past the U.S. Navy but ran into trouble sixty miles from the Central American coast. The ship hit a reef and sank. A British ship rescued Walker and his men and returned them to Mobile.

Persistent, Walker launched a third attempt a year later. The spark, however, was now fading. Only ninety-seven men, almost all Southern youths, answered the call to battle. Traveling in small groups to a rendezvous point in Honduras, they hoped to find additional recruits for a new invasion of Nicaragua. Instead, while marching along the Honduran coast in August 1860, they ran into trouble and had to surrender to a British naval captain. Walker expected to be returned once again to the United States. The British, however, now regarded him as a threat to their interests on the Mosquito Coast and turned him over to the Honduras government. The Hondurans executed him by firing squad, at Trujillo, on September 12, 1860. He died, as he had lived, with no apparent emotion.

Meanwhile, Cornelius Vanderbilt came out smiling. Not only did he get his revenge. He soon received an offer from his two Panama rivals, William Aspinwall and George Law, the owners of Pacific Mail and U.S. Mail lines. They were tired of fighting a price war with him. They offered him money not to compete, first $40,000 a month in 1857, then $56,000 a month in 1858. He took the deal, pocketing $480,000 the first year and $672,000 the next year for doing nothing. These payments ended in 1859. By then the Panama Railroad was well established and Aspinwall's worries were history. No longer did he have to fret about the Nicaraguan route having a competitive advantage over his Panama route. Nor did he have to worry about Vanderbilt building a canal to cover the last twelve-mile leg in Nicaragua. Vanderbilt never did.

6

———◆———

JAMES GADSDEN, EVEN THOUGH HE WAS SEVERAL STEPS BEHIND
William Aspinwall and Cornelius Vanderbilt, still had reason to hope.
Despite their success, nearly every pundit agreed with him. Going
through Central America was dangerous. It exposed Americans to the
whims of foreign rulers and warlords as well as dozens of deadly diseases. It was just a temporary expedient. The best solution was still a
transcontinental railroad within the United States.

Especially adamant were California's newly elected legislators.
Two-thirds had come by way of Panama. Every one, regardless of his
political affiliation, clamored for a transcontinental railroad. In 1850
they called on Congress to finance its construction. A few months later
Senator Gwin presented the legislature's resolution to the Senate. The
resolution then went to the Committee on Roads and Canals. There it
died. The next year a bill calling for land grants for the indigent insane
came before the Senate. To that bill Gwin added an amendment calling
for two railroad routes to the Pacific. The amendment passed, but the
bill itself failed.

Later that same year, Gwin offered a detailed plan that would have
made California an appendage of the South. With San Francisco as the
western terminus (with a later extension up to Oregon), the plan called

for a railroad that went south around the southern end of the Sierras to Albuquerque. There, it split into four branches, one line to Texas, another to New Orleans, another to Memphis, another to Missouri. As soon as Gwin made this proposal, Lewis Cass of Michigan jumped on it. The plan, said the former Democratic candidate for president, was "too grandiose." It necessitated 5,115 miles of track, and the estimated cost was $121,920,000.[1]

Right after Cass's objection, Senator Walker Brooke, a newly elected Mississippi Whig, offered a substitute bill. It was the scheme of the Atlantic and Pacific Railroad Company of New York. Nicknamed the "moonshine" railroad, because it had been chartered at $100 million with only "pennies" in its coffers, the Atlantic and Pacific was headed by Gwin's old friend the ex–treasury secretary Robert J. Walker and his partner, Levi S. Chatfield, the attorney general of New York. Walker and Chatfield also contemplated building a southern railroad, beginning on the Mississippi River or on the Gulf west of the river, but with regards to the exact route they wanted to be able to pick and choose. They also wanted the federal government to grant them land, lend them $30 million, and pay the interest on all the bonds they issued until the project was completed.[2]

It quickly became clear that neither proposal had the votes to pass. The Senate then referred Gwin's bill to a special committee headed by Senator Thomas Jefferson Rusk of Texas. A South Carolinian by birth and a onetime follower of John C. Calhoun, the forty-seven-year-old Rusk had moved to Texas in the winter of 1834 and become its secretary of war in the revolt against Mexico. Since then, he had gained a reputation for always looking out for his constituents, the people of north Texas.[3] Hence, even though he proposed leaving the choice of the route and terminals to President Pierce and called for competitive bidding by contractors, Northern senators immediately assumed that Rusk expected the railroad to be Southern-based and to go through north Texas.

To stop that from happening, Senator James Shields of Illinois slipped in a poison pill. After conferring with Illinois's other senator, Stephen A. Douglas, and Henry S. Geyer of Missouri, he offered an amendment to Rusk's proposal specifying that none of the $20 million appropriated for a railroad could be spent within the limits of "any existing state." The wording put Southern Democrats in a bind. Not only was it impossible to build a southern railroad without going through hundreds of miles of Texas, but the amendment was in keeping with their well-known "principles." For decades, many of them had championed "strict construction" of the Constitution and insisted that spending federal money within a state violated strict-construction doctrine. Would they abide by their principles? Some did, others did not. The amendment passed by a narrow vote, and once it did, Southern senators lost interest in supporting Rusk's proposal. It had become, moaned Rusk, "a useless piece of paper."[4]

At the same time that Thomas Jefferson Rusk watched his bill go down to defeat in the Senate, William A. Richardson of Illinois introduced a bill in the House to organize the Nebraska country. The forty-one-year-old Democrat was Douglas's chief spokesman in the House. He held, in fact, the same seat in the House that Douglas had held before being elected to the Senate. Leaving no doubt where he stood, Richardson said his bill was to facilitate the building of a railroad westward. "Why, everybody is talking about a railroad to the Pacific Ocean. In the name of God, how is the railroad to be made if you will never let people on the lands through which the road passes?"

To kill Richardson's proposal, some of Rusk's fellow Texans brought up the need to terminate Indian titles in the Nebraska country. The costs, they contended, would be prohibitive. Bribes and military force would be necessary. Nonetheless, the bill easily passed the House, 107 to 49.

Richardson's bill then went to the Senate, to the chairman of the Committee on Territories, Stephen A. Douglas himself. Rusk and other Southerners, however, had more political muscle in the Senate than they did in the House. Douglas thus had difficulty getting the Senate to even consider the bill. Finally, two days before Congress adjourned in March 1853, he succeeded. Then, to his dismay, a motion to table the bill passed, 23 to 17, largely by Southern votes. Only two slave-state senators (both from Missouri) supported the bill.[5]

The message was thus clear. Getting any railroad measure through Congress was going to be an uphill struggle. No proposal could please everyone. Was California to become an appendage of the South? Or of the North? Was the railroad's eastern terminus to be in New Orleans? Or Chicago? Or somewhere in between? What city, and what section of the country, was to gain the upper hand? The stakes were high.

One measure, however, got through. On March 3, 1853, Congress appropriated $150,000 for the secretary of war, Jefferson Davis, to survey possible routes. This was a victory for James Gadsden and the South. A huge victory. For Davis was anything but an unbiased observer.

Davis never admitted his bias. Instead, he attributed his enthusiastic support of a southern railroad to two other factors. One was his job as secretary of war. The other was "science." As he saw it, he was just doing his job, and the dictates of his job and "science" happened to coincide with the best interests of the South.

Jefferson Davis, secretary of war. Reprinted from Ben: Perley Poore, Perley's Reminiscences, *2 vols. (Philadelphia, 1886), 1:476.*

As secretary of war, Davis insisted that he had no choice but to support a southern railroad to the Pacific. The war with Mexico had added millions of square miles to the United States. On top of that, millions of dollars in gold had been discovered. How was the vast new national domain and its wealth to be defended? That, said Davis, was the single most pressing issue facing the War Department. And it mandated building a transcontinental railroad. For, in times of crisis, getting troops to the Pacific by sea not only took too long. It also would not be feasible against powerful foreign nations, namely Great Britain and France, as the U.S. Navy had only forty serviceable ships, whereas Great Britain and France had four hundred or more.

This argument, in turn, let Davis run roughshod over his "strict constructionist" past. As a strict constructionist, he had repeatedly argued that the Constitution limited what Congress could do to what was spelled out in the document itself. Where, then, was the clause in the Constitution giving Congress the power to build a transcontinental railroad? There was no such clause. Then didn't laying millions of tracks and ties across the West at federal expense violate strict-construction doctrine? No, argued Davis. The Constitution gave the federal government responsibility for national defense, and the railroad would be constructed largely for military purposes.[6]

Would such a railroad benefit the South? It obviously would. But that, contended Davis, was immaterial. As he saw it, he was a man of "science," and "science" dictated a southern route. The Corps of Topographical Engineers had already spent much time and money surveying and mapping the Southwest. They had been at it since the war with Mexico. The results, contended Davis, "proved" that the best path was from San Antonio to El Paso and then along the 32nd parallel to the Pacific. It had the fewest mountains, the least snow. The only major problem was the lack of water. But that could be remedied by digging artesian wells.

To preclude the appearance of sectional bias, however, Davis decided that it might be prudent to send out three survey parties to check other routes, from the far north to the 35th parallel. Then, after realizing that there were gaps in the original Southwest study, he decided that it might also be prudent to dispatch still another survey team to study the 32nd parallel route once again. He had no fear. He trusted the surveyors to do their job, to measure the depth of snow and report on the availability of water and timber and the habits of Indians. He was also certain that their reports would "prove" once again that only the 32nd parallel route was feasible.[7]

With that in mind, as soon as Congress appropriated the money, Davis leaped at the opportunity. On March 3, 1853, he ordered the chief of the Corps of Topographical Engineers to "make such explorations and surveys as he may deem advisable, to ascertain the most practicable and economical route for a railroad from the Mississippi River to the Pacific Ocean."[8]

The chief of the Corps of Topographical Engineers, William H. Emory, had been a classmate of Davis's at West Point. The son of a wealthy Tidewater family on Maryland's Eastern Shore with strong military and political connections, Emory had been appointed to the academy by none other than John C. Calhoun. He was only eleven or twelve years old at the time. Upon graduating, he had married Benjamin Franklin's great-granddaughter. Now fifty, he still stood out at any social gathering because of his ostentatious red whiskers. He also liked to dress and act like a dashing cavalry officer, even though he had long been a scientist and astronomer by trade.

Like Davis, Emory was anything but an unbiased observer. Part of General Stephen Watts Kearny's invasion of California in 1846, he had become convinced at that time that the Gila River route was the best way to the Pacific. He had sung its praises many times, and he had even bought real estate in San Diego, its likely Pacific terminus. He was also the brother-in-law of Robert J. Walker, the head of the Atlantic and Pacific Railroad, who was pushing for a southern route. On Davis's orders, however, Emory carefully picked men to head the research teams who at least appeared to be impartial. Science, after all, was to prove that Davis was right.[9]

If everything had gone as Davis had anticipated, the four survey parties that Emory sent out would have come back with conclusive evidence "proving" that only the southern route was practicable. That didn't happen. The surveyors found instead that several routes were feasible, not just the 32nd line. They dismissed the 38th parallel route from St. Louis to San Francisco as "impractical," spoke highly of the 41st parallel route from Omaha, also touted the 35th parallel route from Fort Smith, Arkansas, and especially showered praise on Davis's favorite, the 32nd. Their work, overall, was impressive. It was published in eleven large volumes with elaborate drawings and maps, and the faults were well hidden. No one seemed to realize at the time that they underestimated the distance of the 32nd by 102 miles and overestimated the distance of all the others by 50 to 257 miles.[10]

Even though the surveys indicated that several routes were viable, Davis forged ahead with his original plan. He told Congress that the 32nd line was by far the best choice, downplaying its negative features, emphasizing them in all the rest.

By then, Davis had also taken one other key step in behalf of a southern line. In May 1853, just months after the surveyors went to work, he had urged President Pierce to purchase from Mexico land strategic to the construction of a southern railroad. To negotiate the purchase, he got his friend James Gadsden appointed minister to Mexico.

Gadsden eagerly accepted the assignment. His thinking had changed since the days of the Memphis convention. While he still touted a southern railroad, he no longer focused on building it through Arkansas and north Texas. He now envisioned a more southern route along the Gila River. He had been told many times by army engineers that it was the shortest and most practicable of the southern routes. And for several years he had been actively pushing for the acquisition of more Mexican land to make this route more feasible. He also knew that the desired territory, a strip of land south of the Gila River, was regarded by the Mexican government as hostile Indian country and that the Mexican dictator, General Santa Anna, might be willing to sell it if the price was right. He thus set off for Mexico with a strong desire to acquire the land necessary to fulfill his dream of building a transcontinental railroad that would bind the West to the South.

On July 15, Gadsden received from Secretary of State William L. Marcy a list of official instructions.[11] His main task was to secure sufficient land south of the Gila River for the building of a railroad. In addition, he was to try to resolve several other ticklish problems that had plagued the State Department. One concerned a pledge that the federal government had made at the end of the war with Mexico. In the Treaty of Guadalupe Hidalgo, the United States had promised to police the Apaches and other tribes along the New Mexico border and keep them from launching attacks into Mexico. It had proved impossible to do, and the State Department now hoped to find a way to escape financial liability. Also, several well-connected New Orleans entrepreneurs wanted the right to cross the Isthmus of Tehuantepec. They had visions of building a canal or a railroad across Mexico and thus providing transport to California that would be some twelve hundred miles shorter than the Panama route. They also had friends in high places, at least three in the Senate, one or two in the Pierce administration.[12]

Gadsden barely paid lip service to these secondary matters. To him all that really mattered was getting enough land to build a railroad and having a defensible border. In preparing for his negotiations, he conferred at length with Andrew Belcher Gray, a thirty-two-year-old Virginian who had moved to Texas when he was nineteen and had become one of the region's top surveyors. In these talks, Gadsden was single-minded. He only wanted to know what land, precisely, would be necessary for a railroad—and what additional land would be necessary for its defense. He also wanted Marcy to send Gray as his agent to the Gila River region to determine to the mile exactly what land was needed.[13]

The White House, however, had larger goals. On November 14, while Gadsden was negotiating with Santa Anna's government, Christopher L. Ward, a special messenger, arrived with new instructions. The Pierce administration now wanted Gadsden to buy a much bigger slice of northern Mexico. The president had dreams of acquiring the northern part of Tamaulipas, Nuevo León, Coahuila, Chihuahua, Sonora, and all of Baja California, and Gadsden was to offer $50 million for it. Then, if that proposal failed, Gadsden was to offer $35 million, $30 million, and $20 million for progressively smaller chunks of northern Mexico. And then, if none of these four offers worked, he was to get sufficient territory for a transcontinental railroad.[14]

To Gadsden only the last instruction was worth an all-out effort. But he followed the president's wish list nonetheless and tried to get Mexico to part with Baja California and the northern part of Tamaulipas, Nuevo León, Coahuila, Chihuahua, and Sonora. Failing miserably, he blamed the outcome on William Walker's invasion of Baja California. Had it not been for Walker, contended Gadsden, he would have had more success. Walker had hardened General Santa Anna against further land concessions.[15]

This defeat, however, never distracted Gadsden from his main goal. In negotiations, according to Mexican sources, he remained single-minded. With most items on the State Department's agenda, he tended to be lackadaisical. He tried, for example, to get the Mexican government to uphold the Garay and Sloo grants that seemingly would have enabled the well-connected New Orleans entrepreneurs to build a canal or railroad across the Isthmus of Tehuantepec. But when the Mexican minister did not do so, Gadsden did not push it. He agreed instead to have the U.S. government compensate the aggrieved Americans.

On land for a railroad, however, Gadsden gave no quarter. He was not just a tough negotiator. According to the Mexican dictator, General Santa Anna, he was downright nasty and belligerent. Said Gadsden: "The projected railroad from New York to California must be built by way of the Mesilla Valley, because there is no other feasible route. The Mexican government will be splendidly indemnified. The valley must belong to the United States by an indemnity, or we will take it." This infuriated Santa Anna. But he was desperate for money, and the promise of $15 million caused him to turn the other cheek.[16]

Gadsden concluded negotiations on December 30, 1853. For $15 million, the United States was to get about forty-five thousand square miles in the Mesilla valley, south of the Gila River.

The deal disappointed President Pierce. He expected more land. Nonetheless, he backed the Gadsden Purchase in his first annual message and submitted it to the Senate for ratification on February 10. Even more distraught was Senator Augustus Caesar Dodge of Iowa. He deemed the Gadsden Purchase outrageous. He opposed a southern railroad. He wanted one built from Omaha west. Hoping to block the purchase, and to rally others to his cause, Dodge introduced a bill for the organization of Nebraska.

The Senate considered the treaty in secret session. Hence the record of who said what and when is sparse. But judging from offhand remarks made by senators in other debates and newspaper "leaks," the treaty initially fell well short of the necessary two-thirds majority. Opposition came from several quarters. Three senators, including William Gwin of California, wanted more land. Three objected to the United States' agreeing to pay up to $5 million to American entrepreneurs who had once held Mexican franchises, now repudiated by Mexico, for building a railroad or canal across the Isthmus of Tehuantepec. Several Southern senators opposed expansion. The main opposition, however, came from Northern senators who saw the treaty as a gain for the Slave Power. The debate was thus largely sectional.[17]

To dampen Northern disapproval and to win a few key Southern votes, the treaty's backers decided amendments were necessary. They proposed paying less money, $10 million, for less land, roughly twenty-nine thousand square miles. Then, to make sure that they could still build a southern railroad, they had to redraw the boundary. Taking the lead in this effort was Senator James M. Mason of Virginia. For assistance, he relied heavily on his fellow Virginian and Gadsden's trusted expert, Andrew Belcher Gray. The changes infuriated Gadsden, so much so that he lobbied against the finished product.

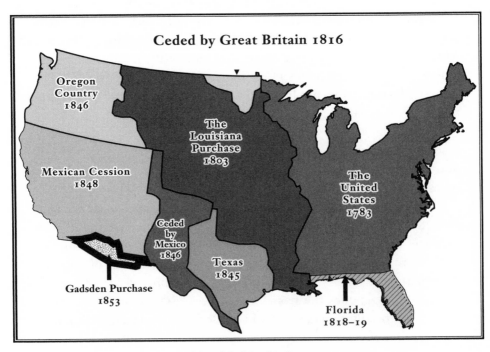

Map of Gadsden Purchase

Even with the changes, it still took weeks of hard work to get the necessary two-thirds vote. Hostile senators not only denounced the treaty. They also lambasted the railroad surveys provided by the Corps of Topographical Engineers that had been used to justify the purchase. Joining the angry senators, once it became time to appropriate money, were members of the House. In both chambers nearly every critic assumed that the surveys were biased. That they were done under Jefferson Davis, said Thomas Hart Benton, "was proof enough for most men" that that was the case.

The most savage criticisms came from Benton. He had lost his seat in the Senate but now sat in the House. Flaying Davis and his handiwork, Benton described the area south of the Gila River as "so utterly desolate . . . and God-forsaken that Kit Carson says a wolf could not make his living on it." Was it worth $10 million? No, Robert J. Walker and his "moonshine" railroad could have bought the same scrubby land for $6,500. As for the "expert" advice from the Corps of Engineers, said Benton, "it takes a grand national school like West Point to put national roads outside of a country and leave the interior without one." Then, waving a map of San Diego, he added: "It is said to belong to the military—to the scientific corps—and to be divided into many shares, and expected to make fortunes of the shareholders or lot holders as soon as Congress sends the Pacific railroad to it." And the biggest crook of the bunch, thundered Benton, was undoubtedly Davis's chief engineer, William Emory. Not only was Emory tied to the "paper city." He was also the brother-in-law of Robert J. Walker, the president of the "moonshine" railroad.[18]

To official Washington, Benton's harsh words came as no surprise. Not only did the Missouri congressman want a railroad running from St. Louis west; he also had a well-known grudge to settle against Emory and the Corps of Engineers. Emory was among the West Point officers who had testified against his son-in-law John C. Frémont. And West Pointers in the Corps of Engineers had always resented Frémont's reputation as the "Pathfinder" and treated him shabbily.

Yet even though Washington insiders realized that Benton had scores to settle, many thought his points were valid. Among them was Zedekiah Kidwell, a forty-year-old Democrat from the hills of western Virginia. A lame-duck congressman, Kidwell later wrote the House minority report on the Pacific railroad surveys. In his eyes, Jefferson Davis blew it. He was so biased in favor of the 32nd parallel route that he not only failed to serve the interests of the nation but also failed the South. He failed to see that the 35th parallel route had the best chance of uniting the various interests, particularly if the eastern terminus was far enough west so that forks could be run to St. Louis, Memphis, and Fort Smith. The 32nd route, in Kidwell's eyes, had no chance of passing. It was just too far south and too controversial, and it infuriated too many rival interests.[19]

Was Kidwell right? The supporters of the 32nd line knew that to have even a chance to prove him wrong, they had to get the treaty passed. On April 17, they were still three votes shy of the necessary two-thirds majority. On ratification, they came up short, 27 to 18. But Southern senators wouldn't let the matter drop. Nor would the Pierce administration. Together, they wooed the wavering—and the corrupt—with sweetheart deals and patronage.[20] And by April 25 they had an additional six votes, the three votes they needed and then some. The amended treaty was thus ratified, 33 to 12.

Had it solely been in the hands of Northern senators, it would have gone down to defeat. Twelve Northern senators voted yes; twelve no. But in the end, the twelve Northern yes votes were decisive. All but one were Democrats, members of President Pierce's party. Only their willingness to vote with a solid bloc of twenty-one Southern senators led to the treaty's approval.[21]

Jefferson Davis thus got the land he needed. But getting the land, as Kidwell knew, was just the first step in developing a southern transcontinental railroad. Would Congress go the next step and appropriate money for building a railroad?

As time passed, Davis became bolder and more determined. The only problem with the 32nd parallel route, in his judgment, was the lack of water. Every other complaint was bogus. So he focused on water. How could that problem be solved? The answer, he decided, lay in artesian wells. So, at his direction, the Corp of Engineers began boring artesian wells near the mouth of the Pecos River in Texas. This experiment ended in failure and provided even further data for his critics.

That didn't stop Davis. His obsession with a southern route, along with the water problem, led to an even more bizarre experiment. As a senator, he had heard about the military advantage of camels. As secretary of war, he came across a book on desert warfare that further touted the military advantage of camels. It "proved" that they traveled twice as fast as horses, ate less, went three days without water, and carried as much as twelve hundred pounds. Would camels solve the transportation problem until a railroad was developed? Davis thought so. The book, however, was in French. So to make his case, Davis stayed up late, night after night, translating the book into English. Then, armed with this "scientific" information, he argued that a camel corps was a military necessity, that it would benefit the U.S. Army anywhere and everywhere, not just in the Southwest.

On March 3, 1855, Congress appropriated $30,000 for a camel corps. Davis then sent Major Henry C. Wayne to the Levant and Egypt to buy shiploads of camels, thirty-three in 1856, thirty-two in 1857. Transported to Indianola, Texas, they were taken inland to Camp Verde, Texas. From there, a few made their way to California, but most disappeared to parts unknown. What happened to the lost camels? No one knows for certain. But they became the subject of one wild story after another as "eyewitnesses" all over the Southwest claimed to have spotted them. What if Davis's experiment had succeeded? Would it have tied the Far West to the South until a railroad was developed? That was clearly Davis's intent. And he, at least, never regarded it as a pipe dream.[22]

While Davis and Gadsden tried to work their magic to get the federal government to build a southern railroad, northern railroad promoters were equally busy. Leading the effort was Stephen A. Douglas.

In January 1854, the diminutive Illinois Democrat introduced the Kansas-Nebraska Act. The bill called for organizing the northern half of the Louisiana Purchase, every inch of soil between the southern border of Missouri and the Canadian border. That, in turn, would make a northern railroad to the Pacific more feasible. It would silence all those who said that the federal government could not build a railroad through unorganized "Indian country."

The bill, however, was divisive. Indeed, it was incredibly divisive, undoubtedly the most divisive piece of legislation presented to Congress before the Civil War, maybe in all of American history. For it also called for repealing the Missouri Compromise, the ban on slavery in the northern half of the Louisiana Purchase, the land above the famous 36°30′ line. In its place, Douglas inserted language that would allow the settlers to vote slavery up or down.

The repeal sparked an outburst of anger and resentment from

Maine to Missouri. A sacred agreement, after thirty-four years, had been violated. Free soil was now open to slavery. The richest acres might end up in the hands of slaveholders. How could this abomination be stopped? When could the settlers make a decision? When could they vote slavery up or down? While the area was still a territory? Or only at the time it became a state? That was uncertain. And that sparked even more fury.

Stephen A. Douglas, "the Little Giant." Reprinted from Ben: Perley Poore, Perley's Reminiscences, 2 vols. (Philadelphia, 1886), 1:315.

What motivated Douglas? That has long been a matter of dispute. On the one hand, Douglas undoubtedly had a strong belief in popular sovereignty. He never doubted the virtues of the people and their capacity for self-government. And he especially rejected the notion that frontier settlers needed to be taught the rudiments of government.[23] He had grown up in Vermont, in a state in which ordinary white males had governed themselves since frontier days. There had been no property qualifications for voting or holding office and no statewide governing authority that even tried to tell local communities what to do. Even if a Vermont governor had been so inclined, the mountainous terrain and harsh winters made it all but impossible for much of the year. In the dead of winter and long into spring, each mountain valley was cut off from its neighbors, and each Vermont village was largely on its own. The only governing bodies that truly mattered, therefore, were the local town meetings. And in Douglas's judgment, they had worked well, much better than any distant government.

Douglas was also a political animal. On moving to Illinois, he had become a kingpin in the state Democratic Party and quickly risen to the top of state politics. Did he seek the presidency? Most of his biographers think he did. And if that was the case, the only way he could have gotten the Democratic nomination was with strong Southern support. The Democratic Party, unlike its Whig rival, required the party nominee to have the support of a two-thirds majority at the nominating convention. And that rule, as Douglas well knew, made it possible for any well-organized minority in the party to stop the choice of the majority from getting the nomination.

That had happened in 1844, when Douglas was a young man just making a name for himself in the Democratic Party. In that year, Southern Democrats had used the two-thirds rule to derail the candidacy of Martin Van Buren of New York. Since then, it had become a mighty weapon for Southern Democrats, one that had forced Northern presidential hopefuls to pay heed to their wishes or suffer the fate of Van Buren. Only Northern Democrats like Lewis Cass and Franklin Pierce, two aspirants who were widely regarded as Northern men with Southern principles, had been able to get the nomination. And in Pierce's case, it had taken him forty-nine ballots to do so.[24]

So as a Democrat who hoped to be president, Douglas knew he had to cater to the South. He had no choice. At the same time, he also probably found it easy to do. He had, after all, Southern interests. For even though he was a free-state politician, he was also a Mississippi slaveholder. In 1847, he had married Martha Martin, the daughter of a wealthy North Carolina planter. As a wedding present, her father had offered Douglas a Mississippi plantation of some twenty-five hundred acres and over one hundred slaves. Douglas thought that would be politically embarrassing. So he convinced his father-in-law to leave the property to Martha in his will. A year later the old man died, and Douglas became the manager of his wife's Mississippi property. She died in 1853, and the property then went to their infant sons. But Douglas continued to manage it and profit from it until the Civil War.[25]

As a Mississippi slave owner and free-state senator, Douglas undoubtedly knew that removing the ban on slavery north of the famous 36°30′ line would make him incredibly popular in the slaveholding South. Slave-state leaders clearly regarded the restriction as a stigma, as an insult to their way of life. The debates in Congress made that abundantly clear. The line was "infamous," declared Senator David R. Atchison of Missouri. It was "a festering thorn" in "the side of the South," said Senator Andrew Butler of South Carolina. It was "a miserable line," as it embodied "a congressional imputation against one half of the states," echoed Representative Philip Phillips of Alabama.[26]

Moreover, in Douglas's judgment, the ban on slavery had hurt his Northern constituents far more than it hurt Southern slaveholders. No slaveholder in his right mind really wanted to settle there, contended Douglas. The land just wasn't fit for slavery. Since 1820, however, the

South had refused to let the land be organized, and at the same time the federal government, through numerous Indian treaties, had encouraged various eastern tribes to relocate there. The ban thus had turned the whole area into "Indian country," which, in turn, not only blocked the development of both a northern and a central railroad route to the Pacific but also stymied the potential growth of Chicago and St. Louis, frustrated commercial interests in both northern and southern Illinois, and by default ensured that New Orleans would become the premier city in the Mississippi basin. Wrote Douglas in 1853: "This policy evidently contemplated the creation of a perpetual and savage barrier to the progress of emigration, settlement and civilization in that direction."[27]

Without question, then, Douglas had multiple reasons for introducing the Kansas-Nebraska Act. But especially pressing, in 1854, was gaining a strip of land for a northern railroad to the Pacific. Time was running out.

Douglas had been promoting railroad development for nearly twenty years. In 1836, as a member of the Illinois legislature, he had introduced a bill proposing two railroads, the Illinois Central, which he expected to run from the terminus of the proposed Illinois and Michigan Canal at La Salle to the mouth of the Ohio River at Cairo, and the Northern Cross, which he envisioned running from the Mississippi River at Quincy to the terminus of the proposed Wabash and Erie Canal at Terre Haute. Later, when he went to Congress, he had tried hard to get federal land grants to build the Illinois Central and complete the Northern Cross.[28]

Douglas had also been an early proponent of a Pacific railroad. In October 1845, he had responded to a scheme put forth the previous year by Asa Whitney, a New York merchant engaged in the China trade. Whitney had promised to build a Pacific railroad for the federal government if Congress would sell to him a strip of land sixty miles wide for 16 cents an acre. As he sold the land, he would plow the money back into laying track. He proposed going from Milwaukee to the mouth of the Columbia River. In an open letter to Whitney, Douglas offered an alternative scheme. Instead of running the railroad west from Milwaukee, he suggested that it begin in Chicago, go through Council Bluffs, and end in San Francisco "if that country could be annexed in time." And instead of using settlers' money to build a railroad, he proposed using the railroad to attract settlers. To facilitate this entire enterprise, he called on Congress to organize the land west of Iowa as the Nebraska Territory.

At the time, however, Douglas lacked the necessary political clout to get Congress to do his bidding. He was just a freshman congressman, just thirty-two years old, with a victory margin in the last election of less than 51 percent of the vote. He also lacked the support of the Illinois legislature, which directed its senators to vote at first for the Whitney route and later for a southern route favored by Senator Sidney Breese. The issue was ticklish, for while half the state wanted a Chicago route, the other half preferred St. Louis. Douglas, meanwhile, bought up property that would skyrocket in value if the Chicago route was chosen. However, not until 1852, the third time that he introduced a bill organizing the Nebraska Territory, did he have the support of his home state legislature. In that year, he bought an additional seventy acres in Chicago and thus increased his economic stake in the outcome.[29]

By this time, the effort to build a Chicago-to-Pacific railroad had become more complicated because of a political dogfight in nearby Missouri.

In 1850, pro-slavery forces had finally gotten their wish. They had succeeded in ousting Thomas Hart Benton from the Senate. The old warrior, who had been in the Senate for thirty years, fought back and in 1852 won election to the House of Representatives. In hustling for votes, he demanded a Pacific railroad and the organization of Nebraska. His pro-slavery enemies, in turn, vehemently objected to his Nebraska proposal on the grounds that Missouri would then be surrounded on three sides by free soil. They insisted that the ban on slavery north of 36°30′ be removed.

Leading them was Senator David Atchison. A forty-five-year-old Transylvania University graduate, Atchison had earned the sobriquet "Bourbon Dave." Tall and imposing, he was a hard-drinking, hard-cussing man, often coarse, sometimes ferocious, usually swaggering. About twenty-five years younger than Benton, Atchison had just gotten started as a lawyer and a planter in the Missouri River valley in 1829, the year Benton became a major player in Jacksonian politics. Fourteen years later, in 1843, Atchison got himself elected to the Senate, emphasizing, among other things, the need for more slaves to work Missouri's river bottomlands.

As a Jacksonian Democrat, Atchison got along with Benton on most economic matters, but not on western expansion. To Atchison, Benton was a traitor to Southern slaveholders. Benton was a slaveholder, and in the 1820s he had often touted the expansion of slavery. But since the 1820s, he had been more concerned with the lot of small farmers. He had authored bill after bill that enabled squatters on government land to buy up to 160 acres for the minimum price of $1.25 an acre. He had also tried to get the federal government to cut the price of federal land that it had a hard time selling. He saw the northern half of the Louisiana Purchase from the same perspective, not as slave country but as a place where the sons and daughters of Missouri's non-slaveholding farmers might someday prosper. And with that and a Pacific railroad in mind, he tried to get it organized as a federal territory.

Atchison objected. He put together a Southern coalition to defeat such bills, ostensibly because Indians had not yet been removed, but in reality because his slaveholding constituents could not bring in their slaves.[30]

So Douglas, if he wanted to achieve a northern or central railroad, had to find some way to neutralize Atchison. And by December 1853, he also felt that time was running out.

Not only did Southerners now seem to have an edge. They also never let Douglas forget that the northern half of the Louisiana Purchase was "Indian country" and thus closed by law to emigration and to travel. That barrier, he concluded, somehow had to be removed. And it had to be done quickly. For if Southerners got a railroad before the Indian barrier was removed, slave-state senators would have the whip hand. They could delay forever a second route "by merely refusing to permit the extinguishment of Indian titles in the Indian country." Thus, as Douglas saw it, he had no choice. He had to organize the land before Congress authorized a southern railroad. Only then would Northerners have a chance of having a transcontinental railroad to the gold country.[31]

So on January 4, 1854, Douglas accepted David Atchison's terms. He agreed to a bill that promised Nebraska eventual admission to the Union "with or without slavery." He tried to keep the language neutral, playing down the assault on the Missouri Compromise. But free-soilers weren't fooled. They knew that Bourbon Dave had emerged victorious.

Yet the wording was too halfhearted and ambiguous to satisfy

Southern hotspurs. They demanded more. Representative Philip Phillips, an Alabama Democrat, called for language that explicitly repealed the Missouri Compromise. So did Senator Archibald Dixon, a Kentucky Whig. Douglas, after taking a carriage ride with Dixon, agreed to an amendment that Dixon had fashioned. He knew it would "raise a hell of a storm."

Douglas also agreed, at the last moment, to divide the land in two, to create two territories instead of one. That, in turn, further convinced Free-Soilers that at least one territory was earmarked for slavery. As a final concession, Douglas also assented to another word change. To say the Missouri Compromise was "inoperative" wouldn't do. His Southern co-authors demanded that it be declared "void."[32]

On January 23, this more drastic version of the bill went before the Senate. The following day all hell broke loose. Two Ohio Free-Soilers, Salmon P. Chase and Joshua Giddings, published an "Appeal of the Independent Democrats in Congress to the People of the United States." They lambasted the proposal as a conspiracy by the Slave

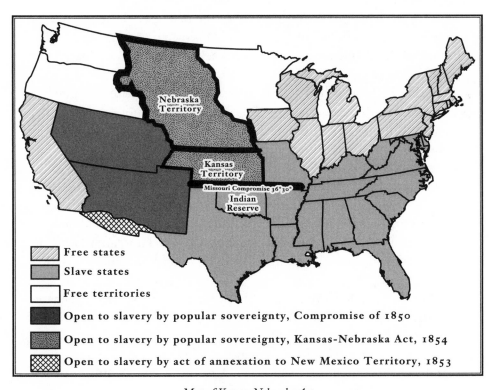

Map of Kansas-Nebraska Act

Power to expand its influence and further dominate the free states. They also branded the bill as a "gross violation of a sacred pledge; as a criminal betrayal of precious rights; as part and parcel of an atrocious plot to exclude from the vast unoccupied region immigrants from the Old World and free laborers from our own States, and to convert it into a dreary region of despotism, inhabited by masters and slaves."[33]

Within days, hundreds of others joined Chase and Giddings in flaying Douglas and his much-amended creation. Anti-Nebraska meetings became everyday news from Springfield, Massachusetts, to Springfield, Illinois. Fiery speeches became commonplace. Abraham Lincoln was just the most memorable of the scores of men who took to the podium. Many castigated the Slave Power for not living up to a sacred agreement. Many blasted Douglas for forcing free laborers to compete with slave labor. Dozens burned Douglas in effigy. Thus the long, nasty battle began.

On January 30, Douglas took the floor in behalf of the Kansas-Nebraska bill. From his remarks, no one in the Senate gallery would have realized that he had lost control of the measure. He spoke as if he were in charge, as if the bill were entirely his own creation, as if he were its sole author. And for the next five weeks, he totally dominated the Senate.

Overall, Douglas had an easy time of it in the Senate. Despite the "Appeal" and the uproar across the North, he had more than enough senators on his side. The only Deep South senator he had to worry about was Sam Houston of Texas. The hero of the Texas Revolution had always been sympathetic to the rights of Indians. At least twice in his life, he had lived as a Cherokee. He also thought it was stupid to provoke free-soilers by reneging on a sacred promise. But every other Deep South senator would vote with Douglas. So, too, would doughface senators like William Gwin and John Weller. Thus, after Houston and others had their say, Douglas had votes to spare. The bill passed easily, 37 to 14.[34]

The House, however, was a different matter. As in the Senate, Douglas could count on all but one or two of the slave-state representatives. Only one, Atchison's enemy, Thomas Hart Benton, was certain to put up a fight. More unexpected was the resistance of Representative John S. Millson of Virginia. A states' rights Democrat of the "strictest sort," Millson opposed squatter sovereignty because it violated common-property doctrine. The argument was simple. If the federal government was just an agent of the states, Congress could not delegate to a territory a power it did not possess. The only power it could delegate "was the power, indeed the obligation, to protect slaveowners in their property rights." Fortunately for Douglas, none of Millson's compatriots were so consistent. In their desire to get rid of the Missouri Compromise, they ignored common-property doctrine.[35]

The problem in the House lay in the numbers. There, free-state representatives outnumbered slave-state representatives by nearly two to one. Douglas thus had to get a substantial number of Northerners to vote with the South. He had just one advantage. Northern members of his own party had always been more sympathetic to the South than Northern Whigs, and he had more Northern Democrats to work with than any previous Democratic leader. His party had scored smashing victories in state after state in the 1852 elections, and as a result ninety-three Northern Democrats now sat in the House, nearly forty more than at the time of the California statehood bill. He needed them. He needed every edge he could get.

As it was, Douglas had to work months to whip Northern Democrats into line, to get the necessary majority to repeal the Missouri Compromise and open the northern half of the Louisiana Purchase to the possibility of slavery. Douglas argued that the possibility was remote—indeed, nonexistent—and that all he was doing was giving the South a fig leaf. He grossly underestimated the opposition and treated with contempt all those who disagreed with him. To his angry opponents the Missouri Compromise was not a trivial matter. It was a sacred compact. Initially, it had benefited the South. Now, just as it was about to benefit the free states, the South wanted to renege on the bargain. It was a breach of faith on the South's part.

These sentiments, Douglas predicted, would dissipate in a few weeks. He was dead wrong. Even erstwhile supporters joined the revolt. Some feared that Kansas-Nebraska would upset the settlement of 1850, which allegedly had put the slavery question to rest. Others regarded it as a violation of a sacred covenant. Over the objections of Douglas's friends, the Connecticut Democratic convention officially went on record against the bill and the Pennsylvania Democratic convention refused to endorse the bill. In Chicago, Douglas's friends called a rally and found it jammed with the bill's enemies. Resolutions in support of the bill and the Little Giant were hooted down. Even the Chicago

Democratic Press turned on Douglas and accused him of committing an unpardonable political error.[36]

To prevail in the House, Douglas somehow had to get twenty-seven Northern Democrats to vote with the South. He was tireless. He spent nearly every waking moment trying to line up additional votes. Not all of these potential recruits, however, responded to his herculean efforts. The news from back home convinced many that Douglas's bill was a political disaster and that the storm over Kansas-Nebraska would destroy all before it. The last thing they wanted to do was confront the onslaught. So on March 21, many of them threw their support behind a parliamentary maneuver that buried the bill beneath fifty other bills.[37]

Douglas thus needed help just to bring Kansas-Nebraska up for a vote in the House of Representatives. He got it from the Pierce administration and its control of federal patronage. The president pulled out all the stops, sending Cabinet members to work the halls of Congress, dangling jobs before hesitant Democrats, threatening to cut Free-Soilers off from the spoils, while the administration's official newspaper promised men who supported the measure that they would be "sustained by every means within the power of the party."[38]

The favors were generally small ones. William Marcy Tweed of New York obtained the right to replace a postmaster in his district. Several other New York congressmen received hefty shipbuilding contracts for their districts. An Ohio congressman got a courthouse appointment, a Philadelphia congressman a printing contract for his newspaper, a Milwaukee congressman a lucrative order to publish government mail contracts. But such favors added up. For Massachusetts Democrats, Pierce's attorney general, Caleb Cushing, calculated the dollar value. If they decided to enhance their power in state politics by joining forces with the Free-Soilers, they would gain a mere "$75,000" in state jobs; if they sided with the administration and the South, they would gain "$1,000,000 per annum" in federal patronage.[39]

In the end the combination of presidential pressure, federal patronage, and Douglas's hard work paid off. By early May, most of the bills that preceded Kansas-Nebraska on the House agenda were set aside, one by one. Then, on May 8, the last eighteen were laid aside, and William Richardson, who carried the torch for Douglas in the House, moved to substitute the Senate version of the bill, which had passed in early March, for the measure before the House.[40]

Three weeks of stormy debate then followed. Douglas worked

alongside Richardson, whipping dissident Democrats into line. Indeed, in the eyes of many, the two men from Illinois behaved like dictatorial, insolent "slave-drivers." Finally, on May 22, they had more than the twenty-seven Northern Democrats they needed. They had forty-four, roughly half the Northern wing of the party. Kansas-Nebraska thus passed the House, 113 to 100.[41]

Back in Illinois, Douglas and Richardson's supporters greeted the victory with a 113-gun salute. Douglas was quick to take the credit. "I passed the Kansas-Nebraska Act myself," he later boasted. "I had the authority and power of a dictator throughout the whole controversy in both houses. The speeches were nothing. It was the marshaling and directing of men, and guarding from attacks, and with a ceaseless vigilance preventing surprise."[42]

The forty-four Northern Democrats who made Douglas's victory possible never received the honors that he did. On the contrary, some of them paid dearly for supporting the Atchison-Phillips-Dixon creation.

So, too, did their party. In the fall elections following the Kansas-Nebraska Act, the Democrats lost thirty of the forty-four districts that these men represented, sometimes by just a few percentage points, sometimes by landslide margins. One Indiana incumbent got just 45 percent of the vote, another 44 percent. In Wisconsin, John B. Macy saw his public support plummet from 55 percent of the total vote in 1852 to 39 percent in 1854. Of the party's replacement candidates, most also lost by huge margins. Tweed's replacement in New York's Fifth District, running in a four-man race, finished third with 25 percent of the vote. In Ohio's Ninth District, Frederick Green's replacement in a two-man race won only 40 percent of the vote.

What happened in Green's district was symptomatic. The district had long been a Democratic stronghold. The party had won 92 percent of the vote there in 1850 and 74 percent in 1852. Now, in trying to defend Green's "treasonous" record, they got trounced. They lost over half their previous support. Across the North, Democrats experienced the same travail. They saw one safe seat after another go over to the opposition. Entering the 1854 election holding ninety-three Northern seats, they emerged with only twenty-two seats. The total losses were staggering.[43]

Douglas refused to accept the blame for this debacle. It was not Kansas-Nebraska, he argued, that led to his party's demise. It was the rise of anti-Catholic and anti-immigrant fervor. Nearly three million immigrants had poured into the United States since 1845, totaling about 13 percent of the nation's population, and the vast majority had settled in the North. Well over one million of these newcomers were Catholic Irish. Not only were the Irish poor and desperate, but their church had long been anathema in Protestant circles. Hundreds of thousands of Northerners had learned at their mother's knee about the "whore of Babylon," the Spanish Inquisition, the Gunpowder Plot, and the "awful disclosures of Maria Monk." For years Protestants had attacked convents and fought with Catholic workers on the streets of Philadelphia, New York, and Boston. And for years most Northern Whigs had catered to Protestant animosity and helped drive Catholic newcomers into the Democratic Party.

In 1852 these new Democrats made a difference. They undoubtedly helped Franklin Pierce win the presidency and tipped the balance in scores of races for congressman, assemblyman, and alderman. And some of the Democrats they helped elect, like Mike Walsh of New York, were not only pro-slavery but blatantly so.

Whig strategists, moreover, were distraught. They knew that the Irish vote, growing by the thousands every day, had to be nullified or the Whig organization would be destroyed at the polls. Some Whigs wanted to compete against the Democrats for Irish support. Others wanted to make it harder for the Irish to vote, called for a residency requirement of twenty-one years for naturalization, and launched a drive to make the Whig Party into a nativist party.

Hence by the time of the Kansas-Nebraska Act, hundreds of thousands of Northern voters now indiscriminately blamed the "Irish menace" and "popery" on the Northern Democracy. Douglas thus had a point in blaming his party's losses on nativism. But hundreds of thousands of Northern voters also indiscriminately blamed the Northern wing of his party, doughfaces and Free-Soilers alike, for the repeal of the Missouri Compromise. Not a single Northern Whig, not a single Northern Free-Soiler, had voted for the bill. Only Northern Democrats.

Who could miss that fact? Nearly every critic blamed Douglas and his followers. He could have traveled home to Chicago, as he himself admitted, by the light of his own burning effigies. Some of his critics spoke about the moral evils of slavery. More railed about the possible expansion of slavery and Southern power. Douglas, as usual, underestimated their resentment.

In this general tumult, ninety-three Democratic House seats were at risk in the fall of 1854. Democrats faced not just the old familiar Whigs and Free-Soilers. Also confronting them were newcomers and old foes who ran under new labels and sometimes two labels at the same time. The nativists usually called themselves Know-Nothings, while the opponents of the Kansas-Nebraska Act often called themselves Anti-Nebraska men or Republicans. Democrats lost some seats to men who ran as Know-Nothings, some to men who ran as Anti-Nebraska men, and many to men who had a foot in both camps. In addition, several seats were lost because the local Democratic Party split in two and ran two men for the same office.[44]

Two years later the battle lines became clearer. In some districts, the Democratic Party's fortunes revived, and fifty-three Northern Democrats won seats in the House. Meanwhile, the Know-Nothing Party, whose program had skyrocketed in popularity at the Democrats' expense in 1854, collapsed almost as fast as it had risen in late 1856. More viable was the new Anti-Nebraska party, which now settled on the name "Republican." After rising in the unstable atmosphere of the 1854 elections, the new Republican Party had stumbled for a year or so, and then soared in the 1856 elections. Even New Hampshire, once the banner state of the Democracy, turned Republican. In 1853, the Democrats had won every district in the state by at least twelve hundred votes. Now the Republicans won every district by at least a thousand votes.[45]

In New Hampshire, as everywhere else, Republicans hammered on the theme that the party of Douglas had betrayed white Northerners to the great slave masters of the South. The new party, moreover, had an obvious advantage over the old Whig Party. Northern Whigs, even though they repeatedly voted against the South, had to cooperate with their Southern colleagues to win national elections.

The new Republican Party had no such restraints. Based entirely in the North, the party had no need, much less desire, to maintain a working arrangement with the planter-politicians of the South. On the contrary, the stock-in-trade of the Republicans was to attack the political influence of the plantation aristocracy at every opportunity. The Slave Power, contended one Republican after another, had long ruled the nation, and now it was conspiring to expand its power by annexing Cuba, capturing the West, and extending slavery onto "free soil."

Having brought havoc to his party, Douglas tried at the next session of Congress to regain the upper hand and resolve the perplexing railroad problem. On January 9, 1855, he introduced a Pacific railroad bill in the Senate. It called for three roads: one west from Texas, another west from Missouri or Iowa, and a third west from Minnesota. The middle one would be linked to Chicago. But many cities—and many states—would benefit. He and his followers saw it as a major piece of statesmanship.

At the time another bill was pending in the House. For it, Representative William Dunbar of Louisiana moved to substitute Douglas's proposal. Two days later John G. Davis of Indiana moved to amend the substitute bill by having only a single road west, from Missouri or Iowa. Thomas Hart Benton, still hoping for a road from St. Louis straight west, rallied the opposition in the House and blocked approval by one vote. Douglas, meanwhile, got the measure through the Senate on February 19, but it was not taken up again in the House. Thus in the end, as one historian put it, Douglas's intention behind the Kansas-Nebraska Act was foiled "by a single vote in the House."[46]

———◆———

THE NEW REPUBLICAN PARTY QUICKLY SOARED TO DIZZYING HEIGHTS in many of the free states. By 1856, it had captured 78 percent of the vote in Vermont, 64 percent in Massachusetts, 61 percent in Maine, 58 percent in Rhode Island, 57 percent in Michigan, 55 percent in Wisconsin, and 54 percent in New Hampshire. That was not the case in California, however. In the gold country, the Republican Party struggled. It barely polled 19 percent of the vote.

The poor showing was especially glaring because the state's one-time hero John C. Frémont had headed the Republican ticket. At the party's nominating convention in Philadelphia on June 17, 1856, the delegates had been united in their opposition to the Pierce administration and their determination to keep slavery out of the West. They had differed, however, over which of the party's luminaries should be the presidential nominee.

Most thought the party's best choice was Senator William H. Seward, a proven winner in New York politics and a firm antislavery man. But he had been persuaded by his longtime political sidekick, Thurlow Weed, that 1856 was not a Republican year and had decided to wait until 1860 before making a presidential bid. In Seward's absence, some delegates touted former Senator Salmon Chase of Ohio, the author of the "Appeal of the Independent Democrats," while Abraham Lincoln and many former Whigs championed Supreme Court Justice John McLean, a perennial favorite in Whig circles. Others, however, regarded Chase as too extreme and the seventy-one-year-old McLean as too old and too unreliable.

That had left the door open for Frémont. The party, said his backers, needed a fresh face. None of the other aspirants had even half his appeal. Not only was he a well-known folk hero; he was young and dashing and a nominal Democrat. On the second day, during the sultry afternoon session, the party leaders orchestrated an informal ballot. Frémont outpolled McLean, 359 to 190, with 4 scattering. The delegates then made the Frémont vote unanimous. Then, as a sop to conservatives, they picked William L. Dayton of New Jersey for vice president.[1]

The Pathfinder undoubtedly had voter appeal in much of the North. Yet he was more a symbol of the new Republican Party than an active participant in it. In the election campaign, he stayed at home, mainly at 56 West Ninth Street, in New York City, while his wife, Jessie, along with John Bigelow and Isaac Sherman, ran his campaign. Jessie's role got extensive coverage. All the major politicians knew that she had been raised in Washington politics, and they soon realized that she understood it far better than her husband. Accordingly, many treated her as a professional, her husband as an amateur. She also got far more public attention than potential First Ladies normally received. Republican publications constantly celebrated her presence. References to "Our Jessie" became commonplace, as did this lyric: "We go for our country and Union, and for brave little Jessie forever."[2]

Jessie and the Republican propaganda machine ran an astute campaign. Yet they couldn't get her father, Thomas Hart Benton, to back the ticket. He supported the party of his youth and gave twenty-one speeches endorsing his son-in-law's opponent. Even more crippling was their lack of money and their newness as a party organization. So they didn't bother to put Frémont's name on the ballot in most of the slave states. Running on "Free Soil, Free Labor, Free Men, Frémont, and Victory," they concentrated solely on the sixteen free states.

From the outset, they knew that they could count all of New England, New York, Ohio, Michigan, Wisconsin, and Iowa as safe for Frémont. To win the presidency, they needed just two of the four swing states—Pennsylvania, New Jersey, Indiana, and Illinois. To these four

"Frémont and Our Jessie." Republican campaign poster, 1856. Library of Congress.

states they dispatched the party's luminaries to keep attention focused on the Democratic Party's attachment to the "Slave Power" and its repeal of the "sacred" Missouri Compromise. But their Democratic rivals, with more money and a better organization, poured cash into these four states, ran rough media campaigns, and in Pennsylvania illegally naturalized thousands of alien immigrants. As a result, the Democratic candidate, James Buchanan of Pennsylvania, emerged victorious.

The election, however, undoubtedly gave Buchanan—and the South—a scare. For in the free states, a whopping 83 percent of the eligible voters went to the polls, and the vast majority voted for someone other than the Pennsylvania Democrat. Among lifelong Democrats in the northern tier of free states, probably one in five voted against the party's nominee, in the lower tier, maybe one in ten. The new Republican Party won eleven of the sixteen free states, 114 electoral votes, and roughly one-third of the total popular vote. Had they carried Pennsylvania and Indiana, or Pennsylvania and Illinois, they would have won the election.

Of the five free states that Frémont lost, the one he lost by the biggest margin was California. Not only did he lose the state to Buchanan by a five-to-two ratio, but he also ran far behind the Know-Nothing candidate, ex-president Millard Fillmore. He barely got 19 percent of the California vote.

Why did Frémont do so poorly in California? At the time, much was made of his "Mariposa problem."

Frémont, along with other officers stationed in California during the Mexican War, had participated in the mad scramble to buy a Mexican land grant. Spanish and Mexican officials had bestowed 813 such grants on their favorites. One was Las Mariposas, a "floating grant" of ten leagues that belonged to a heavily indebted Californio, Juan Bautista Alvarado, and his wife, Martina Caston de Alvarado. On February 10, 1847, Frémont purchased Las Mariposas through an intermediary, Thomas Larkin, for $3,000. He had no idea where the property was located but hoped it was near San Francisco or Monterey. To his disappointment, the seventy-square-mile grant was farther inland, near the Yosemite valley, within the hunting and gathering grounds of the Sierra Miwoks. Also, there was a legal problem, as Alvarado had never taken possession of the property as required by Mexican law.

Nonetheless, after his court-martial in 1848, Frémont decided to move to Las Mariposas and become a cattle rancher. He borrowed money from Thomas Hart Benton and Senator John Dix to build a house, corral, and barn. He also shipped to Las Mariposas farm implements and an entire sawmill via the Aspinwall steamer *Fredonia*. Then he got lucky. Gold was discovered on Las Mariposas, a quartz vein of over five miles in length. In addition, Sonoran miners on his property were washing out hundreds of pounds of placer each month. Overnight he became a rich man.[3]

But what did Las Mariposas include? Where, precisely, was its southern border? Its northern border? Since Las Mariposas was a "floating grant," and the Mexican government had been anything but precise in defining its borders, there was plenty of room for argument. Did the grant include three prosperous mining districts that some thought to be public domain? Land being mined by the Merced Mining Company? By various squatters? And was the grant even valid, as

Alvarado had failed to fulfill its terms by living on the property? The lawyers had plenty to fight about, and the matter remained in court for years. Finally, in 1856, the U.S. Supreme Court decided in Frémont's favor. That added to Frémont's wealth but hardly made him popular with his neighbors.[4]

In the 1856 election, the Chivs made the most of it. Their Stockton newspaper, the *San Joaquin Republican*, continually trashed Frémont as a "nigger-loving" absentee owner with "no friends in the mines," as a man who was so obnoxious that it would be "perfect madness" for any miner to support him.[5] And on Election Day he did poorly, not getting a single vote in some mining-county precincts, and only 165 votes to Buchanan's 1,254 in Mariposa County.[6]

Yet the "Mariposa problem" only partly explains the troubles the Republicans had in California. For Frémont was not the only Republican candidate who did badly on Election Day. Statewide, the Republicans showed strength in only a few districts.

The state party got off to a late start, much later than its eastern counterparts. It was not organized until March 8, 1856, when seven friends got together in Sacramento. All seven were from New England or upstate New York. Several were destined to become railroad tycoons: Collis P. Huntington, Mark Hopkins, Leland Stanford, Edwin B. and Charles Crocker. The chief organizer was Cornelius Cole, a former New Yorker and a Wesleyan College graduate who had studied law in the office of William H. Seward.

The thirty-four-year-old Cole served as secretary and agreed to write the party's manifesto. Article 3 stated: "The principles we advocate are the complete withdrawal of all support to slavery by the federal government, without disturbing that institution as it now exists in the present slave states; firm and uncompromising opposition to the extension of slavery, and the admission of any more slave states." On March 29, the members met again and ratified the manifesto and "entered into a written pledge to oppose the aggressions of slavery."[7]

A month later, on April 30, the seven organizers rounded up enough like-minded men to hold a "state" convention. Meeting at the Congregational church in Sacramento, 125 men attended. Nearly all were from just two towns, Sacramento and San Francisco. Twenty-seven of the state's forty counties were not represented. For president, the delegates favored Cole's mentor, William H. Seward, but when the national party chose Frémont, they enthusiastically threw their support behind the Pathfinder. Unlike Pennsylvania and Indiana, where the party sent out dozens of luminaries touting "Free Soil, Free Labor, Free Men, Frémont, and Victory," the California party relied largely on just two stump speakers, Frederick P. Tracy, a Connecticut Yankee, and Edward Dickinson Baker, an English-born Mexican War veteran who had once whipped Abraham Lincoln in an 1844 Illinois congressional race. Meanwhile, out of his small office on K Street in Sacramento, Cole founded a newspaper, the *Daily California Times.*[8]

Shorthanded, the fledgling party won three of the thirty-two state senate races and eleven of the seventy-nine assembly races. Otherwise, the entire ticket did poorly. In the contest for one of the two seats in the House of Representatives, L. P. Rankin won 20.3 percent of the vote. In the battle for the other seat, J. D. Turner polled 19.5 percent.[9] That was better than Frémont's 18.8 percent, but not by much.

After 1856, the Republicans continued to struggle. In July 1857, the party nominated for governor Edward Stanly. A forty-seven-year-old North Carolinian, Stanly had one notable characteristic. He hated Democrats. He had been taught by his father, a Federalist congressman and accomplished orator, to hate Democrats and had learned his lessons well. Elected to Congress as a Whig by his North Carolina neighbors, he had repeatedly blistered House Democrats and became widely known for his fiery temper and sarcastic tongue. He had also been one of the few Southern Whigs to recognize the constitutionality of the Wilmot Proviso and to follow Zachary Taylor's lead in calling for immediate admission of California as a free state. In 1853, he had not sought reelection to the House. Instead, he had moved to San Francisco and established a successful law practice. He supported Frémont in 1856, but as late as 1857 he still owned slaves in North Carolina.[10]

For a party that was against the expansion of slavery, Stanly was a strange choice for governor. In July, soon after he was nominated, he declared that he could never support "a declaration by Congress that the South should never have any more slave States." He also made it clear that he disagreed with all those who said "that slavery was contrary to the teachings of the Bible." The next day he lambasted his Democratic rival for once defending an abolitionist. A month later, in another speech, he denounced all abolitionists and contended that slavery in his home state of North Carolina was so benevolent that slaves there regarded their condition as "paradise." And, in recognizing Congress's right to prohibit slavery in a territory, he also endorsed the right of the settlers to choose to become a slave state.[11]

Edward Stanly. Reprinted from Ben: Perley Poore, Perley's Reminiscences, *2 vols. (Philadelphia, 1886), 1:293.*

Yet even though Stanly was a slaveholding Southerner, that didn't stop the opposition from calling him a "nigger-loving" abolitionist. That had been the standard Chiv refrain from the day the new Republican Party was founded. In August 1856, after the Republican's chief spokesman, Edward Dickinson Baker, addressed a big audience at the Orleans Hotel in Sacramento, the *Sacramento Journal* reported: "The convention of Nigger worshippers assembled yesterday in this city! This is the first time this dangerous fanaticism has dared bare its breast before the people of California. . . . It is high time that all national men should unite in saving California from the stain of abolitionism." In 1857, the Chiv press played the same tune, repeatedly describing Stanly and his Republican followers as "black Republicans," "abolitionists," "darkey sympathizers," "devotees of the dark faith," and "nigger-worshippers." And in the 1857 election, the Chivs beat Stanly almost as badly as they whipped Frémont. He barely polled 22.5 percent of the vote.[12]

Except for a few local races, no Republican did better than Stanly in the years before the Civil War. In 1858, the party ran L. L. Tracy for a seat in the House of Representatives. He won 14.6 percent of the vote. In 1859, the party chose as their gubernatorial candidate Leland Stanford, a thirty-five-year-old native of New York who later became famous as the president of the Central Pacific Railroad and for naming a university after his son. In his acceptance speech, Stanford declared: "The cause in which we are engaged is one of the greatest in which anyone can labor. It is the cause of the white man—the cause of free labor, of justice, and of equal rights. I am in favor of free white American citizens. I prefer free white citizens to any other class or race. I prefer the white man to the negro as an inhabitant of our country. I believe the greatest good has been derived by having all the country settled by free white men." In the general election, despite the "white only" appeal, Stanford got clobbered, winning only 9.8 percent of the vote.[13]

In 1860, with Abraham Lincoln heading the national ticket, the California Republicans finally got past the 30 percent barrier. In a tight race, Lincoln won the state with 32.3 percent of the vote, barely beating the Northern Democratic candidate, Stephen A. Douglas, who had 31.7 percent, and the Southern Democratic candidate, John C. Breckinridge, who had 28.4 percent. In no other free state did so large a proportion of voters cast ballots against the Republican candidate.

Meanwhile, the Know-Nothings, the other party that sprang to life after the Kansas-Nebraska Act, made a better showing in California. The Know-Nothings, whose formal name was the American Party, got off the mark well before the Republicans. In May 1854, two years before the Republicans first met, Lieutenant Sam Roberts founded a Know-Nothing chapter in San Francisco.

Roberts, a former New York Volunteer, had already gained notoriety. Five years earlier, in 1849, he had established the Hounds, a regulator group dedicated to maintaining public order and to hounding Chileans and other foreigners out of California. His followers had been used as deputy policemen by the alcalde of San Francisco, Thaddeus M. Leavenworth. But they had also held drunken parades, shanghaied sailors back to their ships, levied protection money from local merchants, and terrorized Chileans. In response, Sam Brannan and other San Francisco notables decided to crack down on the Hounds. They tried Roberts and eighteen others at Portsmouth Square for rape, murder, arson, and a host of other crimes and banished nine of Roberts's followers from California, on pain of death should they return.[14]

Now, in May 1854, Roberts again launched a crusade against the "foreign" element, this time mainly against Chinese miners and David Broderick's "Irish" machine. His new followers initially seemed to be more interested in clean government than in nativism. For mayor, they even briefly endorsed a Roman Catholic, Lucien Hermann, who had already been chosen by the Citizen's Party to rid the city of corruption. That endorsement, however, lasted only two days. On September 3, at the Metropolitan Theatre, a much larger contingent of Know-Nothings voted 649 to 109 to strip Hermann of the party's support and give it to a Protestant, Stephen P. Webb. The new ticket, while still campaigning for clean government and election reform, then won seven of San Francisco's eight wards.[15]

By May 1855, Know-Nothing hostility to the foreign-born had

become more pronounced. In one of their publications, *The Political Letters of "Caxton,"* William H. Rhodes singled out "poor foreigners and ignorant exiles" for abuse. He accused them of "stuffing the ballot box and violating the right of suffrage" and generally behaving as the "slaves of Broderick." Instead of becoming "independent" citizens, wrote Rhodes, "they band themselves together in cliques and coteries, and vote in solid phalanx for favourite men. They go up to the ballot boxes as 'the Irish vote,' or 'the German vote,' and not as Whigs or Democrats, or States' right men, or nullifiers or abolitionists. They possess no individual opinions. They follow their ringleader, and as he jumps, so precisely do they jump."[16]

At the same time, the Know-Nothings expanded their base throughout the state. Focusing mainly on the "heathen" Chinese, they soon had enough supporters to hold a statewide convention in Sacramento on August 7 and put forth a slate of candidates. For the state supreme court, the new party endorsed David S. Terry, the pro-slavery Texan who subsequently killed Broderick. For governor, the party backed J. Neely Johnson, who had just celebrated his thirtieth birthday. A native of Indiana, Johnson had practiced law in Iowa before moving to California in 1849. As a Whig, he had been elected Sacramento city attorney in 1850 and 1851 and to the state assembly in 1852. His only political assets, according to observers, were his extremely attractive wife and his pro-Southern sympathies.[17]

By September, the Know-Nothings seemed to be well on their way to becoming a major party. In the gubernatorial race, Johnson beat John Bigler, the incumbent Democratic governor, 50,948 to 45,937. That was no easy task, for Bigler had a staunch nativist record. The fifty-year-old Pennsylvanian had vehemently denounced Chinese immigration and even called for naturalization laws to prohibit Asians from ever becoming American citizens. He had also sided with the settlers against Mexican land grants, refused to translate state documents into Spanish, and strongly endorsed taxes on all foreign miners.[18] Nonetheless, Johnson, with virtually no record whatsoever, won by 5,000 votes.

The Know-Nothings also swept much of the state, winning fifty-six of the ninety assembly seats and seventeen of the thirty-three senate seats. In the mining districts especially, they were invincible. They carried El Dorado County by nearly 1,000 votes, Placer by 800, Sierra by 800, Trinity by 600, Tuolumne by 400, Yuba by 400, Nevada by 350, Plumas by 350, and Mariposa by 250. Explained Bigler to his brother:

"The prejudice in the mineral regions was great against foreigners," and "the opposition promised to turn them out of the mines and give claims to Americans by birth." As a result, added Bigler, the Know-Nothings "have carried everything . . . and will most assuredly elect two U.S. Senators."[19]

When the legislature convened in January 1856, Bigler's prophecy seemed more than likely. The Know-Nothings had nearly a three-to-one majority in the assembly and a one-vote edge in the state senate. And if a joint session was called to elect a U.S. senator, they outnumbered the Democrats by a whopping margin, eighty-three to thirty-nine. With a two-to-one majority, they had more than enough votes to get their man elected.

Their first choice was none other than Henry Foote, the feisty Mississippian who had forced Henry Clay to stuff all his compromise proposals into one bill and who later pulled a gun on Thomas Hart Benton. In 1854, Foote had resigned his post as governor of Mississippi and headed west to practice law and get rich. At the time he had vowed to stay out of politics. That lasted but six months. When the Know-Nothing movement blossomed, Foote got into the thick of it and became one of the new party's top speakers. He also helped many of the party's candidates win seats in the state legislature. They now owed him, and on the twenty-seventh ballot of the Know-Nothing caucus they got the majority to endorse Foote for the Senate seat.

Henry Foote. Library of Congress.

California thus seemed destined to be represented by yet another Mississippi slaveholder. And it might have happened had it not been for Wilson G. Flint, one of the more ornery of the newly elected Know-Nothing state senators.

In most respects, Flint was a "good" party man. He despised the Catholic Irish. And he thought the Chinese, the "heathen celestials" as he called them, should be sent back to China. But the Chinese and the Irish weren't the only people Flint hated. A native of New Hampshire, Flint had moved to Texas in 1842. While there, he had developed a deep hatred for the slaveholding elite. He regarded them as deadwood and as a cancer on American society. Under no circumstances, therefore, would he back Foote for the Senate. So, when at Broderick's urging the Democrats proposed a scheme to block the election, Flint went along.

The scheme was simple. In order to elect a U.S. senator, the two houses of the California legislature had to meet in joint session. All that was necessary, then, was for the senate to turn down the assembly's request for a joint meeting. With Flint's support, the schemers had all the votes they needed, and on January 22 they prevailed by a 17-to-16 margin. They didn't reject the assembly's request; they just found excuses not to meet. The two houses thus never met, and Foote never got elected. The former Mississippi governor then campaigned for the Know-Nothing ticket in the presidential election of 1856 and left the state the following year.[20]

The Flint problem turned out to be the Know-Nothing Party's Achilles' heel. The previous June, when the party's national council had met in Philadelphia, Southern delegates, with the help of eleven Northerners, had rammed through a resolution that essentially endorsed the Kansas-Nebraska Act. In protest, the entire delegations of all the free states except New York, New Jersey, Pennsylvania, and California had walked out. Then, in February 1856, at another national meeting, Northern delegates tried to reverse the earlier decision. After they failed to get a resolution passed calling for the restoration of the Missouri Compromise, fifty delegates from eight Northern states stormed out of the convention and called for a separate Northern party. Within just a few months, most of these men threw their support to Frémont, the Republican candidate for president.[21]

In 1856, the California Know-Nothing Party, just like the national party, collapsed almost as fast as it had risen. In the fall elections, California Know-Nothings lost six seats in the state senate, forty-eight in the assembly. Their numbers in the assembly thus fell from fifty-six to eight. No longer were they the strongest party in the assembly. They were now the weakest. To their dismay, the Democrats with sixty-three seats were again back in control, and even the Republicans with eleven seats had more than they did.[22]

Meanwhile, their young governor, J. Neely Johnson, had a horrid time trying to govern the state. Unable to solve the state's financial problems, and unsuccessful in his attempt to suppress the San Francisco

Vigilance Committee of 1856, which was composed mainly of his political supporters, he soon looked forward to the day when his two years were up. On leaving the governor's office, he moved away from the hubbub of Sacramento and took refuge far to the north, in sparsely populated Trinity County. Two years later Johnson left the state for Nevada, where he eventually became a supreme court judge.

California, then, was different. Unlike the other free states, where the Democratic Party generally fell on hard times after the Kansas-Nebraska Act, California Democrats continued to dominate the state. Except for the brief Know-Nothing interlude, they swept every election. Not only did they beat Frémont handily; they trounced virtually every candidate the new Republican Party threw at them.

Was there, then, no free-soil movement in California? There definitely was, and it took place largely within the Broderick wing of the California Democratic Party.

Why the Broderick wing? That is a tough question to answer. For when Broderick ran for Congress in New York, his ties to the free-soil movement were at best "minimal." On the one hand, he had the backing of George Henry Evans, the radical editor of *The Working Man's Advocate*, whose proposal to distribute public lands for free to settlers as homesteads became a key component of the free-soil movement. Also, Evans, in his extensive writings, left no doubt that the slaveholding elite posed a serious threat to the well-being of the American Republic and that the goals and aspirations of the white working class were incompatible with slavery. At the same time, however, Broderick clearly rejected the free-soil movement at the time of the Barnburner revolt in New York.[23] He also had the backing of Mike Walsh's *Subterranean*, which was anything but supportive of the free-soil movement. Not only was Walsh pro-slavery; he was blatantly pro-slavery and a staunch admirer of John C. Calhoun.

Nonetheless, once Broderick reached San Francisco, he moved quickly into the free-soil column. By then, as historians have frequently pointed out, the free-soil movement had a diverse following. Some joined the movement because they opposed slavery or opposed its expansion. Others became free-soilers largely because they wanted free homesteads or because they detested plantation society and the oligarchs who dominated it. Still others joined the movement because they wanted to keep all blacks, free as well as slave, out of the West. For them "free soil" meant "white only."[24]

In Broderick's case, only the last motive clearly did not apply. Elected to the state senate in January 1850, he quickly made his presence known. He was astute and tenacious. He was also often on the losing side. He fought against a tax on foreign miners and lost. He expressed concern for the rights of Californios, Mexicans, French, and Germans, and again found himself in the minority. He also led the fight against a bill—a very popular bill—to prevent "Free Negroes and Persons of Color" from entering the state.

The bill was the brainchild of the state's first governor, Peter H. Burnett. A forty-three-year-old Tennessee native who had spent many years in Mississippi before moving west to Oregon in 1843, Burnett had authored a similar bill in Oregon. He contended that "the colored races" were "inferior by nature to the white" and, given the circumstances in California, could never hope to advance "a single step in knowledge or virtue." He also insisted that slaves had "been manumitted in the slave states by their owners and brought to California bound to service for a limited period as hirelings" and that the state would soon be overrun with "inferior" black men. He wanted the California legislature to put a stop to black increase by passing a law much like the Oregon law. The bill easily passed the assembly and had ample support in the senate.

Broderick initially lacked the votes to kill the measure outright. So he took full advantage of the parliamentary rules and used one delaying tactic after another to keep the senate from voting on the bill. Weeks dragged by, and soon other legislators realized that their pet bills would never be acted upon as long as the governor's bill was before the senate. Worried about the fate of such legislation, several senators thus decided to join Broderick's effort to kill the governor's proposal. So in the end, his motion to postpone the measure indefinitely passed, 8 to 5.[25]

Broderick also used his parliamentary expertise to destroy a Chiv resolution that censured the free-soil movement. Although poorly worded, the resolution clearly characterized David Wilmot and other free-soil congressmen as "unholy, unpatriotic, and partisan." It also asserted that Congress had no right to interfere with slavery in the territories and endorsed popular sovereignty as the best way of settling the slavery question in the West. Again lacking the votes to defeat the resolution outright, Broderick first tried to get the resolution sent to a select committee, where it would hopefully die. When that parliamentary gambit failed, he then called for cleaning up the language of the resolution. In the process, he managed to amend the resolution in such a way that it also endorsed the free-soil cause. Once that was accomplished, the resolution's original supporters wanted no part of it. Some thus supported a second motion to send the resolution to a select committee, and there it died.[26]

Broderick also took up the cause of squatters. The previous summer, on land granted to Johann Sutter by the Mexican governor, Juan Bautista Alvarado, several thousand settlers had ignored Sutter's claim of ownership. They had feasted on his New Helvetia orchards and butchered his cattle. They also squatted on the Sacramento lots he had sold to Sam Brannan and other entrepreneurs. Trouble then followed, as sheriff's deputies destroyed the squatters' houses and fences and jailed James McClatchy, one of their leaders. In an attempt to free McClatchy, an armed band of squatters encountered a posse assembled by Mayor Hardin Bigelow on Fourth and J streets. The city assessor and three squatters were killed, and the mayor was badly wounded, eventually having to have his thumb amputated, then his arm. The next day another battle led to the death of Sheriff Joseph McKinney and several others. The authorities then tried the leaders of the squatters, McClatchy and Dr. Charles Robinson, who later became the governor of Kansas, for the deaths emerging from the riot.[27]

In the legislature, Broderick joined forces with Senator Thomas B. Van Buren in defending the squatters. Contending that no murder had been committed because there was no "premeditation or malice aforethought," he denounced the judge for allowing this trial to take place. Only a twisted interpretation of the law by an unscrupulous judge could have led to such a trial, contended Broderick. The legislature thus had a duty to stop this miscarriage of justice. And if the legislature did not act, said Broderick, he would raise five thousand men and free the defendants.[28]

In championing the squatters, Broderick made it clear that his primary concern was his kind of people—the free white laborer. Like George Henry Evans, he wanted poor and landless whites to reap the benefits of western expansion. For Broderick "free soil" thus included free land for settlers as well as land free from slavery.

Yet despite his free-soil sympathies and his parliamentary expertise, Broderick in the early years lost more battles than he won. Not only was he in the minority in the state senate; he was definitely in the minority wing in his party.

In all the free states, Democrats tended to be soft on the slavery question. That had been true in the 1830s and 1840s as well as the 1850s. Between 1836 and 1844, the key votes to stop antislavery petitions from being read in Congress had come mainly from free-state Democrats. They had also provided the key votes that enabled Southern planters to obtain the lands of the Cherokees, the Creeks, the Chickasaws, the Choctaws, and the Seminoles in the 1830s, and that enabled Texas to come into the Union in 1845 as a slave state with the right to divide into as many as five states. They had also provided the votes needed to defeat the Wilmot Proviso in 1847 and to enact the Fugitive Slave Law of 1850.[29]

California Democrats were no different. In 1852, on Henry Crabb's bill to establish a retroactive fugitive slave law in California, assembly Democrats provided Crabb with far more support than members of his own Whig Party. On the final roll call, thirty of thirty-three assembly Democrats cast aye votes as compared with eleven of eighteen Whigs. When the measure reached the senate, Broderick again had to use parliamentary tricks to keep it from getting through. He offered one amendment after another, raised points of order, even called for adjournment. His Chiv opponents, however, had the votes, waited him out, and eventually surmounted each obstacle. Similarly, in 1854, on a resolution supporting the Kansas-Nebraska Act, sixteen assembly Democrats endorsed the measure and not a single Whig.[30]

By the time of the Kansas-Nebraska Act, however, Broderick's base in California politics was expanding. He still had scores of enemies within the party, men who detested him and his Tammany Hall methods, men who regarded him as a threat to the South and Southern ways, men who even referred to themselves as "Anti-Broderick Democrats." But he also had a growing core of solid supporters, men who owed him dearly. Similarly, his main rival, William Gwin, had a growing list of enemies, men who never trusted him, men who found his loyalty to the South and Southern ways aggravating.

Much of the distrust centered on patronage. Gwin and his Chiv associates had a near monopoly on federal patronage, and they refused to share it with other California Democrats. Thanks to Gwin, the most powerful federal post—San Francisco collector of customs—went to a Chiv stalwart, Richard P. Hammond, the 1852 assembly Speaker from San Joaquin County who allegedly tried to split the state in two and open the southern half to slavery. Similarly, the job of U.S. marshal for northern California went to another Chiv mainstay, William H. Richardson, who held the post until he got killed in a shoot-out with a well-known gambler, Charles Cora.[31]

Hammond and Richardson, in turn, staffed their offices with Gwin's followers. So, too, did every other federal officeholder. And soon virtually every postmaster, marshal, customs service employee, mint appointee, Indian agent, and land office official in California was beholden to Gwin.

Yet, in dispensing patronage, Gwin never treated all members of the party equally. Nearly all the top jobs went to Southerners. In 1859, for example, the collector of San Francisco was Benjamin Franklin Washington, a Virginian. The appraiser general was Richard Roman, a Texan. The surveyor of San Francisco was W. B. Dameron, a Mississippian. The navy agent was Austin E. Smith, another Virginian. The state's two Indian agents, James Y. McDuffie and John T. Eaton, were both Georgians. The superintendent of the mint, Charles Hempstead, was a Missourian. The only non-Southerner to hold a top post was the surveyor general, James W. Mandeville, a New Yorker. He also was a bitter opponent of David Broderick. These men, in turn, hired hundreds of subordinates.[32]

This blatant bias in favor of Southerners drove other Democrats into Broderick's hands. Repeatedly denouncing the San Francisco Custom House as the "Virginia Poorhouse," Broderick convinced many Democrats from the North that they were being discriminated against because of their place of birth. Among the many who responded to his refrain was the state's third governor, John Bigler.

The Pennsylvania-born Bigler actually liked the South and despised Northern abolitionists. Ideologically, he and Gwin should have been soul mates. But Bigler never trusted Gwin. As a member of the first California legislature, he opposed Gwin's election to the U.S. Senate. And later, as governor of California, he abhorred Gwin's appointment policies. As he complained to his brother William, a major force in Pennsylvania politics and also a governor, "the office holders for this state were nearly all taken from the *South*, but few men from the *North* received favors."[33]

Largely because of this bias, Bigler ended up in Broderick's camp. He disagreed with Broderick on some issues. But he never doubted Broderick's contention that the main battle in California politics was over money and power. Money and power. The Chivs had it. They wanted more of it. And they refused to share it, especially with "ple-beans of the North." In Bigler's eyes, Broderick was dead right. Steps to thwart Chiv dominance had to be taken. Broderick, in turn, returned the favor and agreed to help Bigler get reelected governor.

First, however, the two men had to gain control of the state Democratic convention. They did so, largely by driving through a rule that representation would be on the basis of one delegate for each two hundred Democratic votes. By this formula, Broderick's San Francisco had by far the largest delegation. When the delegates convened at Benicia in 1853, Broderick thus was in control. He got the party to adopt a platform that embraced free-soil principles and especially the teachings of George Henry Evans. It called for putting the needs of the settlers first, making sure that the public lands were distributed in "limited quantities to actual settlers," and avoiding any policy that encouraged the formation of plantations and other landed monopolies. It also denounced "monopolies of privileges" and promised to protect "the laborer from degradation and oppression." Broderick also backed Bigler for a second term against the Chiv favorite, Richard Roman, the state treasurer and a Texan, and delivered the vote in Bigler's behalf.[34]

The Chivs were unhappy with the outcome. Many federal office-holders, all Gwin appointees, sat out the entire election and did nothing to help Bigler get reelected. Others, including Richard P. Hammond, collector of San Francisco, suddenly found themselves overwhelmed with "private business" halfway through the election campaign. And a few Chivs, led by the supreme court justice Solomon Heydenfeldt, actively campaigned for the opposition. In the end, the key was San Francisco, a city that Bigler lost in 1851. This time, with Broderick's help, he emerged victorious.[35]

All this had a price, of course. Broderick insisted on having a decisive hand in dispensing state patronage. Together, the two men appointed their cronies—William M. Lent, R. N. Snowden, Charles H. Bryan, Edward McGowan, Moses E. Flannagan—to such positions as commissioner of pilots, state prison inspector, and judge of the supreme court.[36] And once Broderick gained a whip hand in dispensing state patronage, men who had been turned down for federal jobs flocked to his side.

Some of the jobs he controlled, moreover, were lucrative. The state printing contract of 1852 was worth $270,000, while the State Marine Hospital in 1855 provided $166,000 in patronage money. In 1856, the sheriff of San Francisco County, the county clerk, recorder, coroner, and clerk of the superior court hauled in $325,000 in fees. Of this amount, $240,000 was profit. The sheriff's income alone was $100,000— four times as much as the president's. To would-be candidates, Broderick offered his standard deal: the backing of his machine for half the fees. In essence, then, Broderick sold these jobs—but only to loyal followers. And that, in turn, made him even more of an ogre in Chiv circles.[37]

Broderick and Bigler also tried to gain control of Gwin's Senate seat. They had mixed motives. Gwin, in their eyes, had sat on his hands during the gubernatorial election, and some of his men had sabotaged the party effort. Shouldn't there be a price to pay for such treachery? Bigler and Broderick thought so. In addition—and far more important— Broderick wanted the seat for himself.

When the state legislature met in Benicia in January 1854, Gwin still had more than a year to serve. His term didn't expire until March 1855. There was nothing in the law, however, to prevent the legislature from choosing a replacement a year in advance. Other states had done so. Why not California? The plan of action was simple. Since the Democrats controlled both houses of the legislature, all that was necessary was to get all the Democrats into caucus and make a decision. Should there be an early election or not?

Broderick worked diligently to force passage of an election bill. He organized, he intrigued, he bullied. He eventually managed to get forty assemblymen and fifteen senators to sign an address, probably written by his friend George Wilkes, that denounced party members who sat out the last election, "who tried to betray the party on the field of battle." Meanwhile, a minority document was put forth, signed by eleven senators and twenty-six assemblymen, calling for the party to wait until 1855, the year Gwin's term was over.[38]

As the procedure crept along, lawmakers received hundreds of letters and petitions for and against the proposal. Sixteen hundred residents of Tuolumne County thought an early election would be beneficial to them and the state. One Mexican leader told one of his compatriots that Broderick was their only "sincere" friend and deserved their full support. At the same time, others denounced Broderick as a "ruffian," a "plunderer," a "Bullying rowdy fireman," and the keeper of "a three cent grogery." Still others labeled him an abolitionist and thus dangerous to the South.[39]

The legislature initially planned to wrap up the entire matter by February 25. For on that day, they were scheduled to leave Benicia and move north to Sacramento. Surely, said many, the controversy would be settled by then. It wasn't. It dragged on. Finally, on March 6, in their new quarters in Sacramento, the election bill passed the assembly. In the senate, the initial vote ended in a tie. The presiding officer then voted with the Broderick forces. The Broderick men celebrated long into the night.

The victory celebration was premature, however. For the next day, Jacob Grewell, a former Baptist minister who had voted for the bill, called for the bill's reconsideration. His motion passed, and the senate then rejected the assembly bill, 17 to 14.

The Gwin men thus prevailed, but the rift in the Democratic Party was wider than ever before. It became wider still when the state Democratic convention met on July 18, 1854, at the First Baptist Church in Sacramento.

Hours before the meeting time, Broderick packed the church with his supporters, and then had the fire marshal order the doors closed. His followers then nominated and elected Edward McGowan, one of his closest associates, permanent chairman. The Gwin forces, however, refused to recognize this decision and chose the ex-governor John McDougal permanent chairman. Two sets of officers then tried to gain control of the podium. Neither side got the upper hand. One fracas followed another. The church trustees became alarmed. Might their church be destroyed? They finally decided to kick all the delegates out of the church.

The next day the Gwin men met at Musical Hall. They affirmed the Kansas-Nebraska Act, saying that it should have the backing of "every true lover of republican principles" and noting with "regret" that a "few who claim to be democrats" didn't support it. They also endorsed Robert Walker's Atlantic and Pacific Railroad, which would have linked California with the Deep South, as "the greatest national work of the age." They then nominated two Southern men for Congress, Philemon Herbert, a twenty-eight-year-old from Alabama, and James W. Denver, a thirty-six-year-old native of Virginia. Two years earlier, in 1852, Denver had been involved in a duel with one of Broderick's allies and one of the state's first congressmen, the New York–born newspaper editor Edward Gilbert. The weapons had been Wesson rifles, at forty paces, and after two shots Denver had emerged victorious.

Meanwhile, at nearby Carpenter's Hall, the Broderick forces met. They endorsed the party's free-soil platform of 1853 and nominated for two more years in Congress the party's sitting representatives, Milton S. Latham, a twenty-seven-year-old Ohioan, and James A. McDougall, a thirty-six-year-old New Yorker. They had no idea, however, if either man would accept a second term, as the two men were in transit back to California.[40]

The election campaign was even more divisive. With half the Democratic candidates campaigning as "Anti-Broderick Democrats," half as "Broderick Democrats," brawls and fistfights were the order of the day. Then, at the last minute, Latham withdrew, and the Gwin forces won easily, roughly 36,000 votes to 10,000. One of the two Chiv victors, Philemon Herbert, eventually disgraced his backers. After a night of debauchery in the nation's capital, he went to Willard's Hotel for breakfast, got into an altercation with Thomas Keating, an Irish waiter, and shot him dead. That ended Herbert's legislative career. He later fought for the Confederacy.[41] The other victor, James Denver, had a more illustrious career. He became an important figure in Democratic politics, and years later the city of Denver was named after him.

The Broderick forces not only got clobbered in the congressional elections of 1854. They then had to cope with the nativist crusade of the mid-1850s. Both the Know-Nothing Party and the San Francisco Vigilance Committee of 1856 singled out the Broderick men for attack. In doing so, they often had help from the followers of Gwin.

Vigilantism, which had been prevalent in 1851, enjoyed a rebirth in 1856 thanks largely to two incidents.[42] One involved Gwin's hand-picked U.S. marshal, General William H. Richardson. The general took his wife to the opening of the American Theater in San Francisco. To his shock, the gambler Charles Cora and his mistress, Arabella Ryan, the wealthy owner of a notorious brothel, took a seat in a nearby box. Richardson was furious. Several days later, in a drunken rage, he accosted Cora with a drawn pistol, and Cora shot Richardson dead. Cora's lawyers then argued that he had acted in self-defense, and the trial ended in a hung jury.

The other incident involved a supporter of Broderick. Thanks largely to Broderick, James P. Casey had more than his share of city posts, including deputy county treasurer for two years and inspector of elections. In the spring of 1856, he won a seat on the County Board of

Supervisors. The editor of the San Francisco *Evening Bulletin*, James King of William, then went on an editorial rampage. Never one to mince words, he characterized Casey as a former Sing Sing convict who had been imported by Broderick from New York to stuff ballot boxes. Casey tried to get a retraction. Failing to do so, he then openly shot King on the street. Badly wounded, King died a slow death.

King had been a key member of the first Vigilance Committee of 1851. The very hour he was buried, a second committee came into being. Backed by over two thousand men, they seized Casey and Cora from an unresisting sheriff, tried them hastily, and publicly hanged them four days later. The hangman, Sydney Hopkins, reportedly gloated as he put a hood over Casey's head. The vigilantes then forcibly seized arms from the state militia and held a huge parade, some six thousand strong. They also set about to purge the city of "corruption," singling out twenty-nine "cancerous" men to be eliminated through hanging, prison, or exile.

Nearly all twenty-nine were Democrats. Most were Irish Catholic and friends of Broderick's. On the list was Edward McGowan, Broderick's choice to head the 1854 state Democratic convention. Thanks to Broderick, he had also been a justice of the peace, associate justice of the San Francisco Court of Sessions, and commissioner of emigration. Also

Hanging of Charles Cora and James P. Casey. Reprinted from The San Francisco Daily Town Talk, *May 25, 1856.*

on the list were John W. Bagley, who had been an assemblyman in 1854; Charles P. Duane, chief engineer of the fire department; William Mulligan, collector of state and county licenses, deputy sheriff, and jailer; Billy Carr, member of the Charter Convention and general inspector and manager of the First Ward polls; Martin Gallagher, judge of elections in the First Ward; Terence Kelly, judge of elections at the Presidio; James Cusick, judge of elections in the Sixth Ward. Also to be banished were Michael Brannegan, John Cooney, John Crowe, T. B. Cunningham, James Hennessey, James R. Maloney, Billy Mulligan, and Thomas Mulloy.[43]

Broderick, along with everyone else of Irish ancestry, took the list seriously. Yet if his opponents thought that vigilantism would weaken his hold on the city, they were sadly mistaken. Within days, he and his men put together an organization to resist the Second Vigilance Committee. They called themselves the Law and Order Party. The rank and file of this party, according to the *Alta California*, were "without exception, natives of Ireland." They especially detested the committee's hangman, Sydney Hopkins, who they claimed was a lowlife who had once pimped for both his wife and his mother. They were soon joined by another largely Irish organization, the Jackson Guards, and gained the support of several notable San Franciscans, including William Tecumseh Sherman.[44]

In time, the Vigilance Committee overplayed their hand. Within a month, seventeen men had been deported, all Irish, all friends of Broderick's. Then, in June, the committee called for the banishment of Thomas McGuire, the owner of the Jenny Lind Theater, with whom Broderick had once lived. To many San Franciscans, McGuire was a model citizen, a good, hardworking, law-abiding man. Why was he chosen for banishment? Was it because he was Irish and a friend of Broderick's? Were the banishments politically inspired? Were the vigilantes simply doing dirty work for Gwin and the Chivs? For Foote and the Know-Nothings?

And then, on July 19, the committee ordered the arrest of Broderick himself. That convinced Gerritt W. Ryckman. A prominent leader of the 1851 committee, Ryckman was still a powerful man in San Francisco. He had also suspected all along that the leaders of the 1856 committee were politically motivated. Storming into their headquarters, he gave them an ultimatum. "I told you, you were going to make a political engine of it," said Ryckman. "If you don't rescind that order for the arrest of Broderick, I will tap the bell and order an opposition and arrest every damn one of you." The committee leaders then rescinded the order, Broderick went to talk with them, and they treated him with kid gloves.[45]

In the short term, the Vigilance Committee and the Know-Nothings undoubtedly made life difficult for Broderick. In the long term, however, they probably strengthened his hand.

By the fall of 1856, many committee members thought the battle was all but over. They were certain that they had created a new San Francisco, that they had rid the city of "ruffians, shoulder-strikers, and ballot-box stuffers," and that elections were now in the hands of "the most responsible men in the city." If that was the case, they had used a sledgehammer to kill a flea. For in the fall elections, the changes were minimal. The men still congregated in taverns and marched to the polls in ranks. And out of twelve thousand votes cast, the difference from the previous election was fewer than two hundred votes.[46]

The Broderick men lost some key districts to the People's Party, a new organization that had arisen during the vigilante crusade. But with the shift of a few votes in the next election, the Broderick organization would be back in full control. Broderick himself knew that was the case. Before the election, he reported the situation to Pablo de la Guerra, a political ally: "The efforts of my enemies, Gwin, Foote, Bailie Peyton, etc., to direct the aim of the Vigilance Committee against me, have signally failed, to their great discomfiture."[47]

Of the same opinion was Milton Latham, the twenty-nine-year-old Ohio-born politician who had defected from Broderick's ranks in the 1854 congressional election. Latham had spent his formative years in Alabama before moving to California, knew Southerners well, and now spent much of his time trying to line up Chiv support for a seat in the U.S. Senate. As he explained to one Chiv stalwart, Broderick still was in a position of power. Not only did he have the support of some thirty men in the state legislature, but these men were tied to him "in the most wonderful degree." They would do anything for him. And with these thirty-odd men as his base, all he had to do was pick up a handful of votes to be in complete control.[48]

These words were hardly welcome in Chiv circles. The Chivs had been busy celebrating Broderick's demise. One Chiv had indicated that Broderick had been shorn of his power in San Francisco, Sacramento, and Santa Clara. Another had said that several of his former "wire-pullers" had become "Republican Blacks." Gwin himself had been especially upbeat. After analyzing the makeup of the new legislature, he had predicted glorious days ahead. "We have the materials to achieve a complete and brilliant triumph," wrote Gwin.[49]

By Christmas Day 1856, Gwin knew better. In just six weeks, it had become clear to him that he had celebrated too soon. The claim that Broderick had been stripped of his power by the San Francisco Vigilance Committee through the deportation of his political aides was obviously just wishful thinking. In reality, Broderick was now stronger than ever. He clearly had over thirty legislators in his pocket. No one could get elected to the U.S. Senate without his backing. Two seats were now available, and the only man Broderick was certain to support was himself. All the other potential candidates—Latham, Weller, and Gwin—could stop him only if they worked together. And that was unlikely to happen. Thus they had to scramble for the second seat.[50]

Gwin was a realist. "I care not who my colleague is if I am elected," he wrote. "I do not think Broderick can be defeated, and if elected who so important to our section of the party to be his colleague as myself? . . . A half a loaf is better than no bread."[51]

The legislature convened in the first week of January 1857. Sacramento was cold, wet, and gray. The nearby Sierras were buried in snow. Nonetheless, exciting days lay ahead.

At stake were two U.S. Senate seats. One had remained empty since 1855, when Gwin failed to be reelected and the Know-Nothings came one vote shy of turning the seat over to Henry Foote. That seat entailed a four-year term in the Senate, two years having already gone by. The other post was that of John B. Weller, whose term expired in March 1857. Whoever got that seat would be in office for a full six years.

In the normal course of events, the short term would have been filled first. But in the Democratic caucus, a Broderick man moved to reverse the order. The Gwin men fought the motion, offered substitute motions, called for adjournment. So, too, did Weller's representatives. But with the help of Latham's supporters, the motion passed. The caucus then selected Broderick as the party's nominee for the long term. He received forty-two votes, his various opponents thirty-four. The nomination, according to party ritual, was then made unanimous. The caucus then turned to selecting a candidate for the short term. One vote was taken with no winner. Then, after a second vote and still no winner, the caucus adjourned.

Who among the also-rans had Broderick's ear? Many thought it was Milton S. Latham. For it was his men who provided the votes on the agenda question that enabled Broderick to get the six-year term. Rumor also had it that Latham had agreed to give Broderick his share of federal patronage in return for Broderick's support. But the pundits soon found that they were mistaken. Latham, in fact, had refused to grant Broderick such power.[52]

The pundits had also underestimated William Gwin. On Sunday night, around midnight, January 11, Gwin and a "friend" left Gwin's apartment in the Orleans Hotel by the rear stairway, snuck across J Street into an alley, and then ascended two or three stairs to the door of the Magnolia Hotel, rapped lightly on the door, and were admitted by Colonel A. J. Butler. They then ascended the stairs to room 6, tapped on the door, and were admitted by Broderick. The "friend" then left the room.

There, in room 6, Gwin and Broderick came to an understanding. In exchange for Gwin giving Broderick control of all federal patronage in California, Broderick would support Gwin for the second Senate seat. Gwin agreed and signed a letter to that effect. Dated January 11 and addressed to Broderick, the letter began with a long lament by Gwin on how his control of federal patronage had brought upon him much unhappiness, much criticism, and many "untold evils." He then promised that "while in the senate I will not recommend a single individual to appointment to office in this state. Provided I am elected you shall have the exclusive control of this patronage, so far as I am concerned; and in its distribution I shall only ask that it may be used with magnanimity and not for the advantage of those who have been our mutual enemies and unwearied in their efforts to destroy us."

In addition, Gwin had to write a public letter acknowledging his indebtedness to Broderick. Dated January 13, and addressed to "the People of California," the letter began with Gwin's giving another long account of the troubles he had endured during his senatorial career and especially the "malice" he had suffered as an "indirect dispenser of federal patronage." He also faulted some of his "friends" for deserting him in his time of need. Then, some three hundred words later, he got to the heart of the matter. He made it clear that he owed his election to the Senate to the "timely assistance" provided by "Mr. Broderick and his friends." And he praised Broderick for his magnanimity, for putting aside "all grounds of dissension and hostility" and taking a step that was "necessary to allay the strifes and discords which had distracted the party and the State."[53]

Hence Gwin got a second term in the U.S. Senate. The public letter to "the People of California" appeared in the press the very day Gwin and his wife, Mary, threw a huge victory celebration in San Francisco. Her entertainments had become legendary, noted for their elegance and extraordinary cuisine.

The letter ruined the occasion. More than one Chiv stalwart realized that Broderick had triumphed, that the Chivs undoubtedly had lost their monopoly of federal patronage, and that Gwin probably "had sold out his friends for the sake of being elected."[54]

Fortunately for Mary Gwin, the press did not get a copy of the letter in which her husband signed away all federal patronage. It was hidden from the public, kept under lock and key.[55] It came to be known as the "Scarlet Letter," and everyone who held it came to a bad end. The first was William T. Ferguson, who had arranged the midnight interview in room 6 of the Magnolia Hotel. To him was entrusted the Scarlet Letter. Months later, in the summer of 1858, "a trivial political dispute" in a San Francisco barroom led to Ferguson's being challenged to a duel by George Pen Johnston, "a Democrat of the southern school" and a skilled duelist. The two dueled with rifles on Angel Island, and Johnston emerged the victor.

The night after Ferguson's death, his office desk was found broken open and rifled. To get the letter? Broderick's men believed so. Ferguson, however, had turned the letter over to General James Estell, an assemblyman from Marin County, for safekeeping. In 1858, Estell was also killed in a duel. But he, too, no longer had the letter. He had given it to David Broderick.[56]

8

TRAVELING TOGETHER, THE NEWLY ELECTED SENATORS LEFT San Francisco in late January 1857, crossed Panama in near-record time, and steamed into New York harbor the evening of February 13. On hand to greet Broderick were several hundred men, women, and children. He also received a hundred-gun salute. The fanfare for Broderick, the former stonecutter from Greenwich Village, continued long into the night and for the next several days.

Leaving Broderick to bask in the homage, Gwin made his way to Washington. Since his term as senator theoretically had begun in 1855, he had no need to wait until March to be sworn in. He took the oath of office immediately and cast the deciding vote in favor of an appropriation to lay a transatlantic cable. The vote was of little interest to his California constituents, but Gwin saw it as a good sign. He was back in Washington, in the Senate, doing what he always felt he had been cut out to do.

Gwin also used the occasion to gain leverage over Broderick. He had several advantages. Not only was the nation's capital a Southern city; it was largely run by Southerners, by men like himself. This had often been true in the past, and it was to be especially true in the incoming Buchanan administration.

James Buchanan, in fact, was the consummate doughface—a Northern man with Southern principles.[1] A sixty-five-year-old veteran of many political wars, he had represented Pennsylvania in both the House and the Senate. Yet even though he was a Pennsylvania Democrat, his closest associates in Washington had generally been Southerners or men with deep Southern connections. He roomed for many years with Senator William King of Alabama, a fellow bachelor. His chief advisers included Governor Henry Wise of Virginia, Senator John Slidell of Louisiana, and Robert Tyler of Virginia. Even his most trusted Northern advisers had Southern ties: Representative J. Glancy Jones of Pennsylvania had been a Southern preacher and lawyer; and Senator Jesse Bright of Indiana owned land and slaves in Kentucky.

Ideologically, Buchanan also had much in common with the Southern wing of his party. He was, in most instances, a strict constructionist of the Constitution. He detested abolitionists and "black Republicans." He opposed slavery only in the abstract. He assumed that most slave masters were humanitarians at heart and dismissed all those who argued differently. He thought most slaves were well treated and downplayed the slave pens and slave auctions in the nation's capital that told a different story. And, for all practical purposes, he saw no great wrong in slavery's continued existence.

Buchanan also sympathized with Southern expansionists who hungered for Cuba and wanted to add slave territory to the United States. He had been secretary of state when the Polk administration in 1848 tried to buy Cuba from Spain for $100 million. And in 1854, while minister to Great Britain, he had joined the ministers to Spain and France in issuing, under orders from President Pierce, the Ostend Manifesto, urging the United States to immediately buy Cuba from Spain "at any price" up to $120 million, and also proclaiming that if Spain refused to sell and its possession of Cuba "should seriously endanger" the "internal peace" of the slave states, then the United States would be justified in seizing Cuba "upon the very same principle that would justify an individual in tearing down the burning house of his neighbor if there were no other means of preventing the flames from destroying his own home."[2]

While news of this saber-rattling manifesto had horrified many Northern Democrats, it had hardly hurt Buchanan with zealous Southern expansionists and most Southern Democrats. They were delighted with him and had little trouble supporting his presidential candidacy.

Without these Southern backers, moreover, Buchanan would have lost the 1856 presidential election. He won only five free states, losing eleven to the Republican candidate, John C. Frémont. In contrast, in the fifteen slave states, Buchanan won handsomely, losing only Maryland to the Know-Nothing candidate, Millard Fillmore. All in all, the slave states provided the Pennsylvania Democrat with nearly two-thirds of his electoral votes.

Southern Democrats, needless to say, never let Buchanan forget these facts. Nor was he able to forget that the Democratic majority in both the House and the Senate was dominated by Southerners. In forming a Cabinet, he acted accordingly. He chose four Southerners and three Northern men with Southern principles. Omitted entirely was anyone who understood, much less represented, the free-soil wing of the Democratic Party. Gwin was thus certain to receive a friendly welcome in the White House.

Another asset was Gwin's wife, Mary. The daughter of a well-known Kentucky tavern keeper, she had a knack for entertaining the rich and the powerful. And among those she found it easy to enchant was the Pennsylvania bachelor James Buchanan.

In 1857, when the Gwins returned to Washington, Mary Gwin was forty-one years old. She was also "fashionable, liberal, dashing, generous, and full of Southern partialities." Christened Mary Elizabeth Hampton Bell, she had at age fifteen married William Logan and moved to Houston, Texas. Three years later she met Gwin when he came to Texas to check out some land for one of his many land speculation schemes. The next year, 1835, Logan died. When Gwin learned of Logan's death, he returned to Texas to woo Mary. A year later, in Vicksburg, they married. She was twenty-one at the time, Gwin thirty-one. The couple eventually had four children.

Gwin's wealth enabled Mary to make full use of her social skills. With little effort, she turned their home into a center of hospitality, and thanks to her expertise as a hostess, invitations to the Gwin mansion became highly coveted, first in Vicksburg, then in New Orleans. When Gwin told her of his plans to go to California to become a senator, she encouraged him, apparently looking forward to life in the nation's capital. And at her urging, Gwin purchased a mansion in Washington, at Nineteenth and I streets, three blocks from the White House. There Mary and William Gwin entertained and dazzled the Washington elite.

In March 1858, one observer noted that the Gwins spent about $75,000 per year, roughly three times the president's salary, on entertainment.[3]

Of all Mary Gwin's guests, no one appreciated her hospitality more than James Buchanan.[4] The president's own social life was largely in the hands of his niece Harriet Lane, who had played the same role when he was minister to Great Britain. In a sense, Harriet Lane dictated style, and what she preferred—silk gloves that reached halfway to the elbow, bare shoulders, and plunging necklines—became the rage of Washington. Her uncle, meanwhile, always had a liking for small talk and elegance—as well as anyone who could furnish "in profusion" wild turkeys, prairie hens, partridges, quails, reed birds, chicken and lobster salads, terrapins, oysters, ice creams, various sweets, champagne, sherry, and punch.

In short, elite Washington was a world in which Mary and William Gwin found it easy to operate—and one in which David Broderick, the stonemason's son, was clearly out of his element.

Broderick arrived in Washington several weeks after the Gwins, in March 1857, and took a room in a boardinghouse. He didn't like his living quarters. Nor did he like the nation's capital. It was just too Southern for his taste. He expected, however, to be well received by the White House. After all, he had been an early supporter of Buchanan in the 1856 presidential contest and had been central in the Pennsylvania Democrat's carrying California by a five-to-two margin. Surely the president would be happy to see him.

But there was no warm welcome, and within a month the two men were at loggerheads. The rupture stemmed partly from Buchanan's decision to openly support pro-slavery interests. Two days after his inauguration, the Supreme Court in the Dred Scott case declared the Missouri Compromise unconstitutional, thus opening all federal territories to slavery, and the Buchanan administration's official organ, the Washington *Union*, immediately joined Southerners in singing the praises of the Court.[5]

Free-soilers, in contrast, not only denounced the decision but blamed it on Buchanan. Had Frémont been elected president, said one New York Republican, the Supreme Court would not have dared to violate "the principles we have received from our forefathers."[6] An exaggeration? Not as much as it might at first seem. The Southern judges, historians later discovered, had wanted all along to issue a pro-slavery decision, but knew that the authority of such a decision would be weak if they had only a one-vote majority and no Northern judge was on their side. They set about to persuade one of the Northern Democrats on the Court, Robert C. Grier of Pennsylvania, to join them. Unbeknownst to his Republican critics, Buchanan helped them in this effort, and his intervention undoubtedly contributed to Grier's decision to join the Southern majority in declaring the Missouri Compromise unconstitutional.[7]

Buchanan's decision to cast his lot with pro-slavery doctrine infuriated Broderick. Far more important, however, was the way Buchanan handled California patronage. In March, soon after taking the oath of office, Broderick tried to schedule an appointment with the president. He had difficulty doing so. Frustrated, he turned to John W. Forney, a Philadelphia newsman and powerful figure in Pennsylvania politics. Forney sent a note to the president, reminding him that Broderick was now "the most important man from California" as well as "a man of the people" and Buchanan's "devoted friend in the last struggle."[8]

With Forney's help, Broderick finally got an opportunity to talk with Buchanan. The president wanted to engage in small talk. Broderick didn't. Instead, he immediately presented his recommendations for federal appointments. To his chagrin, he was told to submit them in writing. He did.[9] That, however, did him little good. For the president had already been bombarded with counterproposals from Chiv leaders who were determined to destroy Broderick's influence, and each day's mail brought more Chiv challenges. From California, Milton S. Latham and John B. Weller contacted Buchanan, hoping to undercut Broderick. From Washington, Representatives Philemon Herbert and James Denver did the same thing. What about Gwin? Did he keep his word? No! Despite what several of his biographers claim, he plunged into the fray.[10]

The key post was collector of the port of San Francisco. It was easily the most powerful federal office in California. For it, Broderick recommended his old ally Governor John Bigler. The recommendation, he felt, should have pleased the president. The former governor, after all, was a Pennsylvanian, a native of the president's own state. His brother William, moreover, was a powerful figure in the Pennsylvania Democratic Party. Not only had William been governor of the state; he now represented the state in the U.S. Senate. And William left no doubt where he stood. He made it clear to Buchanan, and everyone in

Buchanan's administration, that his brother John wanted this appointment badly.[11]

Was there any way, then, that the president could ignore Broderick's recommendation? The Chivs initially expected Broderick to get his way. Nonetheless, they offered an alternative. Their choice was Benjamin Franklin Washington, a native of Virginia who had often presided over Chiv meetings and had been the editor of a Chiv newspaper, the *Times and Transcript*. If the Virginian got the collector's office, the message would be loud and clear. There would be no mistaking the significance. Everyone would realize that the president was placing the tremendous power of the collector's office in the hands of Broderick's enemies as well as in the hands of the pro-Southern wing of the California Democratic Party. And that is exactly what Buchanan did.[12]

To make matters worse, Buchanan made Bigler minister to Chile. Years before, Bigler had sought the post, and thus he accepted the appointment. But while in Chile, he was to be six thousand nautical miles from California and no longer a force in state politics. Without question, then, Buchanan dealt Broderick a double blow, stripping him of one of his most important political assets while giving the San Francisco Custom House to his political enemies. To add insult to injury, Buchanan told Broderick that it was only "fair" to give Benjamin Franklin Washington the San Francisco office as two of Broderick's "friends" had received appointments to the custom service in Stockton and San Diego.

Broderick was furious. Did the president take him for a fool? "I will not cross the threshold of the White House while the present incumbent occupies it," he declared. Gwin in turn celebrated. "Washington's appointment was the final stab," he explained to his followers, and Broderick's "denunciations of the President and Cabinet are gross in the extreme." The rift, he noted, also gave him the opportunity to spend "yesterday in visiting the Cabinet and the President with whom I had [patronage] talks."[13]

The first week of April, after less than a month in the nation's capital, Broderick hustled back to California. To offset his Washington misadventure, he hoped to gain control of the state Democratic convention and nominate his friends for state office. He desperately needed another supportive governor who could do for him and his men what John Bigler had done a few years before.

Upon arriving in San Francisco, Broderick immediately learned that the Chivalry had regained much of their former strength. No longer would he be able to play one Chiv faction off against another as he had done during the 1857 Senate election. They were now all united against him. They also realized that Gwin was once again in control of federal patronage. They thus looked to Gwin for leadership and for favors. And so did other party operatives, including some who had once regarded Broderick and Bigler as their only patrons.

Chiv numbers had also increased with the collapse of the Know-Nothing Party. Henry Foote and other Know-Nothing leaders had been delighted with Buchanan's Cabinet picks, and they had announced that Buchanan's Cabinet and his political views made their party unnecessary. Many rank-and-file Know-Nothings, in turn, had taken that as a signal to join the Democratic Party. Virtually none, however, had joined the Broderick wing of the party. Few had any desire to be led by an Irish Catholic. In contrast, many affiliated with the Chivs.[14]

Would these former Know-Nothings be allowed to have a voice in the state Democratic convention in July? That became the telling issue. On opening day, the Broderick men moved to bar all delegates who had voted for anyone other than James Buchanan in the 1856 election. Only "true" Democrats, they argued, should be seated at the convention. William Van Voorhies, a Chivalry Democrat, then offered a substitute motion that welcomed "all national men, of whatever party heretofore, to unite with us in finally and forever destroying within the limits of our state, the evil spirit of disunion and sectionalism." The substitute motion passed, 224 to 81. The convention then went on to nominate for governor a Chiv mainstay, John B. Weller. The vote on the first ballot was overwhelming, 254 to 61.[15]

The Chivs thus emerged triumphant. The rival free-soil wing of the California Democratic Party was in shambles, and the man who had once had Chiv leaders begging for his help was now all but pushed out of the state party.

In early October, Broderick left San Francisco for Washington and the December meeting of Congress. He was in a foul mood. Fearing the worst, Governor-elect Weller suspected that Broderick intended to use the rules of "senatorial courtesy" to block Chiv appointments that came before the Senate for confirmation. In anticipation, Weller wrote his old friend Stephen A. Douglas and asked him to stop Broderick in his tracks.[16]

Weller was right. Broderick had a bit in his mouth when it came to the Chiv power base. On one occasion, he even accused Weller's brother, a San Francisco postmaster, of overcharging customers and pocketing the ill-gained income. He also accused a former Chiv collector of customs of being "a defaulter to the amount of $430,000" and a Chiv melter and refiner and assayer of the mint of being "a defaulter of about $175,000." And he especially zeroed in on a Gwin scheme to have the War Department buy Lime Point, a piece of land at the mouth of San Francisco Bay, for $200,000. Gwin claimed the purchase was necessary to protect the port city from military attack. Broderick said that the transaction amounted to an "enormous fraud." The land, he said, wouldn't bring even $7,000 at auction, and the deal's only purpose was to enrich Chiv speculators.[17]

Douglas, however, couldn't provide Governor Weller with the assistance he requested. For Douglas desperately needed Broderick's help when the first session of the Thirty-fifth Congress convened on December 7. There was a new issue on the agenda, one of the many that had grown out of Douglas's Kansas-Nebraska Act. This one had been started by pro-slavery lawmakers in Kansas. Knowing that Congress would not pass legislation enabling them to form a state, they had decided to force the issue. Over the governor's veto, they had passed legislation calling for a census, the election of delegates to a constitutional convention, and a convention in the fall of 1857. The free-state forces, assuming with good reason that the census would be rigged, boycotted the entire affair.[18]

As predicted, the census was rigged. In over half the counties pro-slavery officials either never took a census or never bothered to register voters. All in all, half the eligible voters never had a chance to register, and the eight counties bordering slaveholding Missouri ended up with two-thirds of the delegates.

At this juncture, President Buchanan appointed Gwin's old friend Robert Walker territorial governor. A Pennsylvanian who had migrated to Mississippi as a young man, Walker had long been a major figure in Deep South politics. Not only had he worked hand in hand with the Gwin brothers in Mississippi; he had also advocated the acquisition of both slaveholding Texas and slaveholding Cuba. He had, in short, strong Southern credentials. But he was not foolhardy. He estimated that Democrats in Kansas outnumbered Republicans by two to one, but more than half of them would go over to the Republicans if the Democracy tried to turn Kansas into a slave state. In his view, Kansas was bound to be a free state, and his party simply had to accept that fact. Otherwise, they would lose the people of Kansas to the "abolitionists." He set about to have honest elections in Kansas and get the free-state majority to participate.

Despite Walker's pleas, the free-state men refused to partake in the rigged election to choose constitutional delegates. Pro-slavery forces thus prevailed easily and at Lecompton drafted a pro-slavery constitution. It proclaimed that "the right of property is before and higher than any constitutional sanction, and the right of the owner of a slave to such slave and its issue is the same and as inviolable as the right of the owner of any property whatever." It also prohibited any constitutional amendment for seven years, and declared that even after seven years had passed, "no alteration shall be made to affect the rights of property in the ownership of slaves."[19]

Robert Walker. Reprinted from Ben: Perley Poore, Perley's Reminiscences, *2 vols. (Philadelphia, 1886), 1:334.*

Knowing that their handiwork would be rejected if submitted to a fair vote, the delegates first decided to send the document straightway to Washington without a referendum of any kind. But, on sober second thought, a majority decided that such a move was just too brazen to succeed. The delegates then worked out a bogus referendum whereby the voters would not have the opportunity to vote down the fundamental constitution, just the opportunity to choose between two alternative clauses, one that would legally permit additional slaves to be brought into Kansas, the other that would legally bar the future importation of slaves. But here again there was a rub. The election was to be conducted not by Governor Walker but by officials named by the convention, the same men who had rigged the constitutional convention. That further convinced free-state men that the whole constitutional movement was a sham.

Walker then set off for Washington to enlist Buchanan's support against the Lecompton Constitution. The president had wavered for nearly half a year. Maybe he could now be persuaded to support honest government. But before Walker got to the nation's capital, Buchanan decided to follow the advice of his Cabinet and his pro-slavery friends in Congress. He threw his full weight behind the Lecompton constitution. Sharing his friends' hatred of abolitionists and Republicans, he apparently saw no great wrong in extending slavery into Kansas. He also knew that he had enough votes to get the admission bill through the Senate, and he was confident that with executive pressure he could bring enough Northern Democrats in line to get the measure through the House.

Once the Washington *Union* announced Buchanan's decision, many Northern Democrats panicked.[20] The administration, as they saw it, had handed the Republicans another issue with which to beat down any chance they had of recapturing their home districts. They were already being lambasted for the Supreme Court's action in Dred Scott. Now they were expected to defend fraudulent elections in Kansas as well as a pro-slavery constitution that even the territorial governor, a onetime Mississippi slaveholder, deemed unacceptable.[21]

The president then formally asked Congress to endorse his decision in early December 1857. The next day, Stephen A. Douglas rose in the Senate and attacked the administration's Kansas policy. A few days later, Walker resigned in protest. And a few days after that, the referendum called by the Lecompton convention took place. With most of the free-state men abstaining, the official results showed some six thousand votes for Lecompton with additional slavery, and some five hundred for it without additional slavery. Of the pro-slavery votes, nearly three thousand came from areas along the Missouri border that had yet to be settled. Towns with six buildings and forty settlers had over four hundred voters. Two weeks later there was still another election in Kansas, this one called by the state legislature. This time the pro-slavery men abstained, and Lecompton was voted down by over ten thousand votes.

Buchanan nevertheless pushed ahead. Denouncing the actions of the free-staters in Kansas and announcing that "Kansas is . . . at this moment as much a slave State as Georgia or South Carolina," he sent the Lecompton constitution to both houses for adoption.[22] What followed was a dramatic contest, with long sessions, filibusters, and fistfights on the floor. Much attention was focused on the Senate, where the Little Giant of Illinois led the revolt against the Buchanan administration.

For Douglas, political principle as well as political survival was at stake. Lecompton's rigged convention and fraudulent votes had made a mockery out of popular sovereignty. Accepting Lecompton was thus out of the question. Yet rejecting it outright meant going against a president of his own party. And, as everyone in Washington knew, Andrew Jackson had crushed two party members who had openly opposed him. Would Buchanan do the same to Douglas? The Pennsylvania Democrat left no doubt. He promised to crush Douglas and any other Democrat who dared to cross him.[23]

Douglas thus had trouble finding Democratic allies. Although many agreed with him in principle, few were willing to take on the administration. In the Senate, there were now twenty Republicans, all from the free states, and thirty-seven Democrats, all but twelve from the slave states. Douglas had the support of nearly all the Republicans but only two members of his own party. One was Charles Stuart of Michigan. The other was David Broderick. Like Douglas, Stuart was cautious. He tried to downplay the fact that he was going against the president. He focused mainly on the fraud and illegalities in drafting the Lecompton constitution. He did not attack the president directly.

In contrast, Broderick singled out Buchanan and his Cabinet for blame. On December 23, he addressed the Senate. It was his maiden speech, and he began by emphasizing that he was a "regular" Democrat, one who had rejected free soil at the time of the Barnburner revolt in New York, and that he had supported Buchanan in the last election—indeed, supported him even before Buchanan had been chosen as the Democratic nominee. Broderick then became brutally direct: "If I understand this subject, and I hope I do, I think that the President of the United States is alone responsible for the present state of affairs in Kansas. It is the first time, I believe, in the history of this country, that a President of the United States ever stepped down from the exalted position he held, to attempt to coerce the people into a base submission to the will of an illegalized body of men." As for the delegates who wrote the Lecompton constitution, said Broderick, "the only thing that has astonished me . . . is the forbearance of the people of Kansas." If they had seized these men "and flogged them, or cut their ears off, and driven them out of the country, I would have applauded them for the act."[24]

Broderick, despite the hullabaloo he created with his maiden speech, had little to say for the next three months.

He did, however, push one item on the free-soil agenda. He introduced a resolution, one that his old friend George Henry Evans had been advocating for years. It called on the federal government to survey the public domain and distribute it "for the free and exclusive use of actual settlers not possessed of other lands." The resolution went to the Committee on Public Lands, of which Broderick was a member, but was subsequently defeated by the Senate's Southern bloc.[25]

Then, on March 22, the last day of the Lecompton debate, Broderick again made his mark. The previous day James Henry Hammond of South Carolina had given a long speech praising slavery and the South. In words that ended up in some ten thousand pamphlets and were repeated as far west as San Francisco, the South Carolina Democrat had lectured his fellow senators on the moral superiority of slavery as a labor system.

Among other things, Hammond had told his Northern colleagues that they dared not make war on cotton, that no power on earth dared make war on cotton, that "cotton was king." He had also acknowledged that slaveholders had long ruled the United States. Indeed, he boasted about it. He regarded slaveholder rule as "the brightest page of human history." He had also praised California and Oregon as being the only free states that had not run roughshod over the Fugitive Slave Law. Indeed, they were pro-Southern in outlook, and as a result there was "no antagonism between the South and these countries and there never will be."

Hammond had also told his Northern colleagues that every society had a "mud-sill" class to do the menial work and that the South had found a people ideally suited to such work in its black slaves. The North, he insisted, also had a "mud-sill" class. "Yours are white, of your own race, you are brothers of one blood. They are equals in natural endowment of intellect and feel galled by their degradation." Moreover, they have the right to vote, and if they ever made good use of it, think of the consequences. "Where would you be? Your society would be reconstructed, your government reconstructed, your property divided."[26]

The next day Broderick responded to Hammond's long lecture, especially to his characterization of Northern laborers as "white slaves" and the "mud-sills" of Northern society. He first supposed that Hammond didn't mean to insult him or any other senator. He then pointed out that he was the second-youngest senator, that he was the son of an artisan, and that he had been a stonemason's apprentice for five years.

Then he said: "I am not proud of this. I am sorry it is true. I would that I could have enjoyed the pleasure of life in my boyhood's days . . . I have not the admiration for the men of the class from whence I sprang that might be expected; they submit too tamely to oppression, and are too prone to neglect their rights and duties as citizens. But, sir, the class to whose toil I was born, under our form of government, will control the destinies of this nation. If I were inclined to forget my connection with them, or to deny that I sprang from them, this Chamber would not be the place in which I could do either. While I hold a seat here, I have but to look at the beautiful capitals adorning the pilasters that support this roof, to be reminded of my father's talent, and to see his handiwork."

Broderick also defended Douglas and the Kansas-Nebraska Act, arguing that in a free contest the slave states had no chance against Northern freemen. Said Broderick: "How foolish for the South to hope to contend with success in such an encounter. Slavery is old, decrepit, and consumptive; freedom is young, strong, and vigorous. The one is naturally stationary and loves ease; the other is migratory and enterprising. There are six millions of people interested in the extension of slavery; there are twenty millions of free men to contend for these territories, out of which to carve themselves homes where labor is honorable."

Broderick also ridiculed Hammond's "King Cotton" argument. "Why, Sir, the single free State of California exports the product for which cotton is raised, to an amount of more than one half in value of the whole exports of the cotton of the slave States. Cotton king! No, sir. Gold is king. I represent a State, sir, where labor is honorable; where the judge has left his bench, the lawyer and doctor their offices, and the clergyman his pulpit, for the purpose of delving in the earth; where no station is so high, and no position so great, that its occupant is not proud to boast that he has labored with his hands."

Finally, Broderick once again savaged James Buchanan. In his last salvo, he said: "I hope, sir, that the historian, when writing the history of these times, will ascribe the attempt of the executive to force this constitution on an unwilling people to the fading intellect, the petulant passion, and trembling dotage of an old man on the verge of the grave."[27]

The harsh words, even though they further distanced Broderick from the president and his men, had only limited impact. For in the Senate, Buchanan always had the votes he needed—and then some. He prevailed easily in the Senate, 33 to 25. His problem was the House, where he needed another fifteen to twenty votes.

To get those votes, Buchanan had plenty of weapons and used every one of them to the limit. He made conspicuous examples of those who crossed him, firing several of Douglas's allies, including the Chicago postmaster, the state mail agent in Illinois, and the federal marshal of northern Illinois, and replacing them with "good" Lecompton Democrats. At the same time, he had his underlings work the halls of Congress, promising patronage awards to the faithful, supply contracts for firms tied to House members, shipbuilding contracts for firms in which congressmen owned shares, an overseas appointment for a close friend of Garnett Adrain of New Jersey, a similar appointment for a friend of John Hickman of Pennsylvania. And then for some there were less traceable favors—wine, women, and cash. All of these enticements came into play again and again in the battle to get Lecompton through the House.[28]

Yet, in the end, Buchanan failed to get the votes he needed. Indeed, his opponents introduced a substitute motion to resubmit the entire Lecompton constitution to a popular vote in Kansas. The amended bill

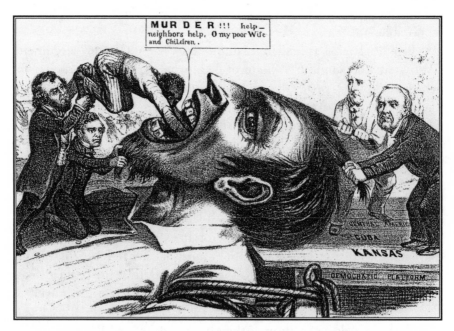

Cartoon of Buchanan administration pushing slavery down a free-soiler's throat. Library of Congress.

passed the House, 120 to 112, on April 1, 1858. For the first time in memory, the South had suffered a crushing defeat.

To mask defeat and deny the anti-Lecompton forces outright victory, the administration scrambled and came up with a "compromise" bill. That measure deliberately subordinated the Lecompton constitution and highlighted a secondary issue, the fact that Kansas had asked for twenty-three million acres of public land grants, about six times the norm for new states. The administration proposed cutting the land grant to about four million acres and asking the voters if they would accept statehood with the reduction. If they ratified this proposal, then Kansas would immediately be admitted as a slave state under the Lecompton constitution. If they rejected it, then Kansas would have to wait until it had a population of ninety thousand before it could become a state. In short, rejection meant the death of the Lecompton constitution and the postponement of statehood for several years.

Republicans railed against these pro-slavery stipulations, said they amounted to a bribe and a threat. Broderick and several other Democrats agreed. But Douglas wavered. He still had presidential aspirations. And he knew that no Democrat could get the party's nomination without the support of its Southern wing. Under the party's two-thirds rule, he had to somehow get two-thirds of the delegates to the next national convention to support his candidacy. He couldn't afford to alienate one-third of the delegates. Needing to make amends, he decided to go along with the administration.

Upon learning of Douglas's decision, Congressman John Hickman of Pennsylvania fumed. The Little Giant had betrayed him. He went to see Broderick. Thunderstruck, Broderick ordered Hickman to bring Douglas to his room. When Douglas arrived, Broderick exploded: "Mr. Douglas, I hear you propose to abandon the fight." Said Douglas: "I see no hope of success; they will crush us; and if they do there is no future for any of us, and I think we can agree upon terms that will virtually sustain ourselves." Said Broderick: "You had better, sir, go into the street and blow your damn brains out. You came to me of your own accord and asked me to take this stand. I have committed myself against this infernal Lecompton constitution. Now, if you desert me, God damn you, I will make you crawl under your chair in the Senate."[29]

Visibly shaken, Douglas subsequently reversed himself and condemned the administration's proposal. Meanwhile, Buchanan and his Southern cronies went all out to save face and win a procedural victory.

There was an army contract for the brother of John Ahl of Pennsylvania, $5,000 for the roommate of Lawrence Hall of Ohio, a township of land for Joseph McKibbin of California, which he refused, the same township for John Haskin of New York, which he also refused. Then there was the threat to fire McKibbin's father from his job as a Philadelphia naval agent. As a result, a handful of anti-Lecompton Democrats joined forces with the administration, and on the last day of April the face-saving "compromise" passed the House, 112 to 103, and the Senate, 31 to 22.

A few months later the voters of Kansas did what everyone had expected. They rejected Lecompton by a six-to-one margin.

Meanwhile, William Gwin was riding high. In California, his men had regained control of state politics and now had the lion's share of state patronage to go along with their continuous monopoly of federal patronage. Gwin thus had ground troops in every district of the state, men who had government jobs largely because of him, and thus men who on Election Day would round up the faithful, provide them with ballots, and march them to the polls.

In Washington, Gwin was also doing well. He had the full support of the dominant wing of the Democratic Party. Often labeled a "dough-face," the term was a misnomer in his case. Unlike James Buchanan, he had never been a Northern man with Southern principles. He had always been a Southern man, first in Tennessee, then in Mississippi, then in California. And, like any good Southern Democrat, he voted consistently with the Southern wing of his party. Accordingly, he had supported the Kansas-Nebraska Act, the Dred Scott decision, the U.S. annexation of Cuba, the Henry Crabb invasion of Sonora, and the William Walker invasions of lower California and Nicaragua. In 1858 he also voted for the Lecompton constitution—as well as against Broderick's resolution to provide free government land for "actual settlers not possessed of other lands."

Not only was Gwin in 1858 riding high in his party. On April 9, his wife, Mary, put on a fancy-dress ball that made him the toast of the town. The ball cost $12,000 and lasted from dusk to dawn. The guests came in costume, as Robin Hood, Friar Tuck, a matador, a gypsy girl, a milkmaid, a Queen of the Night, Red Riding Hood, Byron's "Maid of Athens," and so forth. At the door to greet them was Mary Gwin, dressed as a regal lady, the "Queen of Louis Quatorze." At her side was none other than President James Buchanan. Once all the guests had arrived, the president then escorted Mary out onto the ballroom floor for the first dance of the evening. "All Washington was agog," noted one commentator. Fifty years later the ball was still being hailed as "one of the most brilliant episodes in the annals of ante-bellum days in the capital," and as "far above any similar entertainment ever given at Washington."[30]

By the time of the ball, the Democratic hierarchy knew they could count on Gwin. In most respects, he thought and voted like a typical Deep South senator. Accordingly, they chose him to chair the caucus committee that organized the Senate. From that position, he played a central role in the party's decision to punish the administration's critics. Under his guidance, the committee kicked Broderick off the Committee on Public Lands and stripped Douglas of his chairmanship of the Committee on Territories.

Mary Gwin's fancy-dress party.
Reprinted from Ben: Perley Poore,
Perley's Reminiscences, *2 vols.*
(Philadelphia, 1886), 2:23.

Not only had both men run afoul of Buchanan and Southern Democrats in the Lecompton battle, but Douglas had taken a stance in the famous Lincoln-Douglas debates that had further infuriated Southern Democrats. In his campaign for reelection to the Senate, Douglas had told an audience at Freeport, Illinois, that the people of Kansas could nullify the Dred Scott decision by simply refusing to pass the "police" legislation that slavery needed to exist. Since then, Southern senators had demanded a federal slave code to protect slavery in the territories. At the same time, they had also demanded that immediate action be taken against Douglas for his assertions in the Freeport speech.

From his post as caucus chair, Gwin led the fight. It was Douglas's duty, said Gwin, "to give his reasons to the Senate and to the country" for the tenets that he adopted in the Illinois Senate campaign. And since Douglas had not done so, at least to the satisfaction of Senate Democrats, he should be stripped of power. He should no longer serve as chairman of the Committee on Territories. And so it came to pass that the Little Giant, the most powerful Northern Democrat and the one that many regarded as the party's best choice for president, was reduced to a mere cog in the party hierarchy.[31]

Gwin also chaired the committee on the Pacific railroad. From that position, he continued to push for multiple roads across the country, even though it was evident that many senators were unwilling to support one road, let alone three or four. At the same time, he made it clear that he was willing to leave the question of routes up to the president and the railroad financiers. And since Buchanan had said that he favored the Gila River route, and the Chivs had touted the plans of Robert Walker's Atlantic and Pacific Railroad Company, that was widely interpreted to mean that Gwin favored a Southern route.

On this issue, too, Gwin battled Broderick. In late September 1858, Broderick again made the long trip from San Francisco to Washington. This time he purposely went by stage to get a firsthand look at the highly publicized "central route." It took him six weeks to get to St. Louis, the stage flipped over on the last leg of the journey, and Broderick ended up with a cracked rib and frostbitten toes.

Nonetheless, when Gwin introduced his railroad bill, Broderick took him to task. The only logical route, he said, was the central one. It had long been the chief route for most migrants to the Far West. The surrounding countryside provided more than enough timber and stone to build the road. The grade was easy. And it led directly to the major cities of the West—namely, Sacramento and San Francisco. The southern route, in contrast, ended up in Guaymas. And that was ridiculous. Who wanted to go to Guaymas? It would be equally logical, said Broderick, to make Mexico City the western terminus.[32]

When Congress adjourned in early March, the two warring senators began their long trip back to California. On the agenda of both men was another battle, the upcoming state election on September 7.

Broderick stopped briefly in Philadelphia on his way to catch a steamer out of New York. While waiting for an omnibus at the corner of Sixth and Chestnut streets, he had a long talk with John Forney, the Philadelphia newsman who had aided him in getting a meeting with Buchanan. Forney found him "much depressed." The campaign against Lecompton, said Broderick, had caused "the worst elements" in California to organize against him. Broderick then told Forney: "I feel, my dear friend, that we shall never meet again. I go home to die. I shall abate no jot of my faith. I shall be challenged, I shall fight, and I shall be killed." Then, after Forney tried to console him, he responded with a "sad smile" that Forney would never forget: "No, no, it is best; I am doomed. You will live to write of me and keep my memory green; and now good-by forever."[33]

Did this actually happen? Or was it just a good yarn that Forney later devised after Broderick's death?[34] Oddly enough, by the time this meeting took place, predictions of Broderick's coming death had become almost commonplace. A few months earlier, in a hotel lobby in New York, two men from New Orleans had accosted Broderick. They repeatedly baited him. He tried to ignore them, but they kept at it until he finally turned upon them with his cane. Some bystanders then intervened, and nothing further came of this incident. Several onlookers, however, thought that the two men were hit men, hired to provoke a duel or a gunfight, and rumors soon spread that there was a price on Broderick's head.[35]

Whether there was a price or not, Broderick had a good reason to be "much depressed." For Gwin undoubtedly now had a decisive edge in California politics. Broderick's most powerful ally, John Bigler, was off in Chile, and the Chivs now had the lion's share of all patronage jobs. Only in San Francisco did Broderick still control the regular party machinery. There the Chivs were at a disadvantage, and there he might force the Chivs to organize from scratch. But elsewhere the Chivs had well-built machines that could mobilize hundreds of state and federal employees on Election Day.

And that, as Broderick knew, was the key fact. In an age when parties provided voters with ballots on Election Day, he had no chance of winning unless he had an army of dedicated workers to hand out ballots and march men to the polls. He could be eloquent. He could give rousing campaign speeches. He could have the support of dozens of newspapers. Yet if he was short of men with ballots on Election Day, it was all for naught. There was simply no way that men who responded to his message could vote for the men on his ticket.

That fact had been proven beyond doubt in the 1858 election. Broderick's strongest candidate in 1858 had been John Currey, who had run for a seat on the state supreme court. Currey, a free-soil Democrat, not only had the backing of Broderick and his men. He had also been endorsed by the Republicans. In the state's population centers, in San Francisco and Sacramento, Currey had won handily. He had carried San Francisco by a two-to-one margin. But in the diggings and the "cow counties," where the Chivs had far more men handing out ballots on Election Day, Currey had received just a handful of votes. And as a result, he lost the election.[36]

By 1859, moreover, the Chiv organization was stronger than ever before. Strengthened mainly through patronage, it had also been strengthened by an all-out effort by Stephen A. Douglas to pretend that Lecompton hadn't ripped the party apart. The Illinois Democrat had his eye on the presidency, and more particularly on the Democratic National Convention in Charleston, South Carolina, scheduled for the spring of 1860. Somehow, he had to get two-thirds of the delegates to that convention to support his candidacy. For years, Broderick and his followers had criticized Douglas for destroying the Missouri Compromise. Yet it had been Gwin and his Southern colleagues who had stripped Douglas of his chairmanship of the Committee on Territories.

Among Gwin's followers, however, were a sizable minority who saw no inconsistency in supporting Gwin and the Illinois senator at the same time. And since Douglas desperately wanted to have their support, he pretended that the California Democratic Party was still one big happy family. Lecompton? It was just a passing irritant, and at heart they all had been "good" Douglas Democrats and strong supporters of popular sovereignty.

The Chivs thus found it easy to walk a crooked path, supporting Lecompton to the hilt one day, Douglas and popular sovereignty the next. From reading their campaign literature, no one would realize that they had lambasted Douglas over the Lecompton constitution. Not one word was said about that "old" fight.

Also complicating the 1859 election was a hot state issue. Once again, a movement was afoot to split the state in two. This time its primary sponsor was Andrés Pico, a forty-eight-year-old assemblyman from Los Angeles.

Pico was a member of one of the state's most distinguished Mexican families. His older brother had been governor of Mexican California at the time of the U.S. conquest, and he himself had led troops against both General Kearny and Frémont. Since the conquest, Pico had represented Los Angeles in the state legislature, first as a Whig, later as a Chiv. He, along with Joseph L. Brent and Tomás Sánchez, now ran the Los Angeles branch of Gwin's statewide political machine.[37]

In May 1858 and again in February 1859, Pico introduced legisla-

tion to divide the state in half. Like earlier legislation, it essentially called for lopping off the southern half of the state at San Luis Obispo and turning it into a new territory, the "Territory of Colorado." Pico himself probably hoped to become the governor of this new territory, and prominent Mexican families like his claimed that they needed separation to be free from unfair California taxes. So, too, did other southern California landowners.[38]

But such concerns had little, if any, impact on the California legislature. For the legislature was totally dominated by northern Californians. That had been the case since the gold rush, and it would remain that way for many years to come.

Andrés Pico. Courtesy of The San Fernando Valley Historical Society.

In 1859, legislators from northern California outnumbered legislators from the southern half of the state by more than twelve to one. At best only a handful cared about the plight of the Picos and other Mexican ranch owners. A few may have wanted to increase the power of the West in national affairs, to have the opportunity to create yet another state on the Pacific. But, according to most observers, the bill's main backers were Chivs who wanted to turn southern California into slave country.

In any event, the Chivs had the votes to get the Pico bill through both houses of the legislature in the spring of 1859. The measure first passed the assembly, 34 to 26, and then the state senate, 15 to 12. Of the total aye votes, 4 came from legislators representing the southern half of the state, 45 from legislators representing the northern half. The Chiv governor, John B. Weller, then signed the bill on April 19. The question of dismemberment was then to go to the voters, but only the voters in the affected districts, where the measure was certain to pass in the September elections.

Was this the first step in turning southern California into a slave state? One Chiv leader, Milton Latham, in explaining the measure to James Buchanan, attributed the Pico bill mainly to the desire of Mexican landowners to be free from unfair taxes. But Elisha Crosby and most other observers dismissed the tax argument as balderdash. As they saw it, the Chivs had been wanting to divide the state in two for years. They now had the votes to do it, and thus they had succeeded in taking a gigantic first step in making southern California into slave country.[39]

Agreeing with them was none other than Henry Foote. By this time, Foote had returned to Mississippi, but he still followed California politics. Delighted with the reports he received from California, he told a Vicksburg convention in 1859 that in two years the South would have a slave state in southern California because the state had been divided "for that purpose."[40]

Much was thus at stake in the September 7 election. The Republicans met first, in early June. Lincoln's friend and the party's chief orator, Edward D. Baker, called for fusion with the Broderick Democrats. He made the case that there was no way the free-soilers could win unless they combined forces and agreed to a single slate of candidates. But he was outvoted. The majority insisted on remaining "independent" and put up a full slate of Republican candidates.

A week later the Broderick men gathered in Sacramento. They seemed to be better organized than a year before, when they lacked representation in fourteen counties. Now they had delegates from all but six counties. But the meeting was not harmonious. Five men sought the gubernatorial nomination, two the congressional nomination. Two of the losers blamed Broderick for "poisoning" their chances. One got into a near brawl, then a near duel, with a close Broderick associate, Congressman Joseph McKibbin. Both later campaigned for the Chiv ticket.

By the time the Chivs met in Sacramento in late June, everything was going their way. Among the delegates was Philip A. Roach, a former Mississippi resident, who kept Jefferson Davis abreast on California affairs. He liked what he saw. As he explained the situation to Davis, the only flaw was the Chiv platform. It had been written by men who had not been "fully weaned from Broderickism." A mishmash, it repeatedly sang the praises of the Buchanan administration and came close to condemning the free-soil movement. Yet it also seemed to endorse Douglas and popular sovereignty, and it clearly condemned the demand for a federal slave code for the territories.

What truly pleased Roach, however, was the candidates. They were far better than the platform, he told Davis. They weren't "mild" at all. Many of them were "fire-eating men." And to prove his point, Roach carefully listed their nativity. Nine of the twelve had been born and raised in the South. And of the remaining three, two had lived in the South before migrating to California. Could such "fire-eating men" be elected? Roach was certain they would win—even "over united opposition"—and if Broderick and the Republicans did "not coalesce," they could beat either by twenty thousand votes.[41]

Essentially, Roach was right. In July, Broderick took his case to the people. In his first stump speech, in Placerville, in the heart of the gold country, he challenged Gwin to meet him face-to-face. He then repeated the challenge at Forest Hill, Marysville, and Nevada City. At first Gwin made light of the challenges, but eventually he felt compelled to trail Broderick around the circuit.

Neither man had much experience as a stump speaker. Broderick was a complete novice, and Gwin had never been good at it. But for six weeks, the residents of such obscure gold towns as Downieville, La Porte, Quincy, Yreka, and Weaverville got the chance to see and hear the state's two warring senators. In each town, the meetings were much the same. They were invariably held in front of the town's largest hotel. They were always festive occasions, usually with music and fireworks, and the speaker's stand was always draped in bunting and in signs welcoming the speaker. The speeches began around 8:30 p.m., with the main speaker talking for an hour and a half, and then three or four lesser lights exhorting the crowd for another two or three hours. Broderick's audiences ranged from five hundred to six thousand; Gwin's from three hundred to five hundred.[42]

Each man spent much of his time insulting the other. Gwin called Broderick a dishonest man, a cheat, a pathological liar, a renegade, a traitor, a turncoat, a failure, a vulgarian, a dog. Broderick was more inventive. In addition to calling Gwin a liar, cheat, traitor, leper, and turncoat, he compared Gwin to Pecksniff, Benedict Arnold, Tartuffe, Iago, and Hester Prynne. In the course of insulting each other, the men inevitably made the "Scarlet Letter" an issue. Broderick gave a detailed account of the senatorial election of 1857 and claimed that possession of the letter had led to William Ferguson's death. Gwin eventually had to publish a pamphlet justifying his actions in 1857.[43]

Yet patronage was never the central issue in Broderick's stump speeches. He accused both James Buchanan and William Gwin of "dripping in corruption," not because they had denied him and his followers federal patronage, but because of their pro-slavery bias. The "real issue," he said repeatedly, was their backing of slave labor over free labor. "Can you support," he asked one audience after another, "an administration that would bring slave labor into the West to compete with free labor?" That, he claimed, was the goal of Gwin and his kind. "You, fellow citizens, who are laborers and have white faces, must have black competitors."[44]

Broderick eventually spoke to 22,850 people, Gwin, 2,500. Yet in the end, this fact made little difference. With Free-Soilers divided into two camps, some following Broderick, others the Republicans, winning was out of the question. And with the Gwin forces having far more workers to hand out ballots on Election Day, Broderick and his men never had a chance "in remote little places like Fresno, Tulare, and San Bernardino."[45] In 1858, the Chivs beat them by eight thousand votes; in 1859, the margin swelled to twenty thousand. Thus Milton S. Latham, who had been born in Ohio but politicized in Alabama, easily won the governorship.

Yet even though the election ended as Philip Roach had predicted, the Chivs soon found themselves in deep trouble. At the Chiv nominating convention, one speaker after another had gone after Broderick. Ripping him apart, coming up with the nastiest invective, had been the order of the day.

Especially effective had been the state's chief justice, David S. Terry. In his speech, the chief justice had denounced California's anti-Lecompton Democrats as "a miserable remnant of a faction sailing under false colors." Far from being free men, said Terry, they were "the personal chattels of a single individual, whom they are ashamed of. They belong, heart and soul, body and breeches, to David C. Broderick." But because they were "ashamed to acknowledge their master," they called themselves "Douglas Democrats." Perhaps they did "sail under the flag of Douglas." But it was "the banner of the black Douglass," Frederick Douglass, the black abolitionist, and not the banner of Stephen A. Douglas, the loyal Democrat.[46]

When Broderick learned of this speech over breakfast at the International Hotel in San Francisco, he was seated next to a large group that included a wealthy lawyer friend of Terry's, Duncan W. Perley. He had little respect for Perley. He regarded the thirty-three-year-old New Brunswick native as an effeminate shill for the rich and wellborn. After reading the newspaper account, he tossed the newspaper at Perley. "I see your friend Terry has been abusing me at Sacramento," said Broderick.

Perley played dumb and pretended he didn't know what Broderick was talking about. Broderick then exploded: "The damned miserable wretch, after being kicked out of the convention, went down there and made a speech abusing me. I have defended him at times when all others deserted him. I paid and supported three newspapers to defend him during the Vigilance Committee days, and this is all the gratitude I get from the damned miserable wretch for the favors I have conferred on him."

Perley continued to play dumb. "Mr. Broderick, who is it you speak of as a 'wretch'?" "Terry," snapped Broderick. "I will inform the Judge of the language you have used concerning him," threatened Perley. "Do so," said Broderick. "You would not dare to use this language to him," snarled Perley. "Would not dare," said Broderick. "No, sir!" exclaimed Perley. "You would not dare to do it, and you know you would not dare to do it; and you shall not use it to me concerning him. I shall hold you personally responsible for the language and the menace you have used."

Subsequently, Perley challenged Broderick to a duel. Broderick rejected it. He had no interest in getting into a duel with an upper-class Chiv lawyer, especially one he regarded as a fop, and especially during an election campaign. He just wanted "to kill old man Gwin." And on the stump, he invited Gwin to challenge him. "If Dr. Gwin felt aggrieved at my conduct," he said repeatedly, "he knew his remedy." And even more pointedly: "If I have insulted Dr. Gwin sufficient to induce him to go about the State and make a blackguard of himself, he should seek the remedy left to every gentleman who feels offense."

But Gwin never challenged him. The challenge instead came from David S. Terry. On September 8, one day after the election, the judge sent Broderick a note demanding a retraction. Broderick refused, and on September 13 the two men met at Lake Merced. The hair trigger on Broderick's pistol caused him to misfire. Three days later he was dead.

The question of Terry's motivation later became important to many scholars. Was he a typical Southern gentleman, a proud man who was quick to respond to insults and felt obliged to defend his honor? Or was he an "assassin," as the Broderick camp claimed?

At the time, however, such questions hardly mattered. Those who believed that Terry was the chosen instrument of the Gwin cabal to eliminate Broderick from the political scene suddenly gained the upper hand. Declared Edward D. Baker, the great orator of the new Republican Party: "His death was a political necessity, poorly veiled beneath the guise of a private quarrel." "What was his public crime? The answer is in his own words: 'I die because I was opposed to a corrupt administration and the extension of slavery.' "[47] Those words were repeated endlessly, on every political podium in California—and probably in every barroom, brothel, and dance hall as well.

The Chivs now had a problem. They were constantly on the defensive. They were constantly under attack. Was Terry their assassin? Did they intentionally kill Broderick? They said no. But the question just wouldn't go away.

Free-soilers, in turn, suddenly had an edge, a story that no one would ever forget. A dead senator. A faulty pistol. A pro-slavery assailant. They made the most of it and used it to frame debate for years to come. Chivs fought back, quarreled with one detail after another, and continued to denounce Broderick. Wasn't he a thug? Didn't he rely on Tammany Hall methods? But their attacks invariably reinforced the basic story. Thousands heard them, and thousands still went to their graves believing that the Chivs were guilty of a "murder most foul."[48]

Years later, even one of Judge Terry's seconds, Samuel H. Brooks, seemed to endorse that interpretation. On being asked to explain what happened, Brooks told the San Francisco *Examiner:* "It had its origins in politics."[49]

Epilogue

THE DEATH OF BRODERICK SENT SHOCK WAVES THROUGH CALIFORNIA politics, framed all political debate, and kept Chivs constantly on the defensive. Yet its full impact came slowly. For while the Chivs' popularity plummeted, they had more power than ever before. They had won the September 7 election by some twenty thousand votes. They controlled the statehouse as well as the state's entire congressional delegation.

Thus few Chivs immediately ran for cover, and only a handful wavered. Most stuck by their guns and hoped to weather the storm.

Among them was their leader, William Gwin. Four days after Broderick's death, Gwin left San Francisco for Washington. Accompanying him was Charles L. Scott, one of the two House members. The state now had two House members who were much like Gwin, Southern men with strong Southern biases. The tamer of the two was John C. Burch, a native of Missouri who had attended Kemper College. Scott, who prided himself on being a "fire-eater," was a Virginian and a graduate of the College of William and Mary. Both men were in their early thirties, Burch thirty-three, Scott thirty-two. Both had come to California to mine gold. Both had ended up practicing law and holding one political office after another. And both had benefited from Gwin's success in getting patronage.

The departure was anything but a joyous occasion. Even the *Alta California*, long Gwin's supporter in San Francisco politics, was now critical. The paper, in large black letters, now referred to Gwin and his followers as "jackals" whose "lion hunt" had finally ended "after their feast of blood." It also advised Gwin to look at the empty seat near him in the Senate chamber and then consult his conscience, "if he still had one." Even worse was the crowd that saw the Chiv contingent off at the dock. Where were Gwin's supporters? None were in sight. The men on the dock looked like they were there for a hanging. They also bore a sign: "The Will of the People—May the Murderers of David C. Broderick Never Return to California."[1]

Fortunately, when the two men arrived in Washington, they found that Broderick's death was old news. The nation's capital was in a furor, but not over the death of the California senator. In October 1859, John Brown, a fifty-nine-year-old Connecticut Yankee, had led twenty-one men, including five black men, across the Potomac to Harpers Ferry, Virginia. They had seized the federal arsenal and held several local citizens as hostages. Brown's plan was to instigate a slave insurrection in Virginia, then establish a free state in the southern Appalachians and spread the rebellion southward. The plan never got off the ground. No slaves joined Brown's men, and after two days of battle, a force of U.S. Marines led by Colonel Robert E. Lee captured Brown and his surviving followers.

Indicted for treason against the state of Virginia, Brown had been sentenced to hang on December 2. Four of his followers were to be hanged two weeks later, and two more the following March. The raid, meanwhile, sent a chill of terror through the white South. And while most Northern newspapers had joined Southerners in denouncing Brown and his raid, some antislavery men and women now treated Brown as a hero and a martyr.

The nation's capital was also bitterly divided. Southern leaders now called for revenge, not only revenge against New England and New York abolitionists who had provided Brown with money, but revenge against all "black Republicans." Members of Congress were armed to the teeth. In both the House and the Senate, noted Senator James Henry Hammond, "the only persons who do not have a revolver and a knife are those who have two revolvers."[2]

In Mississippi, where Gwin still owned several plantations, Jefferson Davis addressed the possibility of a Republican president. Rather than recognize a "black Republican" in the White House, he told the state legislature, the Mississippi star should be ripped out of the American flag and placed "on the perilous ridge of battle as a sign round which Mississippi's best and bravest should gather to the harvest-home of death."[3] A month later, in Washington, Senator Clement Claiborne Clay of Alabama echoed the same sentiments. If the black Republicans ever got hold of the national government, said Clay, "we of the South will tear the Constitution to pieces and look to our guns for justice."[4]

Clay's harsh words triggered a speech from Gwin, one that he would later reprint in his memoirs. He spoke from a unique position as a senator from the only free state that had never elected a Republican to Congress and the only one that had fully supported the Buchanan administration in the fall election. Aiming his speech mainly at Northern senators, he told them to listen carefully to Senator Clay. For the Alabama senator spoke not just for himself. He spoke for "a vast majority of the people of the slaveholding states." And he spoke the truth. The Republican Party was undoubtedly a sectional party, strictly a Northern party, one that had "no existence in the Southern States, and never can have any existence there." Thus, if the Republicans should ever win the White House, disunion was certain. The South would secede, and there would be nothing the North could do about it.[5]

Meanwhile, to replace Broderick in the Senate, lame-duck governor John B. Weller chose an innocuous pro-slavery man from Marysville, Henry P. Haun. A forty-four-year-old lawyer, Haun was a native of Kentucky and a graduate of Transylvania University, the same school Gwin had attended. Haun had moved to Iowa as a young man and taken part in writing the Iowa Constitution. He had come to California in 1849. He would serve in the Senate for just four months, for in January, the Chiv-dominated legislature chose newly elected governor Milton Latham to replace him.

Why Latham? And why choose a governor who had been in office just five days? Opinions varied. Some said it was because Latham wanted the job, while others said it was to get him out of the governor's office. The thirty-two-year-old Latham was the boy wonder of Chiv politics. He had supporters for the Senate even when he was still in his twenties. He was a handsome man, and one observer claimed that he had been the beneficiary of all of "the world's smiles and favors." His natural instinct, according to this observer, was to be "moderate in politics" and "genial to all."[6]

But to others, especially the former Democratic congressman Joseph W. McCorkle, Latham was anything but a "genial" man. Not only had Latham snatched away McCorkle's congressional seat in 1853; he also snatched away McCorkle's betrothed, Sophie Birdsall.[7] But that, in the view of many Chivs, was history. And McCorkle, moreover, was a Broderick man.

More important was where Latham stood on the issues of the day. Could the Chivalry count on him? Was he trustworthy? Many had their doubts. One moment, he seemed to support Stephen A. Douglas. The next, Douglas's critics. Again and again, he seemed to waver, to speak out of both sides of his mouth at the same time, to take one step forward and then one step back.

A case in point, so many thought, was the Pico bill. Under the terms of the bill, it had to be ratified in the affected districts in southern California by a two-to-one majority. In the September 1859 election, it had passed handily. About thirty-three hundred voters had turned out in the southern counties, and by nearly three to one they had voted to split California in two, roughly at San Luis Obispo, and create a new territory, the Territory of Colorado.

In January 1860, during his five-day stint as governor, Latham sent the Pico bill to Congress for approval. In a letter to President Buchanan, Latham seemed to justify the bill in one breath and condemn it in another. He claimed that the origin of the act was the southern half of the state's longtime dissatisfaction with the northern half's dominance and taxation policies. Dismemberment was thus a matter of justice. Then, to the disappointment of some of his Chiv followers, Latham also pointed out that the people at large were against the Pico bill and "the measure must be deemed, for the present, at least, impolitic."[8]

In fact, the bill had no chance in Congress. The Republicans had scored impressive gains in the 1858 election, and John Brown's raid had exacerbated the loathing Southern leaders had for them. All Washington now worried about the future of the nation. Might those who predicted disunion be right? Might the nation fall apart? In this atmosphere, not even James Buchanan was willing to push for the dismemberment of a state. The Pico bill was thus dead on arrival.

But was Latham's letter typical of the man? Many apparently thought so and were happy to ship him off to Washington. Once Latham left for Washington, John G. Downey took his place. Born in Ireland, the thirty-two-year-old Downey had lived in Mississippi before migrating to California. Arriving penniless, he had made a fortune in his Los Angeles drugstore, the only one in the southern half of the state, and in ranching and real estate. In the September 1859 election, he had been the Chiv candidate for lieutenant governor. Unlike Latham, he was unwavering in his support of Stephen A. Douglas.

In March, Latham took his seat in the Senate. On April 16, 1860, he gave a major speech on "labor and capital." It was nothing like Broderick's defense of free labor. Quite the contrary. In this speech, Latham defended slavery and attacked the capacities of blacks, the economic motives of the North, and the morals of the Republican Party. In it, he also took up the question of the dissolution of the Union. If that were to happen, said Latham, "We in California would have reasons to induce us to become members neither of the southern confederacy nor of the northern confederacy, and would be able to sustain ourselves the relations of a free and independent state."[9]

Did that mean that California would become independent if the Union fell apart? A separate nation? Most observers thought it did.

While Latham was on his way to Washington, many of his fellow Chivs met in Sacramento to choose delegates to the Democratic National Convention in Charleston, South Carolina. Most were pro-South and anti-Douglas.

For president, the majority preferred Daniel S. Dickinson, a New York senator who had supported the South in one showdown vote after another. Also popular was Joe Lane, an Oregonian who was blatantly pro-slavery, and John C. Breckinridge of Kentucky, the current vice president. On March 1, the convention voted to make Dickinson the California Democracy's first choice. The Douglas men made an effort to delete his name. They failed, 21 to 317. Then some anti-Douglas men moved to make it clear that Douglas was the California Democracy's "last choice." They also failed, 65 to 282. Six Chiv stalwarts and two Chiv moderates were then chosen to represent the California Democracy in Charleston.[10]

Arriving in Charleston in mid-April, the eight California delegates found that the city was in an uproar. The leading candidate for the

Democratic nomination was Stephen A. Douglas. He had by far the most delegates pledged to him. But he was the least acceptable to the "fire-breathing ultras of South Carolina, Mississippi, and Alabama." He had come to symbolize Northern duplicity. Partly to stop him, and with the people of Charleston cheering them on, the "ultras" demanded that the platform include a federal slave code for the territories.

The previous year the Chivs had come out foursquare against such a code, deeming it "a desperate trick of unprincipled and renegade politicians." Now, in April 1860, their man on the platform committee voted for such a code. So, too, did the delegate from Oregon. The platform committee, by a 17 to 16 vote, thus recommended that the party advocate police laws to protect slavery in the territories. The Douglas men on the convention floor battled back, said their man couldn't run on such a platform and that he was the only Democrat who could win the election. They prevailed, defeating the recommendation of the committee, 165 to 138.[11]

Eight Southern states then withdrew from the convention. The remaining delegates then tried to put together a presidential ticket. The California delegation championed Daniel S. Dickinson, "the noblest Roman of them all," and supported him as a bloc on the first five ballots. On the next fifty-two ballots, the California delegation divided, but significantly not one California delegate cast a single vote for the front-running Douglas. Finally, having failed to agree on a nominee after fifty-seven ballots, the party adjourned on May 3 and agreed to reassemble in Baltimore on June 18.[12]

At Baltimore, the California delegation again sided with the "fire-breathing ultras." First the California delegate on the Credentials Committee supported a minority report that called for the admission of the original Southern delegates who had walked out of the Charleston convention. When that report was voted down, the Charleston seceders again stormed out of the convention. So did delegates from Virginia, North Carolina, half of Maryland, and Oregon. At this point, the California delegation had a choice. Would they remain with the other free states and nominate Douglas for president? Or join the exodus? They walked out, joining the seceding delegations, well ahead of delegates from Kentucky, Missouri, and Arkansas.[13]

The seceding delegations then met at nearby Market Hall on June 23. In the California delegation were five new men. They were even more pro-slavery than the men they replaced. Among the newcomers was Congressman Charles L. Scott. Also on board was Calhoun Benham, one of Judge Terry's seconds in the Broderick duel. In short order, the delegation agreed to support John C. Breckinridge for president, Joe Lane for vice president, and a platform that called for federal laws to protect slavery in the territories and the acquisition of slaveholding Cuba.[14]

The Chivs thus stuck by their guns. Always pro-South, they remained so in the 1860 presidential election. Their entire delegation in Congress—Gwin, Latham, Scott, and Burch—campaigned for the Breckinridge-Lane ticket. So did twenty-four of the thirty-six members of the state Democratic committee. Of the party's leading lights, only the new governor, John G. Downey, campaigned for the Northern Democratic nominee, Stephen A. Douglas.[15]

That November the choice of Gwin and most Chivs did well in the southern reaches of the state. In Los Angeles, Breckinridge got 39 percent of the vote to Lincoln's 20 percent; in El Monte, 58 percent to Lincoln's 11 percent.[16] But in the more heavily populated districts of northern California, Breckinridge trailed Douglas by 4,000 votes and Lincoln by 5,000. And overall, in the much-divided state, Lincoln beat Douglas by 614 votes.

On November 14, news that Lincoln had won enough eastern states to be elected president reached California. The Chivs now regarded secession of the South as inevitable. In keeping, several boldly raised the possibility of California also seceding from the Union and creating a Pacific republic. On November 28, *The San Francisco Herald* floated the idea. Then, on January 3, the *Herald* published a letter from Congressman John C. Burch endorsing a Pacific republic "if the fates should *force* us to this last sad resort." Two weeks later, the *Herald* published a more forceful letter from Congressman Charles L. Scott. He urged Californians to secede and form "a separate republic" if the Union should split in two.

The number of enthusiasts, however, was small, consisting mainly of the "extreme" Breckinridge men. As a result, in the U.S. Senate, Senator Milton Latham retracted his earlier declaration that California would leave the Union, saying that his earlier statement on April 16, 1860, foreshadowing the Pacific republic had been "premature." Later he would claim that he had always been a good "Union" man.[17]

· · ·

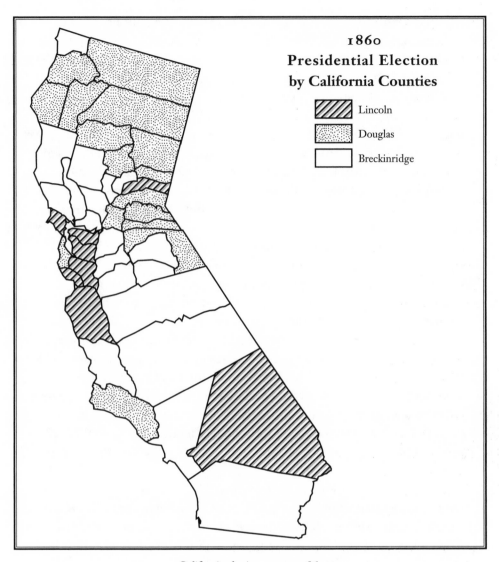

1860
Presidential Election
by California Counties

Lincoln

Douglas

Breckinridge

California election returns, 1860

When the Civil War began in April 1861, the unionists in California quickly gained the upper hand. Making much of the fact that the South, in bombarding Fort Sumter, had fired the first shot, they pushed through the legislature a resolution pledging California's loyalty to the United States. All but five senators and twelve assemblymen supported the resolution. The legislature also agreed to raise two regiments of cavalry and five regiments of infantry for the Union.

The two belligerents, however, were far more interested in California gold than in California regiments. Transporting thousands of raw recruits to the East Coast was deemed too expensive, while transporting gold paid handsome dividends. On each steamer sailing out of the Golden Gate, an average of over $1 million in gold went east. Usually, two or three steamers left per month during the four years of the war. Several times the gold shipments ran over $2 million per steamer, and on one occasion over $3 million. The high point came in 1864, when over $46 million in gold was sent via Panama to support the North's credit and help arm, feed, and clothe one million Union fighting men. Noted General Ulysses S. Grant: "I do not know what we would do in this great national emergency were it not for the gold sent from California."[18]

Of little interest to the belligerents were California's 258,000 males, even though three out of four were of prime fighting age. The North could be choosy. It had a large population to draw upon—nearly four times as many young white men as the eleven states that had seceded from the Union. The South, as time would soon tell, needed every white man it could get. In 1861, about 6 percent of male Californians hailed from the eleven Confederate states and another 7 percent from the border slave states. Would they fight for the Confederacy? Some undoubtedly would.[19] But who would pay to transport them back east? Not the Confederacy. And not the eleven states that had seceded from the Union. They were strapped for money. Maybe these "good" Southern men would pay their own way back? A few gung-ho editors urged them to do so.

Particularly outspoken was Lovick P. Hall, a native of Mississippi. Hall had operated a number of pro-slavery newspapers in both Oregon and California before the war. When war broke out, he established a new paper, the *Equal Rights Expositor*, in Visalia, a town two hundred miles south of Sacramento that had the reputation of being a pro-slavery hotbed. In his editorials, Hall repeatedly encouraged Confederate enlistments. At the same time, he belittled all those who volunteered for the Union cause, and on Thanksgiving Day 1862 he expressed thanks for all the blood that these Union men had shed. In March 1863, in response to another scurrilous editorial, a band of Union volunteers stormed Hall's office, destroyed his press, threw his type out in the street, and put the *Expositor* out of business.[20]

While still operative, the *Expositor* also encouraged "good" Southern men to take California out of the Union and turn it into a Confederate ally. Although Hall undoubtedly exaggerated the number of participants, talk of such plots was commonplace. Most were in sparsely populated southern California, several hundred miles away from the major gold fields.[21] The most famous, however, involved two young northern Californians, Asbury Harpending and Ridgeley Greathouse. Both came from wealthy Kentucky families. And both had visions of glory.

In early 1861, Harpending joined a secret society, the Committee of Thirty, in which each member pledged to recruit one hundred men, take Alcatraz island and other federal strongholds by surprise, and then seize San Francisco. With San Francisco in their clutches, they could then stop all gold shipments to the North. At the same time, they could establish a new gold route "through savage Arizona" into Confederate Texas.

At one point the Committee of Thirty had high hopes that the new military commander of the Department of the Pacific, General Albert Sidney Johnston, would support their cause. Not only was Johnston a secessionist; his native Texas had seceded from the Union. Dispatched to see Johnston were Harpending and two other firebrands. They were much impressed. The general was a "giant of a man with a mass of heavy yellow hair, untouched by age, although he was nearing sixty." To their dismay, however, he told them that he was aware of their "foolish" plot and had taken steps to make sure it didn't happen under his command. Johnston subsequently resigned his commission, went south, taking many Chivs with him, and became one of the Confederacy's leading generals. He was killed at Shiloh in 1862.

After being "squashed" by General Johnston, Harpending traveled across Mexico, caught passage to Charleston, and then made his way to Richmond. There he procured a letter of marque and a captain's commission in the Confederate navy that authorized him to burn, bond, and capture Union ships bearing California gold. The goal was to stop the flow of millions of dollars in gold from San Francisco to the North and thus cripple the Union war effort.

Upon returning to California, Harpending hired Captain William C. Law, "the most repulsive reptile in appearance I had ever set eyes on," to lead the privateers to their prey. The thirty-nine-year-old captain had run slaves from Virginia to New Orleans before the war. He had also worked for the Pacific Mail Line and knew the routes that the gold ships would be following. On his advice, Greathouse then purchased for $6,500 the *J. M. Chapman*, a swift ninety-ton schooner that was in the news for making a trip around the Horn from New York to San Francisco in just 138 days. Greathouse then hired a crew of four seamen and a cook, while Harpending recruited fifteen gunmen.

The plan was to set sail on March 15, 1863, to some islands off the Mexican coast, convert the *Chapman* into a privateer, and lay in wait for Pacific Mail steamers bearing California gold for the Union cause. If all went well, the two Kentuckians would then turn the captured steamers into privateers, seize even more gold shipments, and thus disable Lincoln's war machine. Federal authorities, however, had learned of the plot and were just waiting for the Kentuckians and their men to set sail. So, as soon as the *Chapman* lifted anchor and moved out into San Francisco Bay, two boatloads of seamen from the USS *Cyane* appeared out of nowhere, seized the vessel, and arrested the two Kentuckians and nineteen of their accomplices.[22]

On the Union side, more than sixteen thousand men volunteered to fight for the Northern cause, but only a handful saw action. Since the federal government had deemed the costs of transporting thousands of men through Panama to the East Coast as just too expensive, the vast majority of California volunteers spent the war in local garrison duty, while a minority policed Indians in the Northwest or guarded overland mail routes. The only California units that came close to seeing action were the members of the "California Column," who were sent to New Mexico in 1862 to ward off an impending Confederate invasion.

In July 1861 a group of Texans led by Colonel John Baylor had seized the southern half of the New Mexico Territory and named the region the Confederate Territory of Arizona. That fall Jefferson Davis, as president of the Confederacy, instructed General Henry Sibley to follow up on Baylor's handiwork and open a wide corridor to California and then capture the gold fields in the Sierras. Sibley, however, first had to gain control of the Union forts lining the Rio Grande. As fighting raged up and down the river, the "California Column" was sent east to stop the Confederate invasion. By the time they reached the Rio Grande, in August 1862, Sibley's troops had suffered heavy casualties and withdrawn, and the threat of invasion was effectively over.

None of the California units, in short, saw much blood and gore. Hoping for more action, 500 young Californians turned to Massachusetts. Their leaders, J. Sewall Reed and DeWitt Clinton Thompson, had friends in Boston and managed to get the ear of Governor John Andrew. If Andrew would grant them bounties that they could use for transportation costs, they would recruit able men to fight as Massachusetts volunteers. Andrew agreed, and Reed provided a company of 100 men, and a few months later Thompson provided four companies totaling 400 men. Together, they became members of the Second Massachusetts Cavalry. Known as the California Battalion, they fought in more than fifty engagements, mainly in Virginia. They suffered horrific losses. By war's end, out of the 500 men who began the adventure, only 182 were left. And these men, to their dismay, had to finance their own way home.

Cavalry Company for the East.

THE UNDERSIGNED HAS BEEN authorized by the Secretary of War to raise a Company of Cavalry for service in the East to make a part of the Massachusetts quota.

A Roll of the Company is at Assembly Hall, corner Post and Kearny streets where persons desirous of joining can enroll their names

No one need apply who is not a good horseman and in good health. Men from the country preferred. The Roll will be kept open a reasonable time before selections are made.

All expenses will be paid as soon as accepted.

Further particulars apply to Office, corner Post and Kearny street.

oc28-2ptf   **J. SEWALL REED.**

Advertisement for California troops. Reprinted from Alta California, *October 1862.*

Equally persistent were another group of five hundred men, some from Oregon, most from California. They made their way back east, largely at their own expense, to Pennsylvania and joined the Seventy-first Pennsylvania Volunteers. Known as the California Brigade, they were initially commanded by Colonel Edward D. Baker, who, after presiding over Broderick's funeral, served briefly as a senator from Oregon and then as Lincoln's chief West Coast adviser. At Ball's Bluff in October 1861, the California Brigade suffered heavy casualties. Among the dead was Colonel Baker. The survivors then went on to fight at Antietam in September 1862 and Gettysburg in July 1863. Their final battle was the June 1864 assault at Cold Harbor, where the Union lost seven thousand men in one hour. Having experienced the bloodiest single day of the war, and four of the worst days that followed, well over half the brigade perished, 99 from disease, 160 on the field of battle.[23]

As for the leading Chivs, only a handful saw anything as bloody as Antietam, Gettysburg, and Cold Harbor. Many, however, supported the Southern cause.

Milton Latham, as usual, wavered. Retaining his seat in the U.S. Senate, he endorsed a bill that Californians had long coveted. With the South out of the Union, Free-Soilers in July 1862 finally hammered out the railroad legislation they wanted. Called the Pacific Railroad Act, it provided for federal subsidies for a railroad running from Nebraska to California. Yet while backing the bill, Latham continued to impugn the motives of the North. He also defended slavery and constantly found fault with the Lincoln administration. At the same time, however, he usually supported war measures and the troops on the front line. Branded as disloyal by the Republicans in California, who finally gained control of the state midway through the war, Latham lost his Senate seat in March 1863. Returning to San Francisco, he became a banker and railroad tycoon.

Congressman Burch never went back to Congress. He instead practiced law in San Francisco. Congressman Scott also never returned to Congress. He instead immediately headed South and joined the Confederate army. He became a major in the Fourth Regiment of the Alabama Volunteers and was wounded at Bull Run in July 1861.

With the onset of war, William Gwin and his family also demonstrated their loyalty to the South. Gwin's teenage son enlisted in the Confederate army, his eldest daughter moved to Richmond and became a Confederate belle, and his wife, Mary, was accused at one point of being a Confederate spy. Gwin himself was briefly arrested and, after being released by Lincoln, retired to his Mississippi plantation. He remained there until the Battle of Vicksburg, when his plantation was burned to the ground. After that, he worked for the Confederacy in France and Mexico and upon his return to the United States was imprisoned.

As for Judge Terry, he was never prosecuted for killing Broderick. Another judge threw the case against him out of court.

Months later, in the 1860 presidential campaign, Terry served as an elector for John C. Breckinridge, the Southern contender, and thus gave Free-Soilers still more ammunition to attack Chivs.

Then, when the Civil War broke out, Terry returned to the South, joined the Confederate army, and rose to the rank of brigadier general. After the war, he came back to California and settled again in Stockton. In 1889, exactly thirty years after he killed a U.S. senator, Terry got into

Cartoon displaying disgust with David Terry. Courtesy of The Bancroft Library.

another fracas, this time with a U.S. Supreme Court justice, Stephen Field.[24]

Justice Field, oddly enough, owed his life to the dead senator. Arriving in California in 1849, Field had established himself as a judge in the town of Marysville, made over $100,000 in just six months on the bench, and then had it all taken away from him by a rival judge who almost had him disbarred. Furious, Field had won a seat in the state legislature and there attempted to have the rival judge removed from office. In the process, he narrowly avoided a duel and being killed in a barroom ambush. To his aid had come Broderick. Already a power in the legislature, Broderick had consented to be Field's second in the duel, which was never consummated, and then foiled the ambush by throwing his body between Field and the would-be assassin.

Field later broke with Broderick over national politics, and their intimacy ceased. Yet, Field wrote, "I could never forget his generous conduct to me; and for his sad death there was no more sincere mourner in the state."[25] Nor could Justice Field ever forget the man who was responsible for Broderick's death. He knew Terry well. He had served under Terry on the California Supreme Court, and Terry had opposed him on virtually every decision. Terry, he noted, "had the virtues and prejudices of men of the extreme South."[26]

Then, many years later, in 1888, Field presided over a circuit court case that involved Terry's second wife. Thirty years Terry's junior, and several months pregnant, she had sued the senator of Nevada for alimony. She had won in the state court but now had to cope with Justice Field. Over one of his rulings, she exploded. As she was being forcibly ejected from court, Terry rushed to her aid and drew a knife. Field sentenced her to thirty days in jail, the judge to six months. Both threatened Field.

Months later, the couple encountered Field in a railroad restaurant in Lathrop, just outside Stockton. Terry marched up to Field and slapped him in the face. Field's bodyguard, David Neagle, then shot and killed Terry. Nearly one hundred people saw what happened. Most thought the shooting amounted to murder, that it was unnecessary, especially after a search of Terry's body revealed that he was unarmed. Many also testified that the slaps were light and appeared to be intended as the first steps toward a duel.

Local authorities filed charges, citing Neagle for murder and Field as his accomplice. Field, however, maneuvered to have the case handled by a federal judge. That judge, in turn, took testimony and eventually declared that the federal court had jurisdiction over the matter and the state of California had no right to prosecute Neagle. Then, on the basis of his review of the evidence, he added that Neagle's killing of Terry was not merely justified, it was commendable. The U.S. Supreme Court upheld his decision.

The story was carried in nearly every daily newspaper in the country. Most emphasized Terry's life of violence, and many saw in his death "a useful lesson." Such a man should expect to die as he had lived, they said. The New York *Sun*, along with several other newspapers, gave the story a different twist. After thirty years, proclaimed the *Sun*, David Broderick could now rest in peace. He had finally been avenged.

Notes

PROLOGUE

1. For the story of the duel, see Carroll Douglas Hall, *The Terry-Broderick Duel* (San Francisco, 1939); A. Russell Buchanan, *David S. Terry of California: Dueling Judge* (San Marino, Calif., 1956); David A. Williams, *David C. Broderick: A Political Portrait* (San Marino, Calif., 1969).

2. David S. Terry to Cornelia Terry, June 29, 1852, David Smith Terry Papers, Huntington Library, San Marino, Calif.; Charles R. Boden, "David Terry's Justification," *Wasp* 55 (1933), 3; Buchanan, *Terry*, 93.

3. Donald E. Hargis, "The Issues in the Broderick-Gwin Debates of 1859," *California Historical Society Quarterly* 32 (Dec. 1953), 313–25; Donald E. Hargis, " 'Straight Toward His Heart': George Wilkes' Eulogy of David C. Broderick," *California Historical Society Quarterly* 38 (Sept. 1959), 196–217; L. E. Fredman, "Broderick: A Reassessment," *Pacific Historical Review* 30 (Feb. 1961), 39–46; Hall, *Terry-Broderick Duel*.

4. Arthur Quinn, *The Rivals: William Gwin, David Broderick, and the Birth of California* (New York, 1994), 41–42; James O'Meara, *Broderick and Gwin* (San Francisco, 1881), 4–5.

5. Hargis, "George Wilkes' Eulogy of David C. Broderick," 196–217; Fredman, "Broderick: A Reassessment," 39–46; Hall, *Terry-Broderick Duel*.

6. James J. Ayers, *Gold and Sunshine: Reminiscences of Early California* (Boston, 1922), 170–78.

7. "Oration of Col. E. D. Baker," in Jeremiah Lynch, *The Life of David C. Broderick* (New York, 1911), 229–38; Oscar T. Shuck, *Masterpieces of E. D. Baker* (San Francisco, 1899).

8. Charles A. Barker, ed., *Memoirs of Elisha Oscar Crosby* (San Marino, Calif., 1945), 62–63.

CHAPTER I

1. Erwin G. Gudde, ed., *Bigler's Chronicle of the West: The Conquest of California, Discovery of Gold, and Mormon Settlement as Reflected in Henry William Bigler's Diary* (Berkeley, Calif., 1962), 66ff.; David L. Bigler, ed., *The Gold Discovery Journal of Azariah Smith* (Salt Lake City, 1990), 108.

2. Anne Dismukes Amerson, "Jennie Wimmer Tested Gold in Her Soap Kettle," www.goldrushgallery.com.

3. The story of Sutter and his mill has been told many times. Among other sources, see Mary Hill, *Gold: The California Story* (Berkeley, Calif., 1999), 24; Kenneth N. Owens, ed., *John Sutter and a Wider West* (Lincoln, Nebr., 1994), 21; Rodman Wilson Paul, *California Gold: The Beginning of Mining in the Far West* (Cambridge, Mass., 1947), 18; Hubert Howe Bancroft, *History of California, 1848–1859*, 6 vols. (San Francisco, 1888), 6:38–40.

4. The story of Marshall's discovery has been told many times and in many different ways. See, for example, Henry William Bigler diary, Jan. 24, 1848, Society of California Pioneers, San Francisco; Malcolm J. Rohrbough, *Days of Gold: The California Gold Rush and the American Nation* (Berkeley, Calif., 1997), 7; Rodman Wilson Paul, *Mining Frontiers of the Far West, 1848–1880* (New York, 1963), 13; Hill, *Gold: The California Story*, 23–24.

5. JoAnn Levy, *They Saw the Elephant: Women in the California Gold Rush* (Hamden, Conn., 1990), xix–xxi.

6. The story of Brannan's life, like Sutter's, has been told many times. For details, see Rodman Wilson Paul, *California Gold Discovery: Sources, Documents, Accounts, and Memoirs* (Georgetown, Calif., 1967), 69–80; Bancroft, *History of California*, 6:56; Hill, *Gold: The California Story*, 26–27, 33; James Austin Brown Scherer, *The First Forty-niner and the Story of the Golden Tea-Caddy* (New York, 1925); *Sutter County Historical Society* 13 (Jan. 1974), entire issue.

7. Walter Colton, *Three Years in California* (New York, 1851), 246–48, 251–52, 253.

8. James Lynch, *With Stevenson to California, 1846–1848* (New York, 1882); Francis D. Clark, *Stevenson's Regiment in California, 1847–1848* (New York, 1896). These two books have also been reprinted together as *The New York Volunteers in California* (Glorieta, N.Mex., 1970).

241

9. Larkin to James Buchanan, June 28, July 20, 1848, in George P. Hammond, ed., *The Larkin Papers*, 10 vols. (Berkeley, Calif., 1951–68), 7:304, 321; John A. Hawgood, *America's Western Frontier: The Exploration and Settlement of the Trans-Mississippi West* (New York, 1967), 172.

10. For further details on the Chilean migration, see Jay Monaghan, *Chile, Peru, and the California Gold Rush* (Berkeley, Calif., 1973); Edwin A. Beiharz and Carlos U. López, eds. and trans., *We Were 49ers! Chilean Accounts of the California Gold Rush* (Pasadena, Calif., 1976); Carlos U. López, *Chilenos in California: A Study of the 1850, 1852, and 1860 Censuses* (San Francisco, 1973).

11. Vicente Pérez Rosales, *California Adventure*, trans. Edwin S. Morby and Arturo Torres-Rioseco (San Francisco, 1947), 271–79.

12. Edward H. Hargraves, *Australia and Its Gold Fields* (London, 1855), 75. For further details on Australian migration, see Jay Monaghan, *Australians and the Gold Rush: California and Down Under, 1849–1854* (Berkeley, Calif., 1960); Charles Bateson, *Gold Fleet for California: Forty-niners from Australia and New Zealand* (East Lansing, Mich., 1964).

13. T. A. Rickard, "The Gold-Rush of '49," *British Columbia Historical Quarterly* 14 (Jan.–April 1950), 48–51; Ralph J. Roske, "The World Impact of the California Gold Rush, 1849–1857," *Arizona and the West* 5 (Autumn 1963), 195–96; H. W. Brands, *The Age of Gold: The California Gold Rush and the New American Dream* (New York, 2002), 463–66; Hargraves, *Australia and Its Gold Fields*, 86–117; Robert Hughes, *The Fatal Shore: A History of the Transportation of Convicts to Australia, 1787–1868* (New York, 1987), 561–65.

14. For the conflicting accounts on Chinese migration, see Stephen Williams, *The Chinese in the California Mines, 1848–1860* (San Francisco, 1930); Frederic Wakeman, Jr., *Strangers at the Gate: Social Disorder in South China, 1839–1861* (Berkeley, Calif., 1966); Ping Chiu, *Chinese Labor in California, 1850–1880: An Economic Study* (Madison, Wis., 1967); Yong Chen, *Chinese San Francisco, 1850–1942* (Stanford, Calif., 2000), 11–41.

15. Alexander McLeod, *Pigtails and Gold Dust: A Panorama of Chinese Life in Early California* (Caldwell, Idaho, 1947), 23.

16. *Daily Alta California*, May 15, 1852. These three individuals were clearly not the first Chinese to come to California. For conflicting details regarding earlier migrants, see Thomas W. Chinn, H. M. Lai, and Philip P. Choy, *A History of the Chinese in California: A Syllabus* (San Francisco, 1969), 8–16; Bancroft, *History of California*, 7:336; *San Francisco Chronicle*, July 21, 1878.

17. *Daily Alta California*, May 15, 1852.

18. *San Francisco Chronicle*, Dec. 5, 1869; Herbert Asbury, *The Barbary Coast* (New York, 1933), 172–73; Curt Gentry, *Madams of San Francisco* (New York, 1964), 50–59; McLeod, *Pigtails and Gold Dust*, 175–77; Benson

Tong, *Unsubmissive Women: Chinese Prostitutes in Nineteenth-Century San Francisco* (Norman, Okla., 1994), 6–9, 11–12; Judy Yung, *Unbound Feet: A Social History of Chinese Women in San Francisco* (Berkeley, Calif., 1995), 33–34. One account has Ah Toy returning to California and living until age ninety-nine.

19. David Roberts, *A Newer World: Kit Carson, John C. Frémont, and the Claiming of the American West* (New York, 2000); William Goetzmann, *Army Exploration in the American West, 1803–1863* (New Haven, Conn., 1959), 77–78, 97.

20. *Memoirs of General William Tecumseh Sherman, by Himself* (New York, 1875), 70–77.

21. Henry Blumenthal, "The California Societies in France, 1849–1855," *Pacific Historical Review* 25 (Aug. 1956), 251–60; Abraham P. Nasatir, "Alexandre Dumas fils and the Lottery of the Golden Ingots," *California Historical Society Quarterly* 33 (June 1954), 125–42; Karl Marx, *The Eighteenth Brumaire of Louis Bonaparte* (New York, 1852; repr., New York, 1963), 84–85.

22. Cardinal Goodwin, *The Establishment of State Government in California, 1846–1850* (New York, 1914), 56; Bancroft, *History of California*, 6:121; R. W. G. Vail, "Bibliographical Notes on Certain Eastern Mining Companies of the California Gold Rush, 1849–1850," *Papers of the Bibliographical Society of America* 43 (3rd Quarter), 247–78; Octavius T. Howe, *Argonauts of '49: History and Adventures of the Emigrant Companies from Massachusetts, 1849–50* (Cambridge, Mass., 1923), 174–75, 189, 209; James P. Delgado, *To California by Sea: A Maritime History of the Gold Rush* (Columbia, S.C., 1990), 7, 18–21.

23. Howe, *Argonauts of '49*, 189, 209.

24. Lynch, *With Stevenson to California*, 5–18; Howe, *Argonauts of '49*, 173, 189, 191.

25. Howe, *Argonauts of '49*, 64.

26. Brian Roberts, *American Alchemy: The California Gold Rush and Middle-Class Culture* (Chapel Hill, N.C., 2000), 74–78.

27. Donald Dale Jackson, *Gold Dust* (New York, 1949), 98, 103; "Petrel," Bancroft Library, Berkeley; Howe, *Argonauts of '49*, 75–76, 204–5; Roberts, *American Alchemy*, 102–12.

28. Thomas Jefferson Matteson diary, April 15–19, 1849, Bancroft Library.

29. For more details on Farnham, see JoAnn Levy, *Unsettling the West: Eliza Farnham and Georgiana Bruce Kirby in Frontier California* (Santa Clara, Calif., 2004); and the introductions to two Farnham reprints, *Life in Prairie Land* (1846; repr., Urbana, Ill., 1988) and *California In-Doors and Out* (1856; repr., Nieuwkoop, 1972). Also see Roberts, *American Alchemy*, 221–44.

30. Farnham, *California In-Doors and Out*, 1–21.

31. Hill, *Gold: The California Story*, 43–45; Rohrbough, *Days of Gold*, 59–60; Oscar Lewis, *Sea Routes to the Gold Fields: The Migration by Water to California in 1849–1852* (New York, 1971), 170–82; John Haskell Kemble, *The Panama Route, 1848–1869* (Berkeley, Calif., 1943), 167–76.

32. Lewis, *Sea Routes to the Gold Fields*, 171; Kemble, *Panama Route*, 167; Jeremiah Lynch, *A Senator of the Fifties: David C. Broderick of California* (San Francisco, 1911), 36–38.

33. Lewis, *Sea Routes to the Gold Fields*, 190–95; Kemble, *Panama Route*, 176–77; J. S. Holliday, *The World Rushed In: The California Gold Rush Experience* (New York, 1981), 428–31.

34. Duncan S. Somerville, *The Aspinwall Empire* (Mystic, Conn., 1983); Fessenden Nott Otis, *History of the Panama Railroad . . .* (New York, 1867).

35. Lewis, *Sea Routes to the Gold Fields*, 168; Kemble, *Panama Route*, 37.

36. Kemble, *Panama Route*, 37–38.

37. David A. Williams, *David C. Broderick: A Political Portrait* (San Marino, Calif., 1969), 28–29; Arthur Quinn, *The Rivals: William Gwin, David Broderick, and the Birth of California* (New York, 1994), 55–56; Edgar H. Adams, "Private Gold Coinage in California," *American Journal of Numismatics* 45 (1911), 174–78, 189; James O'Meara, *Broderick and Gwin* (San Francisco, 1881), 22–23.

38. Williams, *Broderick*, 28–29; Quinn, *Rivals*, 55–56; Adams, "Private Gold Coinage in California," 174–78, 189; O'Meara, *Broderick and Gwin*, 8–9, 22–23.

39. Augustine F. Costello, *Our Firemen: A History of the New York Fire Department* (New York, 1887), 145–60 and passim; Sean Wilentz, *Chants Democratic: New York City and the Rise of the American Working Class, 1788–1850* (New York, 1984), 259–62; Tyler Anbinder, *Five Points: The 19th-Century New York City Neighborhood That Invented Tap Dance, Stole Elections, and Became the World's Most Notorious Slum* (New York, 2001), 183–85.

40. Robert Ernst, "The One and Only Mike Walsh," *New-York Historical Society Quarterly* 36 (Jan. 1952), 43–65; Wilentz, *Chants Democratic*, 326–35; Anbinder, *Five Points*, 156–58; O'Meara, *Broderick and Gwin*, 7–8, 10.

41. What sparked the 1842 riot is a matter of dispute. The poet Walt Whitman, an admirer of Walsh, blamed it on Tammany Hall. The merchant Philip Hone, who despised Walsh, blamed it on religious tensions. See Joseph J. Rubin and Charles H. Brown, eds., *Walt Whitman of the "New York Aurora"* (State College, Pa., 1950), 77–80; Allan Nevins, ed., *The Diary of Philip Hone, 1828–1851* (New York, 1936), 596. For further details, see also Anbinder, *Five Points*, 154–58.

42. Alexander Saxton, *The Rise and Fall of the White Republic: Class Politics and Mass Culture in Nineteenth-Century America* (New York, 1990), 206–10;

Helene S. Zahler, *Eastern Workingmen and National Land Policy, 1829–1862* (New York, 1941), 1–49.

43. Williams, *Broderick*, 13; O'Meara, *Broderick and Gwin*, 6.

44. O'Meara, *Broderick and Gwin*, 18–21. Lynch, *A Senator of the Fifties*, 31–34, tells the same story but says the president was John Tyler.

45. Marcus Lee Hansen, *The Atlantic Migration, 1607–1860* (Cambridge, Mass., 1940), chaps. 7–13; Robert Greenhalgh Albion, *The Rise of New York Port* (Devon, U.K., 1970), apps. 27, 28; Robert Ernst, *Immigrant Life in New York City, 1825–1863* (New York, 1965); Leo Hershkovitz, "The Native American Democratic Association in New York City, 1835–36," *New-York Historical Society Quarterly* 46 (Jan. 1962), 41–60; Amy Bridges, *A City in the Republic: Antebellum New York and the Origins of Machine Politics* (New York, 1984), 83–84, 99–100, 148.

46. Williams, *Broderick*, 22–25.

47. Broderick to Robert J. Walker, Nov. 1846, Miscellaneous MSS, New-York Historical Society; Broderick to Mary and Bridget Colbert, April 19, 1847, in *People of California v. McGlynn*, California State Archives, file 3494, 167, Sacramento; *Congressional Globe*, 35th Cong., 1st sess., 1857–58, app., 193.

48. O'Meara, *Broderick and Gwin*, 9, 22–23.

49. Affidavit of George Wilkes, n.d., Bancroft Library; Adams, "Private Gold Coinage in California," 174–78; Saxton, *Rise and Fall of the White Republic*, 206–9; Williams, *Broderick*, 21–25; Quinn, *Rivals*, 42–45; Lynch, *A Senator of the Fifties*, 11–13.

50. Saxton, *Rise and Fall of the White Republic*, 209; Williams, *Broderick*, 25–30; O'Meara, *Broderick and Gwin*, 17–19.

51. Adams, "Private Gold Coinage in California," 174–78, 189; David A. Williams, "The Forgery of the Broderick Will," *California Historical Society Quarterly* 40 (1961), 203–14.

52. Lynch, *A Senator of the Fifties*, 68–71.

53. *California Senate Journal*, 1st sess., 1850, 108–9; R. A. Burchell, *The San Francisco Irish, 1848–1880* (Berkeley, Calif., 1980), 121–22; Roger W. Lotchin, *San Francisco, 1846–56: From Hamlet to City* (New York, 1974), 219; Andrew J. Newman, "The Formation of the First Political Parties in California, 1849–51" (master's thesis, University of California, Berkeley, 1918), 30–33.

CHAPTER 2

1. Craig Simpson, *A Good Southerner: The Life of Henry A. Wise of Virginia* (Chapel Hill, N.C., 1985), 5.

2. Waldo W. Braden, ed., *Oratory in the Old South, 1828–1860* (Baton Rouge, La., 1970), 119.

3. Simpson, *Wise*, 20–21, 91.

4. Ibid.; J. D. B. DeBow, *Statistical View of the United States . . . : Being a Compendium of the Seventh Census* (Washington, D.C., 1854), 320; Celestine G. Koger, *The 1850 Slave Inhabitants Schedule of Accomac County, Virginia* (n.p., 1995).

5. Simpson, *Wise*, 87, 104, 124–25; Henry A. Wise, *Speech on the Basis Question, Delivered in the Virginia Reform Convention* (Richmond, 1851), 31, 36; Wise to Nehemiah Adams, Aug. 22, 1854, in *Washington Union*, Sept. 13, 1854; *Richmond Enquirer*, June 17, 1856; Henry A. Wise, *Territorial Government and the Admission of New States into the Union* (Richmond, 1859), 130–35; Henry A. Wise, *Seven Decades of Union* (Philadelphia, 1871), 240, 242.

6. Edwin Arthur Miles, *Jacksonian Democracy in Mississippi* (Chapel Hill, N.C., 1960), 49–54, 170, 112; Edwin Arthur Miles, "Andrew Jackson and Senator George Poindexter," *Journal of Southern History* 24 (Feb. 1958), 63–64; J. F. H. Claiborne, *Mississippi as Province, Territory, and State* (Jackson, Miss., 1880), 427–46.

7. 1840 Warren County Tax Roll, Mississippi Archives, Jackson; Roy S. Bloss, "Biography of William McKendree Gwin and Supporting Documents, 1856–1873," MS, Bancroft Library, Berkeley; Lately Thomas, *Between Two Empires: The Life Story of California's First Senator, William McKendree Gwin* (Boston, 1969), passim; Arthur Quinn, *The Rivals: William Gwin, David Broderick, and the Birth of California* (New York, 1994), 12–16; Mary Agnes Oyster, "Gwin in the Constitutional Convention of California of 1849" (master's thesis, University of California, Berkeley, 1928), 8–10; *Re-union of the Passengers on the Fourth of June, 1874, Being the Twenty-fifth Anniversary of the Arrival of the Steamship Panama at San Francisco* (San Francisco, 1874).

8. Oyster, "Gwin in the Constitutional Convention," 14–16.

9. Robert W. Johannsen, *Stephen A. Douglas* (New York, 1973), 211.

10. William H. Ellison, ed., "Memoirs of the Hon. William M. Gwin," *California Historical Society Quarterly* 19 (1940), 1–2.

11. *Re-union of the Passengers*, passim.

12. The details of Benton's life are ably covered in William N. Chambers, *Old Bullion Benton: Senator from the New West* (Boston, 1956); Elbert B. Smith, *Magnificent Missourian: The Life of Thomas Hart Benton* (Philadelphia, 1958); Thomas Hart Benton, *Thirty Years' View*, 2 vols. (New York, 1856).

13. Benjamin C. Merkel, "The Slavery Issue and the Political Decline of Thomas Hart Benton, 1846–1856," *Missouri Historical Review* 38 (July 1944), 390–94.

14. The literature on Frémont is extensive. For various accounts of his life and character, see Allan Nevins, *Frémont: Pathmarker of the West*, 2 vols.

(New York, 1955); Andrew Rolle, "Exploring an Explorer: Psychohistory and John Charles Frémont," *Pacific Historical Review* 51 (May 1982), 135–63; Andrew Rolle, *John Charles Frémont: Character as Destiny* (Norman, Okla., 1991); Tom Chaffin, *Pathfinder: John Charles Frémont and the Course of American Empire* (New York, 2002). For his own account, see John C. Frémont, *Memoirs of My Life* (New York, 1887).

15. The literature on Jessie Benton Frémont is also extensive. For various perspectives, see Pamela Herr, *Jessie Benton Frémont: A Biography* (New York, 1987); Catherine Coffin Phillips, *Jessie Benton Frémont: A Woman Who Made History* (San Francisco, 1935); Rolle, "Exploring an Explorer," 153–54. For her own perspective, see Jessie Benton Frémont, *Souvenirs of My Time* (Boston, 1887); Pamela Herr and Mary Lee Spence, eds., *The Letters of Jessie Benton Frémont* (Urbana, Ill., 1993).

16. Much of the information in this paragraph has been disputed. See Richard Stenberg, "Polk and Frémont, 1845–1846," *Pacific Historical Review* 7 (1938), 211–27; George Tays, "Frémont Had No Secret Instructions," *Pacific Historical Review* 9 (1940), 151–71; John A. Hussey, "The Origins of the Gillespie Mission," *California Historical Society Quarterly* 19 (1940), 43–58; William H. Goetzmann, *Army Explorations in the American West* (New Haven, Conn., 1959), 116–18; Donald Jackson and Mary Lee Spence, eds., *The Expeditions of John Charles Frémont*, 3 vols. and supps. (Urbana, Ill., 1970–84), 2:469.

17. Samuel J. Bayard, *A Sketch of the Life of Com. Robert F. Stockton* (New York, 1856), microform; Dwight L. Clarke, *Stephen Watts Kearny, Soldier of the West* (Norman, Okla., 1961); *Proceedings of the Court Martial of Colonel Frémont*, 30th Cong., 1st sess., 1847–48, Senate Executive Document 33.

18. Rolle, *Frémont*, 112; Kenneth M. Johnson, *The Frémont Court Martial* (Los Angeles, 1968).

19. Chaffin, *Pathfinder*, 391–404; John C. Frémont to Jessie Benton Frémont, Jan. 27, 1849, in Jackson and Spence, *Expeditions of Frémont*, 3:76, 80.

20. Joaquin Miller, *Overland in a Covered Wagon*, ed. Sidney G. Firman (New York, 1930), 42–43.

21. The full Lewis and Clark journal, available to us today, had yet to be printed.

22. Jackson and Spence, *Expeditions of Frémont*, 1:xx.

23. Sarah Royce, *A Frontier Lady: Recollections of the Gold Rush and Early California*, ed. Ralph Henry Gabriel (New Haven, Conn., 1932), 3.

24. Mary McDougall Gordon, "Overland to California in 1849: A Neglected Commercial Enterprise," *Pacific Historical Review* 52 (Feb. 1983), 18–19.

25. For details on the 1849 epidemic, see Charles E. Rosenberg, *The Cholera Years: The United States in 1832, 1849, and 1866* (Chicago, 1962), pt. 2; Georgia Willis Read, "Diseases, Drugs, and Doctors on the Oregon-

California Trail in the Gold Rush Years," *Missouri Historical Review* 38 (April 1944), 260–74.

26. Royce, *Frontier Lady*, 34–35.

27. Ibid., 54–55.

28. Niles Searls, *The Diary of a Pioneer and Other Papers* (San Francisco, 1940); David McCollum, "Letters," in Russell E. Bidlack, ed., *Letters Home: The Story of Ann Arbor's Forty-Niners* (Ann Arbor, Mich., 1960); Gordon, "Overland to California in 1849," 17–36.

29. Doris Marion Wright, "The Making of Cosmopolitan California: An Analysis of Immigration, 1848–70," *California Historical Society Quarterly* 19 (Dec. 1940), 324–26; Ralph J. Roske, "The World Impact of the California Gold Rush, 1849–1857," *Arizona and the West* 5 (Autumn 1963), 198–99; Ralph Bieber, ed., *Southern Trails to California in 1849* (Glendale, Calif., 1937).

30. For details, see William B. Griffen, *Utmost Good Faith: Patterns of Apache-Mexican Hostilities in Northern Chihuahua Border Warfare, 1821–1848* (Albuquerque, N. Mex., 1988); William B. Griffen, *Apaches at War and Peace: The Janos Presidio, 1750–1858* (Albuquerque, N. Mex., 1988).

31. Benjamin Butler Harris, *The Texas Argonauts and the California Gold Rush*, ed. Richard H. Dillon (Norman, Okla., 1960), 109; Bieber, *Southern Trails*, 36, 271–75.

32. Harris, *Texas Argonauts*, 110–11; Ralph A. Smith, "John Joel Glanton, Lord of the Scalp Range," *Smoke Signal* (Fall 1962).

33. John Albert Wilson, *History of Los Angeles County* (Oakland, 1880), 90; Henry W. Splitter, "Los Angeles in the 1850's," *Historical Society of Southern California Quarterly* 31 (1949), 118; "Documents: California Freedom Papers," *Journal of Negro History* 3 (Jan. 1918), 45–51; Carvel Collins, ed., *Sam Ward in the Gold Rush* (Stanford, Calif., 1949), 28; Rudolph M. Lapp, *Blacks in Gold Rush California* (New Haven, Conn., 1977), 75–76; Susan Lee Johnson, *Roaring Camp: The Social World of the California Gold Rush* (New York, 2000), 68–69, 115, 190.

34. Thomas J. Green, *Journal of the Texian Expedition Against Mier* (New York, 1845; repr., Austin, Tex., 1935); J. Joseph Milton Nance, *Attack and Counterattack: The Texas-Mexican Frontier, 1842* (Austin, Tex., 1964); Texas House of Representatives, *Biographical Directory of the Texan Conventions and Congresses, 1832–1845* (Austin, Tex., 1941); Walter Prescott Webb et al., *The Handbook of Texas*, 2 vols. (Austin, Tex., 1952), 1:728.

35. Sam Houston's speech, in *Congressional Globe*, 33rd Cong., 1st sess., 1853–54, app., 1214–18.

36. "Sherman Was There: The Recollections of Major Edwin A. Sherman," *California Historical Society Quarterly* 23 (Dec. 1944), 350–52. See also Lapp, *Blacks in the Gold Rush*, 76; John C. Parish, "A Project for a Califor-

nia Slave Colony in 1851," *Huntington Library Bulletin* 8 (Oct. 1935), 171–75; Nathaniel Wright Stevenson, "California and the Compromise of 1850," *Pacific Historical Review* 4 (June 1935), 114.

37. For details on Terry's early life, see Alexander E. Wagstaff, *Life of David S. Terry* (San Francisco, 1892), 33–55; A. Russell Buchanan, *David S. Terry of California: Dueling Judge* (San Marino, Calif., 1956), 3–7; Charles S. Potts, "David S. Terry: The Romantic Story of a Great Texan," *Southwest Review* 19 (Spring 1934), 295–98. For details on his mother's family, which seems to have been both more powerful and more influential than his father's, see May Wilson McBee, *The Life and Times of David Smith* (Kansas City, Mo., 1959).

38. Wagstaff, *Terry*, 147.

39. Randolph B. Campbell, *An Empire for Slavery: The Peculiar Institution in Texas, 1821–1865* (Baton Rouge, La., 1989), 39, 275.

40. *Austin Texas Democrat*, April 19, 1849, quoted in H. Bailey Carroll, "Texas Collection," *Southwestern Historical Quarterly* 48 (July 1944), 92.

41. Harris, *Texas Argonauts*, 111–12.

CHAPTER 3

1. Van Buren to George Bancroft, Feb. 15, 1845, "Van Buren–Bancroft Correspondence, 1830–1845," *Proceedings of the Massachusetts Historical Society* 42 (June 1909), 439–40; Gideon Welles to Van Buren, July 28, 1846, Martin Van Buren Papers, Library of Congress.

2. The literature on the Wilmot Proviso is extensive. See, for example, Charles Buxton Going, *David Wilmot, Free-Soiler* (New York, 1924); Champlain W. Morrison, *Democratic Politics and Sectionalism: The Wilmot Proviso Controversy* (Chapel Hill, N.C., 1967); Eric Foner, "The Wilmot Proviso Revisited," *Journal of American History* 61 (Sept. 1969), 262–79; Leonard L. Richards, *The Slave Power: The Free North and Southern Domination, 1780–1860* (Baton Rouge, La., 2000), 150–59; Jonathan H. Earle, *Jacksonian Antislavery and the Politics of Free Soil* (Chapel Hill, N.C., 2004), 1–3, 131–43.

3. *Congressional Globe*, 29th Cong., 2nd sess., 1846–47, 317.

4. Ibid., 453–55.

5. Ibid., app., 244–46, 455; Robert R. Russel, "The Issues in the Congressional Struggle over the Kansas-Nebraska Bill, 1854," *Journal of Southern History* 39 (May 1963), 188–89.

6. *Congressional Globe*, 30th Cong., 2nd sess., 1848–49, 21, 39, 71, 477–78, 605–9; William J. Cooper, Jr., " 'The Only Door': The Territorial Issue, the Preston Bill, and the Southern Whigs," in William J. Cooper, Jr., Michael F. Holt, and John McCardell, eds., *A Master's Due: Essays in Honor of David Herbert Donald* (Baton Rouge, La., 1985), 67–84.

7. *Californian*, March 15, 1848; *California Star*, March 25, 1848; Peter H. Burnett, *Recollections and Opinions of an Old Pioneer* (New York, 1880), 221, 127–31; Etta Olive Powell, "Southern Influences in California Politics Before 1864" (master's thesis, University of California, Berkeley, 1929), 36–37; Lucile Eaves, *A History of California Labor Legislation* (Berkeley, Calif., 1910), 89–90; Paul Finkelman, "The Law of Slavery and Freedom in California, 1848–1860," *California Western Law Review* 17 (1981), 451.

8. Justus H. Rogers, *Colusa County* (Oakland, 1891), 370–71.

9. "Sherman Was There: The Recollections of Major Edwin A. Sherman," *California Historical Society Quarterly* 23 (Dec. 1944), 350–52; James J. Ayers, *Gold and Sunshine: Reminiscences of Early California* (Boston, 1922), 49–63; Leonard Pitt, *Decline of the Californios: A Social History of Spanish-Speaking Californians, 1846–1890* (Berkeley, Calif., 1966), 57–58.

10. George Tennis, "California's First Election, November 13, 1849," *Southern California Quarterly* 50 (Dec. 1968), 358; Neal Harlow, *California Conquered: The Annexation of a Mexican Province* (Berkeley, Calif., 1982), 318, 323–25; House Executive Document 17, 31st Cong., 1st sess., 1849–50, 744, 748.

11. For T. Butler King and his mission, see Edward M. Steel, Jr., *T. Butler King of Georgia* (Athens, Ga., 1964); Holman Hamilton, *Zachary Taylor: Soldier in the White House* (Hamden, Conn., 1966); Brainerd Dyer, *Zachary Taylor* (Baton Rouge, La., 1946); K. Jack Bauer, *Zachary Taylor: Soldier, Planter, Statesman of the Old Southwest* (Baton Rouge, La., 1985); Elbert B. Smith, *The Presidencies of Zachary Taylor and Millard Fillmore* (Lawrence, Kans., 1988); *Re-union of the Passengers on the Fourth of June, 1874, Being the Twenty-fifth Anniversary of the Arrival of the Steamship Panama at San Francisco* (San Francisco, 1874). On Taylor's slaveholdings, see Dyer, *Taylor*, 55, 72–73, 256–57, 262.

12. *San Jose Pioneer*, March 30, 1878, quoted in Peter V. Conmy, "William Edward Shannon, 1823–1850" (Oakland, 1954), MS, 4, Bancroft Library, Berkeley.

13. Shannon to Bartley Wilkes, Nov. 25, 1846, quoted in Donald C. Biggs, *Conquer and Colonize: Stevenson's Regiment and California* (San Rafael, Calif., 1977), 84.

14. "Members of the Convention of California," in J. Ross Browne, *Report of the Debates in the Convention of California on the Formation of the State Constitution in September and October, 1849* (Washington, D.C., 1850), 478–79; William H. Ellison, *A Self-Governing Dominion: California, 1849–1860* (Berkeley, Calif., 1950), 25, 27.

15. Powell, "Southern Influences in California Politics Before 1864," 31–32; Hubert Howe Bancroft, *History of California, 1848–1859*, 6 vols. (San Francisco, 1888), 6:286.

16. Biggs, *Stevenson's Regiment in California*, 177–96; Frank Soulé, *The Annals of San Francisco* (New York, 1854), 773–78; *Alta California*, Jan. 1–June 14, 1849.

17. Donald E. Hargis, "Pre-convention Speaking, California: 1849," *Western Speech* 18 (May 1954), 167–75.

18. Charles A. Barker, ed., *Memoirs of Elisha Oscar Crosby* (San Marino, Calif., 1945), 40, 61.

19. Ibid., 41; Barbara R. Warner, *The Men of the California Bear Flag Revolt* (Sonoma, 1994), 107–23; Arthur Quinn, *The Rivals: William Gwin, David Broderick, and the Birth of California* (New York, 1994), 67.

20. Cardinal Goodwin, *The Establishment of State Government in California, 1846–1850* (New York, 1914), 242; Merrill Burlingame, "The Contribution of Iowa to the Formation of the State Government of California in 1849," *Iowa Journal of History and Politics* 30 (April 1932), 189–91. One unidentified delegate made margin notes on his copy of the Iowa Constitution detailing the sections cribbed by the California convention (California State Archives, Sacramento).

21. Browne, *Report of the Debates*, 43–44; Barker, *Memoirs of Crosby*, 48–49.

22. *New-York Tribune*, Feb. 20, 1850, quoted in Roy S. Bloss, "Biography of William McKendree Gwin and Supporting Documents, 1856–1873," MS, Bancroft Library, 90.

23. Thomas W. Prosch, *McCarver and Tacoma* (Seattle, 1906).

24. For the debate, see Browne, *Report of the Debates*, 137–62, 330–40. For various scholarly perspectives, see Goodwin, *Establishment of State Government in California*, 112–32; Powell, "Southern Influences in California Politics Before 1864," 38–39; David Alan Johnson, *Founding the Far West: California, Oregon, and Nevada, 1840–1890* (Berkeley, Calif., 1992), 127–30.

25. Browne, *Report of the Debates*, 137–38, 140.

26. Ibid., 333.

27. Ibid., 335.

28. Ibid., 138.

29. Ibid., 138–39.

30. Ibid., 144.

31. Ibid., 149.

32. For legal details, see Norma Basch, *In the Eyes of the Law: Women, Marriage, and Property in Nineteenth-Century New York* (Ithaca, N.Y., 1982). The Basch book, while good on details, is rather poor on the party politics of the period. For the party politics, see Michael D. Pierson, " 'Guard the Foundations Well': Antebellum New York Democrats and the Defense of Patriarchy," *Gender and History* 7 (April 1995), 25–40; Michael D. Pierson, *Free Hearts, Free Homes: Gender and Antislavery Politics*

(Chapel Hill, N.C., 2003). For women's rights generally, see Sylvia D. Hoffert, *When Hens Crow: The Woman's Rights Movement in Antebellum America* (Bloomington, Ind., 1995).

33. Browne, *Report of the Debates*, 257–69, 478–79; Goodwin, *Establishment of State Government in California*, 217–18.

34. For the debate, see Browne, *Report of the Debates*, 167–96, 417–58; Goodwin, *Establishment of State Government in California*, chap. 7.

35. Browne, *Report of the Debates*, 178–79.

36. Ibid., 196; Mary Agnes Oyster, "Gwin in the Constitutional Convention of California of 1849" (master's thesis, University of California, Berkeley, 1928), 113–14.

37. Browne, *Report of the Debates*, 180; Powell, "Southern Influences in California Politics Before 1864," 50; Oyster, "Gwin in the Constitutional Convention of California of 1849," 114.

38. Browne, *Report of the Debates*, 442.

39. Samuel Upham, *Notes of a Voyage to California via Cape Horn, Together with Scenes in El Dorado, in the Years 1849–50* (Philadelphia, 1878), 304.

40. Charles H. Shinn, *Mining-Camps: A Study in American Frontier Government* (New York, 1884); Joseph W. Ellison, "The Mineral Land Question in California, 1848–1866," *Southwestern Historical Quarterly* 30 (July 1926), 9–15; Maureen A. Jung, "Capitalism Comes to the Diggings: From Gold-Rush Adventure to Corporate Enterprise," *California History* 77 (Winter 1998–99), 56–58.

41. Browne, *Report of the Debates*, 136. For more on the individual liability clause, see Ira Cross, *Financing and Empire: History of Banking in California*, 4 vols. (Chicago, 1927), 1:113.

42. Browne, *Report of the Debates*, 135–36.

43. William H. Ellison, ed., "Memoirs of the Hon. William M. Gwin," *California Historical Society Quarterly* 19 (1940), 8, 10.

44. Ralph Mann, *After the Gold Rush: Society in Grass Valley and Nevada City, 1849–1870* (Stanford, Calif., 1982), 10, 13–15.

45. Ibid., 10–12.

46. Jung, "Capitalism Comes to the Diggings," 62–68; *Manhattan Quartz Mining Company, Facts Concerning Quartz and Quartz Mining: Together with the Charter* (New York, 1852), 24.

47. Robert L. Kelley, "Forgotten Giant: The Hydraulic Gold Mining Industry in California," *Pacific Historical Review* 23 (Nov. 1954), 343–46.

48. Edwin Bean, *Bean's History and Directory of Nevada County, California* (Nevada City, Calif., 1867), 65; Harry A. Wells, *History of Nevada County, California* (Oakland, 1880), 171.

49. Kelley, "Forgotten Giant," 343–48.

50. Don Alexander, ed., *History and Mining Techniques of the Empire Mine*

(Grass Valley, Calif., 1994), 5–8; Charles A. Bohakel, *A Brief History of the Empire Mine of Grass Valley* (Grass Valley, Calif., 1968), 1–3.

51. Mann, *After the Gold Rush*, 238.
52. Arthur C. Todd, *The Cornish Miner in America* (Glendale, Calif., 1967); Eliot Lord, *Comstock Mining and Miners* (Washington, D.C., 1883), 382–86; Mann, *After the Gold Rush*, 142–47; Richard E. Lingenfelter, *The Hardrock Miners: A History of the Mining Labor Movement in the American West, 1863–1893* (Berkeley, Calif., 1974), 6–7; John Rowe, *The Hard-Rock Men: Cornish Immigrants and the North American Mining Frontier* (Liverpool, U.K., 1974), 96.
53. Thomas Senior Berry, "Gold! But How Much?" *California History Quarterly* 55 (Fall 1976), 251; David Martin, "1853: The End of Bimetallism in the United States," *Journal of Economic History* 33 (Dec. 1973), 825–44; Barry Eichagreen and Ian W. McLean, "The Supply of Gold Under the Pre-1914 Gold Standard," *Economic History Review* 47 (1994), 294; James Gerber, "Gold Rushes and the Trans-Pacific Wheat Trade: California and Australia, 1848–57," in Dennis O. Flynn, Lionel Frost, and A. J. H. Latham, eds., *Pacific Centuries: Pacific and Pacific Rim History Since the Sixteenth Century* (London, 1999), app. 1, 147; George W. Van Vleck, *The Panic of 1857: An Analytical Study* (New York, 1943), 38–39, 50, 105; E. J. Hobsbawm, *The Age of Capital, 1848–1875* (New York, 1975), 33–34; Kenneth Pomeranz and Steven Topik, *The World That Trade Created: Society, Culture, and the World Economy, 1400–the Present* (Armonk, N.Y., 1999), 123; Mark A. Eifler, *Gold Rush Capitalists: Greed and Growth in Sacramento* (Albuquerque, N. Mex., 2002), pt. 3.
54. Conmy, "Shannon," 4; Biggs, *Stevenson's Regiment and California*, 190.

CHAPTER 4

1. The population figure in the federal census of 1850—92,567—is clearly inaccurate, as it doesn't include the returns of Contra Costa, Santa Clara, and San Francisco counties. For the guesswork in figuring out California's population in 1850, see Warren S. Thompson et al., *Growth and Changes in California's Population* (Los Angeles, 1955), 9.
2. George Tennis, "California's First Election, November 13, 1849," *Southern California Quarterly* 50 (Dec. 1968), 374–75; Elisha Crosby, "First State Election in California," *Quarterly of the Society of California Pioneers* 5 (June 1928), 73.
3. Jennie to Milton, Nov. 11, 1849, in *Apron Full of Gold: The Letters of Mary Jane Megquier from San Francisco, 1849–1856*, ed. Robert Glass Clelland (San Marino, Calif., 1949), 30; Tennis, "California's First Election," 383.
4. Edward M. Steel, Jr., *T. Butler King of Georgia* (Athens, Ga., 1964), 7 and

passim; *Re-union of the Passengers on the Fourth of June, 1874, Being the Twenty-fifth Anniversary of the Arrival of the Steamship* Panama *at San Francisco* (San Francisco, 1874).

5. Elisha Crosby, "Events in California," MS, 29, Bancroft Library, Berkeley.

6. *Reminiscences of Francis J. Lippitt* (Providence, 1902), 81–82.

7. Daniel Knower, *Adventures of a Forty-Niner* (Albany, N.Y., 1895), 115; Tennis, "California's First Election," 367.

8. Cardinal Goodwin, *The Establishment of State Government in California, 1846–1850* (New York, 1914), 260–61; Frederic Hall, *The History of San José and Surroundings* (San Francisco, 1871), 218–21; Hubert Howe Bancroft, *History of California, 1848–1859,* 6 vols. (San Francisco, 1888), 6:309–11.

9. Crosby, "Events in California," 64.

10. Herbert C. Jones, *The First Legislature of California* (Sacramento, Calif., 1950), 10–11; Goodwin, *Establishment of State Government in California,* 256, 258.

11. Charles A. Barker, ed., *Memoirs of Elisha Oscar Crosby* (San Marino, Calif., 1945), 40, 61; Crosby, "Events in California," 29.

12. Toombs to Linton Stephens, March 22, 1850, in U. B. Phillips, ed., "The Correspondence of Robert Toombs, Alexander H. Stephens, and Howell Cobb," *Annual Report of the American Historical Association for the Year 1911* (Washington, D.C., 1913), 2:188.

13. Cobb to his wife, Dec. 20, 1849, ibid., 2:179.

14. *Congressional Globe,* 31st Cong., 1st sess., 1849–50, app., 702.

15. Ibid., 757. See also Etta Olive Powell, "Southern Influences in California Politics Before 1864" (master's thesis, University of California, Berkeley, 1929), 40; William L. Barney, *The Road to Secession: A New Perspective on the Old South* (New York, 1972), 67, 107–8.

16. *Congressional Globe,* 31st Cong., 1st sess., 1849–50, app., 702.

17. Ibid., 27; Joshua Giddings to his son, Dec. 14, 1849, Joshua Giddings Papers, Ohio Historical Society, Columbus, microfilm.

18. *Congressional Globe,* 31st Cong., 1st sess., 1849–50, 28.

19. Ibid., 29.

20. Giddings to his son, Dec. 14, 1849, Giddings Papers.

21. Clay's "Alabama Letter, July 27, 1844," repr. in Arthur M. Schlesinger, Jr., and Fred J. Israel, eds., *History of American Presidential Elections, 1789–1968,* 4 vols. (New York, 1971), 1:855–56.

22. For Clay's resolutions and accompanying remarks, see *Congressional Globe,* 31st Cong., 1st sess., 1849–50, 244–49.

23. Manisha Sinha, *The Counterrevolution of Slavery: Politics and Ideology in Antebellum South Carolina* (Chapel Hill, N.C., 2000), 81–82; Cleo Hearon, *Mississippi and the Compromise of 1850* (Oxford, Miss., 1913),

39–68; Thelma Jennings, *The Nashville Convention: Southern Movement for Unity, 1848–1851* (Memphis, 1980), 25–27, 35–40.

24. Robert E. May, *John A. Quitman: Old South Crusader* (Baton Rouge, La., 1985); John McCardell, "John A. Quitman and the Compromise of 1850 in Mississippi," *Journal of Mississippi History* 37 (1975), 239–66; J. F. H. Claiborne, *Life and Correspondence of John A. Quitman, Major-General, U.S.A., and Governor of the State of Mississippi*, 2 vols. (New York, 1860).

25. "Inaugural Address of Gov. John A. Quitman, Delivered Before Both Houses of the Mississippi Legislature, January 10th, 1850," in Claiborne, *Quitman*, 2:21–25.

26. Jefferson Davis et al. to Quitman, Jan. 21, 1850, in Dunbar Rowland, ed., *Jefferson Davis, Constitutionalist: His Letters, Papers, and Speeches*, 10 vols. (Jackson, Miss., 1923), 1:261, 601–2; *Congressional Globe*, 31st Cong., 1st sess., 1849–50, app., 586.

27. Hearon, *Mississippi and the Compromise of 1850*, 77, 83–86; Claiborne, *Quitman*, 2:34.

28. *Congressional Globe*, 31st Cong., 1st sess., 1849–50, 200–5; T. L. Clingman, *Selections from the Speeches and Writings of Hon. Thomas L. Clingman, of North Carolina* (Raleigh, N.C., 1877), 232–33; John S. Bassett, "The Congressional Career of Thomas L. Clingman," *Trinity College Historical Papers*, ser. 4 (1900), 48–63; Don E. Fehrenbacher, *The South in Three Sectional Crises* (Baton Rouge, La., 1980), 40.

29. Of the many Davis biographies, I am most indebted to Clement Eaton, *Jefferson Davis* (New York, 1977); William C. Davis, *Jefferson Davis: The Man and His Hour* (New York, 1991); and William J. Cooper, Jr., *Jefferson Davis, American* (New York, 2000).

30. Jefferson Davis, "Speech at Holly Springs, October 25, 1849," and "Remarks on Henry Clay's Resolutions, January 29, 1850," in Lynda Lasswell Crist, Mary Seaton Dix, and Richard E. Beringer, eds., *The Papers of Jefferson Davis* (Baton Rouge, La., 1983), 4:49, 66, 67, 69; *Washington Union*, Jan. 30, 1850.

31. Davis to William R. Cannon, Jan. 8, 1850, in Crist, Dix, and Beringer, *Papers of Davis*, 4:56.

32. Davis, "Remarks on Henry Clay's Resolutions, January 29, 1850," ibid., 4:66, 67.

33. *Congressional Globe*, 29th Cong., 2nd sess., 1846–47, 455; Chaplain W. Morrison, *Democratic Politics and Sectionalism: The Wilmot Proviso Controversy* (Chapel Hill, N.C., 1967), 34–35; William J. Cooper, Jr., *The South and the Politics of Slavery, 1828–1856* (Baton Rouge, La., 1978), 253–54.

34. *Congressional Globe*, 31st Cong., 1st sess., 1849–50, app., 149–57; Davis, "Speech on Slavery," in Rowland, *Davis Papers*, 1:263–308.

35. In 1851, a year after Calhoun's death, they would appear in print as *A Dis-*

quisition on Government and *A Discourse on the Constitution and Government of the United States.*

36. *Congressional Globe*, 31st Cong., 1st sess., 1849–50, 451–55; Richard K. Cralle, ed., *The Works of John C. Calhoun*, 6 vols. (New York, 1854–61), 4:542–73.

37. John Wentworth, *Congressional Reminiscences: Adams, Benton, Clay, Calhoun, and Webster* (Chicago, 1882), 23–24.

38. Henry S. Foote, *Casket of Reminiscences* (Washington, D.C., 1874), 81.

39. Ibid., passim; John E. Gonzales, "Henry Stuart Foote: A Forgotten Unionist of the Fifties," *Southern Quarterly* 1 (1963), 129–39.

40. *Congressional Globe*, 31st Cong., 1st sess., 1849–50, 603, app. 267, 1485; Gonzales, "Foote," 129–39; William W. Freehling, *The Road to Disunion: Secessionists at Bay, 1776–1854* (New York, 1990), 505–7.

41. *Congressional Globe*, 31st Cong., 1st sess., 1849–50, 365–69, 416–17, 517–18.

42. Ibid., 760–63; Holman Hamilton, *Prologue to Conflict: The Crisis and Compromise of 1850* (New York, 1966), 92–94; L. A. Gobright, *Recollection of Men and Things at Washington, During the Third of a Century* (Philadelphia, 1869), 114–18; George W. Julian, *Political Recollections, 1840–1872* (Chicago, 1884), 91–92.

43. Ronald C. Woolsey, "A Southern Dilemma: Slavery Expansion and the California Statehood Issue in 1850—A Reconsideration," *Southern California Quarterly* 65 (Summer 1983), app. C, 140; Hamilton, *Prologue to Conflict*, apps. A and C, 190–91, 195–200.

44. See, for example, *Charleston Mercury, Athens Southern Banner, Mobile Daily Register, Jackson Mississippian, Natchez Free Trader, Yazoo (Miss.) Democrat, New Orleans Daily Delta*—all, Sept.–Nov. 1850.

45. John Barnwell, *Love of Order: South Carolina's First Secession Crisis* (Chapel Hill, N.C., 1982), 138; Laura A. White, *Robert Barnwell Rhett: Father of Secession* (New York, 1931), 128; William C. Davis, *A Fire-Eater Remembers: The Confederate Memoir of Robert Barnwell Rhett* (Columbia, S.C., 2000), 185; Betty L. Mitchell, *Edmund Ruffin: A Biography* (Bloomington, Ind., 1981), 73–74; speech of R. B. Rhett, in *Charleston Mercury*, Sept. 25, 1850; *Charleston Mercury*, Sept. 13, Oct. 3–4, 1850.

46. *Columbus Sentinel*, Sept. 2, 1850, quoted in Robert P. Brooks, "Howell Cobb and the Crisis of 1850," *Mississippi Valley Historical Review* 4 (Dec. 1917), 289.

47. Amos Aschbach Ettinger, *The Mission to Spain of Pierre Soulé, 1853–1855: A Study in the Cuban Diplomacy of the United States* (New Haven, Conn., 1932), 116ff.; J. Preston Moore, "Pierre Soulé: Southern Expansionist and Promoter," *Journal of Southern History* 21 (May 1955), 205–15; C. Stanley Urban, "The Ideology of Southern Imperialism: New Orleans

and the Caribbean, 1845–1860," *Louisiana Historical Quarterly* 39 (Jan. 1956), 48–73.

48. Quitman to J. J. McRae, Sept. 28, 1850, in Claiborne, *Quitman*, 2:44–46; McCardell, "Quitman and the Compromise of 1850," 245–46; Claiborne, *Quitman*, 2:35–37; Hearon, *Mississippi and the Compromise of 1850*, 157–58.

49. Seabrook to Quitman, Sept. 20, Oct. 23, 1850, in Claiborne, *Quitman*, 2:36–38.

50. Quitman's Message to the Legislature, Nov. 18, 1850, in Claiborne, *Quitman*, 2:46–51.

51. Foote, *Casket of Reminiscences*, 356; Reuben Davis, *Reminiscences of Mississippi and Mississippians* (Boston, 1889), 317; Christopher J. Olsen, *Political Culture and Secession in Mississippi: Masculinity, Honor, and the Antiparty Tradition, 1830–1860* (New York, 2000), 44–46.

52. May, *Quitman*, 263–64.

53. Lillian Adele Kibler, *Benjamin F. Perry: South Carolina Unionist* (Durham, N.C., 1946), 263.

54. A. M. Friedenberg, "Solomon Heydenfeldt," JewishEncyclopedia.com; *Huntsville Democrat*, Jan. 13, 1849; Oscar T. Shuck, *History of the Bench and Bar of California* (Los Angeles, 1901), 457–59; Arthur Quinn, *The Rivals: William Gwin, David Broderick, and the Birth of California* (New York, 1994), 100–2; Herbert C. Jones, *The First Legislature of California* (Sacramento, Calif., 1950), 10, 13.

55. William H. Ellison, *A Self-Governing Dominion: California, 1849–1860* (Berkeley, Calif., 1950), 271, 276; Royce D. Delmatier et al., *The Rumble of California Politics, 1848–1970* (New York, 1970), 15; Quinn, *Rivals*, 92–93; David A. Williams, *David C. Broderick: A Political Portrait* (San Marino, Calif., 1969), 55–56.

56. James O'Meara, *Broderick and Gwin* (San Francisco, 1881), 42–43, later claimed that Gwin's role in patronage appointments was much exaggerated and that men like Richard P. Hammond obtained federal posts largely because of their own political connections. The federal records, however, don't support O'Meara's claim. See California Appointment Papers, RG 56, National Archives. The *San Francisco News*, June 8, 24, Aug. 18, 1859, ran a series listing some hundred officials who held office because of Gwin. See also Powell, "Southern Influences in California Politics Before 1864," 74–75; Williams, *Broderick*, 227–28; Bancroft, *History of California*, 6:673–74.

57. *Biographical Directory of the American Congress, 1774–1971* (Washington, D.C., 1971); *Alta California*, Aug. 4, 1857; *Hutchings California Magazine*, March 1858, 186–87; James McHall Jones Papers, Bancroft Library; Lewis P. Lesley, "The International Boundary Survey from San Diego to

the Gila River," *California Historical Society Quarterly* 9 (March 1930), 2–15; *Re-union of the Passengers;* Ellison, *Self-Governing Dominion,* 272, 276; Delmatier et al., *Rumble of California Politics,* 15.

58. Gwin's support of Southern independence is well documented by all his biographers. For Weller, see *Speech of Ex-governor John B. Weller Delivered Before the Democratic Club at Petaluma, Cal., June 6, 1863,* Huntington Library, San Marino, Calif.

CHAPTER 5

1. Robert E. May, *John A. Quitman: Old South Crusader* (Baton Rouge, La., 1985), 236.

2. Romulus M. Saunders to Buchanan, Dec. 14, 1848, in W. R. Manning, ed., *Diplomatic Correspondence of the United States: Inter-American Affairs, 1831–1860,* 12 vols. (Washington, D.C., 1932–39), 11:456–59.

3. C. Stanley Urban, "The Ideology of Southern Imperialism: New Orleans and the Caribbean, 1845–1860," *Louisiana Historical Quarterly* 39 (Jan. 1956), 53, 55, 57.

4. *New Orleans Daily Delta,* Sept. 13, Nov. 5, 11, 1850, Aug. 1, 1851. See also *New Orleans Bulletin,* May 9, 1851; *New Orleans Louisiana Courier,* Oct. 21, 1850, June 27, July 1, Aug. 1, 19, 1851.

5. Mrs. Jefferson Davis, *Jefferson Davis: A Memoir by His Wife,* 2 vols. (New York, 1891), 1:412.

6. For information on López and his adventures, see Tom Chaffin, *Fatal Glory: Narciso López and the First Clandestine U.S. War Against Cuba* (Charlottesville, Va., 1996); Robert E. May, *The Southern Dream of a Caribbean Empire, 1854–1861* (Athens, Ga., 1989), 25–29; Charles H. Brown, *Agents of Manifest Destiny* (Chapel Hill, N.C., 1980), 42–88.

7. May, *Quitman,* 239.

8. Brown, *Agents of Manifest Destiny,* 94–95, 103–31; "Articles Between Cuban Junta and General Quitman," in J. F. H. Claiborne, *Life and Correspondence of John A. Quitman, Major-General, U.S.A., and Governor of the State of Mississippi,* 2 vols. (New York, 1860), 2:389.

9. *Congressional Globe,* 32nd Cong., 2nd sess., 1852–53, 338–39.

10. *New York Evening Post,* Aug. 6, 1853; *New York Herald,* Aug. 6, 1853.

11. C. Stanley Urban, "The Africanization of Cuba Scare, 1853–1855," *Hispanic American Historical Review* 37 (Feb. 1957), 29–45; Resolution of the Louisiana Legislature, in *Senate Miscellaneous Documents,* 33rd Cong., 1st sess., 1853–54, no. 63; Quitman to the Cuban Junta, April 16, 1854, in Claiborne, *Quitman,* 2:391.

12. Marcy to Soulé, April 3, 1854, in Manning, *Diplomatic Correspondence: Inter-American Affairs,* 11:175–78.

13. Claiborne, *Quitman,* 2:195–209, 391–92.

14. Marcy to Soulé, June 24, 1854, Soulé to Marcy, Oct. 15, 1854, in Manning, *Diplomatic Correspondence: Inter-American Affairs,* 11:189–90, 825–26; text of manifesto, Oct. 18, 1824, ibid., 7:579–85.

15. Some accounts indicate that Northern Democrats started out with ninety-one seats and ended up with twenty-five. The disparity in the tallies stems largely from discrepancies in the sources and the turmoil that characterized the 1854 election. For the discrepancies in the records, see Kenneth C. Martis, *The Historical Atlas of Political Parties in the United States Congress, 1789–1989* (New York, 1989), 380–90.

16. Jared Ingersoll to Marcy, Jan. 17, 1855, Lewis Cass to Marcy, March 24, April 9, 1855, G. A. Worth to Marcy, March 27, 1855, P. M. Wetmore to Marcy, March 31, 1855, Robert H. Morris to Marcy, April 14, 1855, George Bancroft to Marcy, April 17, 1855, William L. Marcy Papers, Library of Congress; *New-York Tribune,* March 7, 1855; *New York Evening Post,* March 6, 7, 13, April 11, 14, 1855; *Philadelphia Ledger,* March 9, April 9, 1855; Ivor Spencer, *The Victor and the Spoils: A Life of William L. Marcy* (Providence, 1959), 325–28; Amos Aschbach Ettinger, *The Mission to Spain of Pierre Soulé, 1853–1855: A Study in the Cuban Diplomacy of the United States* (New Haven, Conn., 1932), 394–412.

17. For biographical information on Gadsden, see Paul Neff Garber, *The Gadsden Treaty* (Philadelphia, 1923), 76–80 and passim; J. Fred Rippy, *James Gadsden: Biographical Essay* (Farmington Hills, Mich., 2004), 1–2.

18. *DeBow's Commercial Review* 1 (Jan. 1846), 27–33; 3 (Feb. 1847), 485; Jere W. Roberson, "The South and the Pacific Railroad, 1845–1855," *Western Historical Quarterly* 5 (April 1974), 164–66.

19. Gadsden to Green, Dec. 7, 1851, William Leidesdorff Papers, Huntington Library, San Marino, Calif.; Gadsden to Amos Estes, Dec. 10, 1851, *Charleston Daily Courier,* Feb. 7, 1852; John C. Parish, "A Project for a California Slave Colony in 1851," *Huntington Library Bulletin* 8 (Oct. 1935), 171–75; Nathaniel Wright Stevenson, "California and the Compromise of 1850," *Pacific Historical Review* 4 (June 1935), 114.

20. Memorial to the Legislature of California, Misc. Petition Reports (1852), California State Archives, Sacramento. See also Paul Finkelman, "The Law of Slavery and Freedom in California, 1848–1860," *California Western Law Review* 17 (1981), 437–38.

21. *Assembly Journal, 1852,* 159; *San Francisco Daily Evening Picayune,* Feb. 11, 1852; *San Francisco Pacific,* April 23, 1852.

22. *San Francisco Herald,* April 16, 1852; *San Francisco Pacific,* April 23, 1852.

23. Robert H. Forbes, *Crabb's Filibustering Expedition into Sonora, 1857* (Phoenix, 1952), Bancroft Library, Berkeley; Joseph Y. Ainsa, *History of the Crabb Expedition into N. Sonora: Decapitation of the State Senator . . . and*

Massacre of Ninety-eight of His Friends, at Caborca and Sonoita, Sonora, Mexico, 1857 (Phoenix, 1951), Bancroft Library; Rufus Kay Wyllys, "Henry A. Crabb—a Tragedy of the Sonora Frontier," *Pacific Historical Review* 9 (1940), 183–94; Joe A. Stout, Jr., "Henry A. Crabb: Filibuster or Colonizer?" *American West* 8 (1971), 4–9.

24. Leonard L. Richards, *The Slave Power: The Free North and Southern Domination, 1780–1860* (Baton Rouge, La., 2000), 110–11, 179–83.

25. Thomas D. Morris, *Free Men All: The Personal Liberty Laws of the North, 1780–1861* (Baltimore, 1974); Stanley W. Campbell, *The Slave Catchers: Enforcement of the Fugitive Slave Law, 1850–1860* (Chapel Hill, N.C., 1968); Thomas P. Slaughter, *Bloody Dawn: The Christiana Riot and Racial Violence in the Antebellum North* (New York, 1991); Kevin L. Gilbert, "The Ordeal of Edward Greeley Loring: Fugitive Slavery, Judicial Reform, and the Politics of Law in 1850s Massachusetts" (Ph.D. diss., University of Massachusetts, Amherst, 1997).

26. *Statutes of California, 1852*, 67–69; *Senate Journal, 1852*, 277; *General Laws of the State of California, 1850–1864* (Sacramento, Calif., 1865), 459–60; *San Francisco Daily Evening Picayune*, Feb. 6, 1852; *San Francisco Herald*, Feb. 8, 1852; C. E. Montgomery, "The Lost Journals of a Pioneer," entry June 11, 1852, *Overland Monthly* 7 (1886), 180; Rudolph M. Lapp, "Negro Rights Activities in Gold Rush California," *California Historical Quarterly* 45 (March 1966), 11; In re Perkins, 2 Cal 424–58 (1852); Ex parte Archy, 9 Cal 147; Lucile Eaves, *A History of California Labor Legislation* (Berkeley, Calif., 1910), 99–103; Finkelman, "Law of Slavery and Freedom in California," 454–57.

27. *San Francisco Daily Evening Picayune*, Aug. 2, 1851.

28. Antonio Maria de la Guerra to Pablo de la Guerra, Feb. 4, 1852, de la Guerra Papers, Santa Barbara Mission Archives, microfilm; Montgomery, "Lost Journals of a Pioneer," 179; *San Francisco Pacific*, March 19, 1852; *Alta California*, Feb. 29, 1852.

29. *Senate Journal, 1853*, app., doc. 16, 17; David A. Williams, *David C. Broderick: A Political Portrait* (San Marino, Calif., 1969), 35–37; Hubert Howe Bancroft, *History of California, 1848–1859 6 vols. (San Francisco, 1888)*, 6:668–69; *Winfield J. Davis*, History of Political Conventions in California, 1849–1892 (Sacramento, Calif., 1893), 25.

30. *Execution of Colonel Crabb and Associates*, 35th Cong., 1st sess., 1857–58, House Executive Document 64, 71.

31. Ibid., 83.

32. W. O. Croffut, ed., *Fifty Years in Camp and Field: Diary of Major General Ethan Allen Hitchcock* (New York, 1909), 400–3.

33. *Execution of Colonel Crabb and Associates*, 33. For the story of the invasion, see also Forbes, *Crabb's Filibustering Expedition into Sonora*; Ainsa, *History*

of the Crabb Expedition; Edward S. Wallace, *Destiny and Glory* (New York, 1957), 122, 117–19; Wyllys, "Henry A. Crabb—a Tragedy of the Sonora Frontier," 183–94; Stout, "Henry A. Crabb: Filibuster or Colonizer?" 4–9; May, *Southern Dream of a Caribbean Empire*, 148.

34. *Execution of Colonel Crabb and Associates*, 74.

35. Calculated from Thomas Senior Berry, "Gold! But How Much?" *California Historical Quarterly* 55 (Fall 1976), 251; James Gerber, "Gold Rushes and the Trans-Pacific Wheat Trade: California and Australia, 1848–57," in Dennis O. Flynn, Lionel Frost, and A. J. H. Latham, eds., *Pacific Centuries: Pacific and Pacific Rim History Since the Sixteenth Century* (London, 1999), app. 1, 147.

36. Robert R. Russel, *Improvement of Communication with the Pacific Coast as an Issue in American Politics, 1783–1864* (Cedar Rapids, Iowa, 1948), 56–58; *House Reports*, 30th Cong., 2nd sess., 1848–49, vol. 1, no. 26.

37. Russel, *Improvement of Communication with the Pacific Coast*, 58–59; *Congressional Globe*, 30th Cong., 2nd sess., 1848–49, 40, 49–52, 59–60, 398–402, 411–15, 457–63, 626.

38. John Haskell Kemble, *The Panama Route, 1848–1869* (Berkeley, Calif., 1943); Fessenden Nott Otis, *History of the Panama Railroad . . .* (New York, 1867); Joseph Schott, *Rails Across Panama: The Story of the Building of the Panama Railroad* (Indianapolis, 1967), 102.

39. Wheaton J. Lane, *Commodore Vanderbilt: An Epic of the Steam Age* (New York, 1942).

40. *House Executive Documents*, 31st Cong., 1st sess., 1849–50, vol. 10, no. 75, 173–80; Manning, *Diplomatic Correspondence: Inter-American Affairs*, 3:360–74, 193–408; James P. Baughman, *Charles Morgan and the Development of Southern Transportation* (Nashville, 1968), chap. 4; Russel, *Improvement of Communication with the Pacific Coast*, 64–66, 74–75.

41. Baughman, *Charles Morgan and the Development of Southern Transportation*, 73–74.

42. Oscar T. Shuck, *Representative and Leading Men of the Pacific* (San Francisco, 1870), 143–64; Frank Soulé et al., *The Annals of San Francisco* (New York, 1854), 744–47.

43. William Frank Stewart, *Last of the Fillibusters; or, Recollections of the Siege of Rivas* (Sacramento, Calif., 1857), 11, 12.

44. For Walker's life and adventures, see William O. Scroggs, *Filibusters and Financiers: The Story of William Walker and His Associates* (New York, 1916), passim; Wallace, *Destiny and Glory*, passim; Albert Z. Carr, *The World of William Walker* (New York, 1963), passim; Joseph A. Stout, Jr., *The Liberators: Filibustering Expeditions into Mexico, 1848–1862, and the Last Thrust of Manifest Destiny* (Los Angeles, 1973), passim; May, *Southern Dream of a Caribbean Empire*, 77–83, 111–35; and Robert E. May, *Manifest*

Destiny's Underworld: Filibustering in Antebellum America (Chapel Hill, N.C., 2002), passim.

45. *Alta California*, Dec. 15, 1853; Croffut, *Diary of Major General Ethan Allen Hitchcock*, 400–5; Etta Olive Powell, "Southern Influences in California Politics Before 1864" (master's thesis, University of California, Berkeley, 1929), 70; Robert E. May, "Young Army Males and Filibustering in the Age of Manifest Destiny: The United States Army as a Cultural Mirror," *Journal of American History* 78 (Dec. 1991), 872–73.

46. Stewart, *Last of the Fillibusters*, 85.

47. James Carson Jamison, *With Walker in Nicaragua; or, Reminiscences of an Officer of the American Phalanx* (Columbia, Mo., 1909), 15, 58–64.

48. Brown, *Agents of Manifest Destiny*, 378–81.

49. J. Preston Moore, "Pierre Soulé: Southern Expansionist and Promoter," *Journal of Southern History* 21 (May 1955), 205–15.

50. William Walker, *The War in Nicaragua* (New York, 1860), 263.

CHAPTER 6

1. *Congressional Globe*, 32nd Cong., 2nd sess., 1852–53, 280–85; Robert R. Russel, *Improvement of Communication with the Pacific Coast as an Issue in American Politics, 1783–1864* (Cedar Rapids, Iowa, 1948), 97–98; Arthur Quinn, *The Rivals: William Gwin, David Broderick, and the Birth of California* (New York, 1994), 142–43.

2. *Congressional Globe*, 32nd Cong., 2nd sess., 1852–53, 315; 33rd Cong., 1st sess., 1853–54), app. 1031–36. Russel, *Improvement of Communication with the Pacific Coast*, 97–98, 148–49; Mark W. Summers, *The Plundering Generation: Corruption and the Crisis of the Union, 1849–1861* (New York, 1987), 205–6.

3. Mary W. Clarke, *Thomas J. Rusk: Soldier, Statesman, Jurist* (Austin, Tex., 1971).

4. *Congressional Globe*, 32nd Cong., 2nd sess., 1852–53, 469–70, 711, 714, 744; Russel, *Improvement of Communication with the Pacific Coast*, 98–108; Robert W. Johannsen, *Stephen A. Douglas* (New York, 1973), 391–94.

5. *Congressional Globe*, 32nd Cong., 2nd sess., 1852–53, 474–75, 542–44, 556–65, 1111–17; Russel, *Improvement of Communication with the Pacific Coast*, 156–59; Johannsen, *Douglas*, 395–98.

6. Jefferson Davis, speech at Merchant's Hotel, Philadelphia, following banquet, July 12, 1853, in Lynda Lasswell Crist and Mary Seaton Dix, eds., *The Papers of Jefferson Davis* (Baton Rouge, La., 1985), 5:30–31.

7. William J. Cooper, Jr., *Jefferson Davis, American* (New York, 2000), 257–58.

8. Frank N. Schubert, ed., *The Nation Builders: A Sesquicentennial History of*

the Corps of Topographical Engineers, 1838–1863 (Fort Belvoir, Va., 1988), 66–67.

9. William Goetzmann, *Army Exploration in the American West, 1803–1863* (New Haven, Conn., 1959), 128–30, 267–74; James P. Shenton, *Robert John Walker: A Politician from Jackson to Lincoln* (New York, 1961), 129–33; *Re-union of the Passengers on the Fourth of June, 1874, Being the Twenty-fifth Anniversary of the Arrival of the Steamship* Panama *at San Francisco* (San Francisco, 1874).

10. Report of the Secretary of War to President Franklin Pierce, Dec. 1, 1853, in Dunbar Rowland, ed., *Jefferson Davis, Constitutionalist: His Letters, Papers, and Speeches,* 10 vols. (Jackson, Miss., 1923), 2:310–17; Clement Eaton, *Jefferson Davis* (New York, 1977), 85; Goetzmann, *Army Exploration in the American West,* 295; Stephen E. Ambrose, *Nothing Like It in the World: The Men Who Built the Transcontinental Railroad, 1863–1869* (New York, 2000), 31; Russel, *Improvement of Communication with the Pacific Coast,* 180.

11. David Hunter Miller, ed., *Treaties and Other International Acts of the United States of America,* 8 vols. (Washington, D.C., 1942–48), 6:342–47. For the complete correspondence between the State Department, Gadsden, and Mexican officials, see Miller, *Treaties of the United States,* 6:293–437, and William R. Manning, ed., *Diplomatic Correspondence of the United States: Inter-American Affairs, 1831–1860,* 12 vols. (Washington, D.C., 1932–39), 9:134–69, 600–96.

12. For details on the Tehuantepec entrepreneurs, see Merl E. Reed, *New Orleans and the Railroads: The Struggle for Commercial Empire, 1830–1860* (Baton Rouge, La., 1966), 69, 71–72; J. J. Williams, comp., *The Isthmus of Tehuantepec . . . Prepared for the Tehuantepec Railroad Company of New Orleans* (New York, 1852); *Senate Executive Documents,* 32nd Cong., 1st sess., 1851–52, vol. 10, no. 97; *Congressional Globe,* 32nd Cong., 2nd sess., 1852–53, app., 134–47, 160–70; Robert D. Meade, *Judah P. Benjamin: Confederate Statesman* (New York, 1943), 74–75, 122–23; A. L. Diket, "Slidell's Right Hand: Emile La Sere," *Louisiana History* 4 (1963), 189–93.

13. Gadsden to Marcy, July 7, 1853, Gray to Marcy, Aug. 12, Sept. 13, 1853, William L. Marcy Papers, Library of Congress; Odie B. Faulk, *Too Far North, Too Far South* (Los Angeles, 1967), 128–29, 10–11.

14. Miller, *Treaties of the United States,* 6:342–47, 361–62; Faulk, *Too Far North, Too Far South,* 129, 131.

15. Gadsden to Marcy, Nov. 19, 1853, Sept. 2, 1854, in Manning, *Diplomatic Correspondence: Inter-American Affairs,* 9:666–67, 728–30; *Charleston Daily Courier,* Jan. 21, 1854.

16. Quoted in Clarence R. Wharton, *El Presidente: A Sketch of the Life of Gen-*

eral Santa Anna (Austin, Tex., 1926), 189; Faulk, *Too Far North, Too Far South*, 131.

17. Paul Neff Garber, *The Gadsden Treaty* (Philadelphia, 1923), 109–45; Russel, *Improvement of Communication with the Pacific Coast*, 130–49.

18. *Congressional Globe*, 33rd Cong., 1st sess., 1853–54, app. 1031–36; Goetzmann, *Army Exploration in the American West*, 266–74; Summers, *Plundering Generation*, 205–6; Russel, *Improvement of Communication with the Pacific Coast*, 148–49.

19. Zedekiah Kidwell, *Supplementary Report in Reply to the Comments of the Sec. of War*, 34th Cong., 3rd sess., 1857, 44; Goetzmann, *Army Exploration in the American West*, 299, 303–4.

20. Since the treaty was considered in secret session, much of the story on how it was passed comes from "leaks," especially leaks to *The New York Herald*, which published article after article on the deals that were made to get the treaty passed. Were the leaks trustworthy? Some were confirmed by more than one source; others were not. See *New York Herald*, Jan. 6–April 25, 1854.

21. Garber, *Gadsden Treaty*, 109–45; Russel, *Improvement of Communication with the Pacific Coast*, 130–49.

22. Rowland, *Jefferson Davis, Constitutionalist*, 2:288–90, 461–62, 464–66; *The Reports upon the Purchase, Importation, and Use of Camels and Dromedaries to Be Employed for Military Purposes*, 34th Cong., 3rd sess., 1857, Senate Executive Document, 62; Walter Prescott Webb, *The Great Plains* (Boston, 1931), 199–200; Eaton, *Jefferson Davis*, 84–85; Cooper, *Jefferson Davis, American*, 258–59.

23. John W. Burgess, *The Middle Period, 1817–1858* (New York, 1900), 385; Robert W. Johannsen, "The Kansas-Nebraska Act and the Pacific Northwest Frontier," *Pacific Historical Review* 22 (May 1953), 129–41.

24. Richard C. Bain, *Convention Decisions and Voting Records* (Washington, D.C., 1960), 17ff. app.; Congressional Quarterly, *National Party Conventions, 1831–1872* (Washington, D.C., 1976); James S. Chase, *Emergence of the Presidential Nominating Convention, 1789–1832* (Urbana, Ill., 1973), 264–66; David M. Potter, *The South and the Concurrent Majority* (Baton Rouge, La., 1972).

25. Johannsen, *Douglas*, 208–9, 211, 232, 299–300, 337–38, 870–71.

26. *Congressional Globe*, 33rd Cong., 1st sess., 1853–54, 1303, 1309; app. 240, 533.

27. Douglas to J. H. Crane, D. M. Johnson, and L. J. Eastin, Dec. 17, 1853, in Robert W. Johannsen, ed., *The Letters of Stephen A. Douglas* (Urbana, Ill., 1961), 269; James C. Malin, "The Motives of Stephen A. Douglas in the Organization of the Nebraska Territory: A Letter Dated December 17, 1853," *Kansas Historical Quarterly* 19 (Nov. 1951), 351–52; James C.

Malin, *The Nebraska Question, 1852–1854* (Lawrence, Kans., 1953), 18–19, 81–82, 443–48; Don E. Fehrenbacher, *The Slaveholding Republic* (New York, 2001), 273–74.

28. Frank Heywood Hodder, "The Railroad Background of the Kansas-Nebraska Act," *Mississippi Valley Historical Review* 12 (1925), 4–5.

29. Douglas to Whitney, Oct. 15, 1845, in Johannsen, *Letters of Douglas*, 127–33; *Congressional Globe*, 28th Cong., 2nd sess., 1845–46, 41; Frank Heywood Hodder, "The Genesis of the Kansas-Nebraska Act," *Proceedings of the State Historical Society of Wisconsin for 1912*, 69–86; Johannsen, *Douglas*, 163–65.

30. William E. Parrish, *David Rice Atchison of Missouri, Border Politician* (Columbia, Mo., 1961); Benjamin C. Merkel, "The Slavery Issue and the Political Decline of Thomas Hart Benton, 1846–1856," *Missouri Historical Review* 38 (July 1944), 388–407.

31. Malin, "Motives of Douglas: Letter Dated December 17, 1853," 342–43.

32. Henry Barrett Learned, "The Relation of Philip Phillips to the Repeal of the Missouri Compromise in 1854," *Mississippi Valley Historical Review* (1922), 303–17; Mrs. Archibald Dixon, *True History of the Missouri Compromise and Its Repeal* (Cincinnati, 1898), 445.

33. *National Era*, Jan. 24, 1854. The "Appeal" is also printed in *Congressional Globe*, 33rd Cong., 1st sess., 1853–54, 281–82.

34. *Congressional Globe*, 33rd Cong., 1st sess., 1853–54, 532.

35. Ibid., app. 425–29; Robert R. Russel, "The Issues in the Congressional Struggle over the Kansas-Nebraska Bill, 1854," *Journal of Southern History* 39 (May 1963), 188–89, 208–9.

36. *New York Evening Post*, Feb. 21, March 31, 1854; *Hartford Daily Times*, March 17, 1854; *Philadelphia Daily News*, June 5, 1854; *Chicago Democratic Press*, Feb. 16, May 24, 1854; Allan Nevins, *Ordeal of the Union: A House Dividing, 1852–1857* (New York, 1947), 2:146–49.

37. For the details, see Leonard L. Richards, *The Slave Power: The Free North and Southern Domination, 1780–1860* (Baton Rouge, La., 2000), 185–86.

38. Summers, *Plundering Generation*, 211ff.

39. "Notes on Party Spirit," Caleb Cushing Papers, Library of Congress.

40. *Congressional Globe*, 33rd Cong., 1st sess., 1853–54, 1130–33.

41. For details on the vote, see Richards, *Slave Power*, 185–89.

42. Quoted in Johannsen, *Douglas*, 434.

43. Some accounts indicate that the Democrats started out with ninety-one seats and ended up with twenty-five seats. The disparity in the tallies stems largely from discrepancies in the sources and the turmoil that characterized the 1854 election. Not only did Whigs and Free-Soilers run under a host of new labels, and some under two labels, but five incumbent Democrats switched parties, ran against the Democracy, and won. I have

counted these reelections as "losses" for the Democratic Party, but they have sometimes been counted as Democratic victories, even though the party's official candidates were defeated. Another source of confusion is that some documents list two incumbent Democrats as Free-Soilers before the Kansas-Nebraska debacle, while others list them as Democrats. I have counted them as Democrats, which was their party affiliation in the 1852 election. For the discrepancies in the sources, see Kenneth C. Martis, *Historical Atlas of Political Parties in the United States Congress, 1789–1989* (New York, 1989), 380–90.

44. The cause of the Northern Democracy's decline is a matter of much debate. Some historians blame the turn of events mainly on bungling politicians. Others claim that antislavery and anti-Southern sentiment overwhelmed the existing parties and created the new Republican Party of Abraham Lincoln. And still others point to underlying changes in local politics, the demise of the old economic issues of Jackson's day, and the rise of ethno-cultural issues such as temperance and anti-Catholicism. See Avery Craven, *The Coming of the Civil War,* 2nd rev. ed. (Chicago, 1966); Eric Foner, *Free Soil, Free Labor, Free Men* (New York, 1970); David M. Potter, *The Impending Crisis, 1848–1861* (New York, 1976); Stephen E. Maizlish, *The Triumph of Sectionalism: The Transformation of Ohio Politics, 1844–1856* (Kent, Ohio, 1983); Tyler Anbinder, *Nativism and Slavery: The Northern Know Nothings and the Politics of the 1850s* (New York, 1992); Michael F. Holt, *The Political Crisis of the 1850s* (New York, 1978); Paul Kleppner, *The Third Electoral System, 1853–1892* (Chapel Hill, N.C., 1979), 59–74; Joel H. Silbey, " 'There Are Other Questions Beside That of Slavery Merely': The Democratic Party and Antislavery Politics," in Alan M. Kraut, ed., *Crusaders and Compromisers: Essays on the Relationship of the Antislavery Struggle to the Antebellum Party System* (Westport, Conn., 1983), 163–66; William E. Gienapp, *The Origins of the Republican Party, 1852–1856* (New York, 1987).

45. For the rise of the Republican Party in New Hampshire, see Thomas R. Bright, "The Anti-Nebraska Coalition and the Emergence of the Republican Party in New Hampshire, 1853–1857," *Historical New Hampshire* 27 (Summer 1972), 57–88.

46. Hodder, "Railroad Background of the Kansas-Nebraska Act," 17–18.

CHAPTER 7

1. Richard H. Sewall, *Ballots for Freedom: Antislavery Politics in the United States, 1837–1860* (New York, 1976), 279–84; *Proceedings of the First Three Republican National Conventions of 1856, 1860, and 1864 . . . as Reported by Horace Greeley* (Minneapolis, 1893), 15–78; William B. Hesseltine and

Rex G. Fisher, eds., *Trimmers, Trucklers, and Temporizers: Notes of Murat Halstead from the Political Conventions of 1856* (Madison, Wis. 1961), 83–90.

2. Jessie Benton Frémont to Elizabeth Blair Lee, [April 18, 1856], in Pamela Herr and Mary Lee Spence, eds., *Letters of Jessie Benton Frémont* (Urbana, Ill., 1993), 97–98; Whitman Bennett, *Whittier: Bard of Freedom* (Chapel Hill, N.C., 1941), 240–41; William E. Gienapp, *The Origins of the Republican Party* (New York, 1987), 376; Tom Chaffin, *Pathfinder: John Charles Frémont and the Course of American Empire* (New York, 2002), 442–43; Ruhl J. Bartlett, *John C. Frémont and the Republican Party* (Columbus, Ohio, 1930); Margaret Clapp, *Forgotten First Citizen: John Bigelow* (Boston, 1947).

3. Frederick S. Dellenbaugh, *Frémont and '49* (New York, 1914), 385, 464; Paul W. Gates, "The Adjudication of Spanish-Mexican Land Claims in California," *Huntington Library Quarterly* 21 (May 1958), 213–36; Paul W. Gates, "California's Embattled Settlers," *California Historical Society Quarterly* 41 (June 1962), 99–130; W. W. Robinson, *Land in California* (Berkeley, Calif., 1948); Donald Jackson and Mary Lee Spence, eds., *The Expeditions of John Charles Frémont*, 3 vols. and supps. (Urbana, Ill., 1970–84), 2:299, 3:lix–lxiii.

4. Paul W. Gates, "The Frémont-Jones Scramble for California Land Claims," *Southern California Quarterly* 56 (Spring 1974), 37–38; *Alta California*, June 23, 1857, Nov. 6, 1856; Charles Gregory Crampton, "The Opening of the Mariposa Mining Region, 1849–1859" (Ph.D. diss., University of California, Berkeley, 1941), 217n and passim; Susan Lee Johnson, *Roaring Camp: The Social World of the California Gold Rush* (New York, 2000), 259–74; Jackson and Spence, *Expeditions of Frémont*, 2:297–300; 3:xxxvi–lxix.

5. *San Joaquin Republican*, 1852–56, esp. July 20, Aug. 6, 1856.

6. Royce D. Delmatier et al., *The Rumble of California Politics, 1848–1970* (New York, 1970), 48; *Sacramento Daily Union*, Nov. 18, 1856.

7. Cornelius Cole, *Memoirs* (New York, 1908), 97, 112–14; photocopy of the records of the Republican Association of the City of Sacramento, Organized March 8, 1855, MS, 3, California Historical Society, San Francisco. See also Gerald Stanley, "Slavery and the Origins of the Republican Party in California," *Historical Society of Southern California Quarterly* 60 (1978), 1.

8. Cole, *Memoirs*, 112–14; *Sacramento Daily California Times*, Aug. 15, 17, 1856; Ray R. Albin, "Edward D. Baker and California's First Republican Campaign," *California History* 60 (Fall 1981), 280–83.

9. *Sacramento Daily Union*, Nov. 18, 1856; *Congressional Quarterly's Guide to U.S. Elections*, 3rd ed. (Washington, D.C., 1994), 999; Delmatier et al., *Rumble of California Politics*, 48.

10. Norman D. Brown, "Edward Stanly: First Republican Candidate for Governor of California," *California Historical Society Quarterly* 47 (Sept. 1968), 251–72; *Congressional Globe*, 25th Cong., 2nd sess., 1837–38, app., 87; 26th Cong., 1st sess., 1839–40, 526; 31st Cong., 1st sess., 1849–50, app., 339; Gerald Stanley, "The Politics of the Antebellum Far West: The Impact of the Slavery and Race Issues in California," *Journal of the West* 16 (Oct. 1977), 19–20.

11. *Speech of the Hon. Edward Stanly Delivered at Sac. July 17, 1857* (Sacramento, Calif., 1857); *Sacramento Union*, July 18, Aug. 27, 1857; Stanley, "Impact of the Slavery and Race Issues in California," 20.

12. *Sacramento Journal*, Aug. 28, 1856; Albin, "Edward D. Baker," 283–87; Stanley, "Impact of the Slavery and Race Issues in California," 23; *Sacramento Union*, Oct. 6, 1857.

13. *Sacramento Union*, June 9, Oct. 12, 1859; Gerald Stanley, "The Slavery Issue and Election in California, 1860," *Mid-America* 62 (Jan. 1980), 37.

14. *Alta California*, Aug. 2, 1849; Jay Monaghan, *Chile, Peru, and the California Gold Rush of 1849* (Berkeley, Calif., 1973); Peyton Hurt, "The Rise and Fall of the 'Know Nothings' in California," *California Historical Society Quarterly* 9 (March and June 1930), 16–49, 99–128.

15. *Alta California*, Sept. 3–6, 1854; Hurt, "Rise and Fall of the 'Know Nothings' in California," 27–28; R. A. Burchell, *The San Francisco Irish, 1848–1880* (Berkeley, Calif., 1980), 212 n. 54, 127.

16. [William H. Rhodes], *The Political Letters of "Caxton"* (San Francisco, 1855), 14–16.

17. *Sacramento Pictorial Union*, Jan. 1, 1856; Howard Brent Melendy, *The Governors of California* (Georgetown, Calif., 1965), 66–79; Robert Sobel and John Raimo, eds., *Biographical Directory of the Governors of the United States*, 4 vols. (Westport, Conn., 1978).

18. Lionel E. Freedman, "The Bigler Regime" (master's thesis, Stanford University, 1959).

19. California State Capitol Museum Archives, capitolmuseum.ca.gov/english/legislature/history/year1856.html; *Journal of the California State Senate, 1856*, 87, 89; *Sacramento Daily Union*, Oct. 3, 1855; *California Chronicle*, Oct. 4, 1855; Arthur Quinn, *The Rivals: William Gwin, David Broderick, and the Birth of California* (New York, 1994), 172.

20. *Alta California*, Feb. 26, 1854; *San Francisco Daily Herald*, March 1, 1854; *Sacramento Union*, June 25, Dec. 21–24, 1855; Flint obituary, *San Francisco Daily Evening Bulletin*, Jan. 5, 1857; Henry S. Foote, *Casket of Reminiscences* (Washington, D.C., 1874); John D. Carter, "Henry Stuart Foote in California Politics, 1854–1857," *Journal of Southern History* 9 (May 1943), 224–37.

21. Tyler Anbinder, *Nativism and Slavery: The Northern Know Nothings and the*

Politics of the 1850s (New York, 1992), 162–74; Henry Wilson, *History of the Rise and Fall of the Slave Power in America*, 3 vols. (Boston, 1872–77), 2:423–33.

22. California State Capitol Museum Archives, capitolmuseum.ca.gov/english/legislature/history/year1857.html; Delmatier et al., *Rumble of California Politics*, 48.

23. *Congressional Globe*, 35th Cong., 1st sess., 1857–58, 163–64.

24. For the diverse appeal of the free-soil movement, see Eric Foner, "Racial Attitudes of New York Free Soilers," *New York History* 46 (Oct. 1965), 311–29; Eric Foner, "Politics and Prejudice: The Free Soil Party and the Negro, 1849–1852," *Journal of Negro History* 50 (Oct. 1965), 239–56; Eugene H. Berwanger, *The Frontier Against Slavery* (Urbana, Ill., 1967); Leonard L. Richards, *"Gentlemen of Property and Standing": Anti-Abolition Mobs in Jacksonian America* (New York, 1970), 163–65; Frederick J. Blue, *The Free Soilers: Third Party Politics, 1848–54* (Urbana, Ill., 1973); John Mayfield, *Rehearsal for Republicanism: Free Soil and the Politics of Antislavery* (Port Washington, N.Y., 1980); Jonathan H. Earle, *Jacksonian Antislavery and the Politics of Free Soil* (Chapel Hill, N.C., 2004).

25. *Senate Journal*, 1st sess., 1852, 347; Cardinal Goodwin, *The Establishment of State Government in California, 1846–1850* (New York, 1914), 266–67, 318–23; Hubert Howe Bancroft, *History of California, 1848–1859*, 6 vols. (San Francisco, 1888), 6:312–13; David A. Williams, *David C. Broderick: A Political Portrait* (San Marino, Calif., 1969), 34–35; Paul Finkelman, "The Law of Slavery and Freedom in California, 1848–1860," *California Western Law Review* 17 (1981), 451; Peter H. Burnett, *An Old California Pioneer* (Oakland, 1946), 127–31; Lucile Eaves, *A History of California Labor Legislation* (Berkeley, Calif., 1910), 89–90; James A. Fisher, "The Struggle for Negro Testimony in California, 1851–1853," *Southern California Quarterly* 51 (Dec. 1969), 313–24.

26. *Senate Journal*, 1st sess., 1850, 372–80.

27. Josiah Royce, "The Squatter Riot of '50 in Sacramento," *Overland Monthly* 6 (Sept. 1885), 225–46; C. E. Montgomery, "The Lost Journals of a Pioneer," *Overland Monthly* 7 (1886), 173–81; W. W. Robinson, *Land in California* (Berkeley, Calif., 1948), 114–16; Frank W. Blackmar, *The Life of Charles Robinson* (Topeka, Kans., 1901), 43–47; Erwin G. Gudde, *Sutter's Own Story: The Life of General John Augustus Sutter and the History of New Helvetia in the Sacramento Valley* (New York, 1936), 227.

28. *Alta California*, March 15–22, 1851; *Senate Journal*, 2nd sess., 1851, 313–37.

29. For the details, see Leonard L. Richards, *The Slave Power: The Free North and Southern Domination, 1780–1860* (Baton Rouge, La., 2000).

30. *Alta California*, April 8–10, 1852; *Statutes of California, 1852*, 67–69; Stan-

ley, "Slavery and the Origins of the Republican Party in California," 1–16; Cole, *Memoirs*, 112.

31. Williams, *Broderick*, 74–75; Bancroft, *History of California*, 6:673–74; Gwin to Millard Fillmore, Jan. 31, 1853; Gwin to Franklin Pierce, March 18, 1853, California Appointment Papers, RG 56, National Archives; Etta Olive Powell, "Southern Influences in California Politics Before 1864" (master's thesis, University of California, Berkeley, 1929), 74–75.

32. *San Francisco News*, Aug. 18, 1859. See also Williams, *Broderick*, 227–28; Powell, "Southern Influences in California Politics Before 1864," 74–75. *The San Francisco News*, on June 8, provided a list of hundreds of postmasters who held office thanks to Chivs and, on June 24, still another long list of Chiv members who held federal appointments.

33. John Bigler to William Bigler, March 31, April 14, 1854, Bigler Collection, Historical Society of Pennsylvania, Philadelphia, microfilm.

34. Winfield J. Davis, *History of Political Conventions in California, 1849–1892* (Sacramento, Calif., 1893), 24–25.

35. Archibald C. Peachy to J. L. Folsom, Aug. 14, 1853, Leidesdorff Papers, Huntington Library, San Marino, Calif.; James W. Wilson to James W. Mandeville, Aug. 21, 1853, Mandeville Papers, Huntington Library; *Alta California*, Sept. 6, 15, 23, 1853; Powell, "Southern Influences in California Politics Before 1864," 83–84.

36. Williams, *Broderick*, 76; Governor's Appointments, 1850–1940, drawer 1, California State Archives, Sacramento.

37. Roger W. Lotchin, *San Francisco, 1846–1856; From Hamlet to City* (New York, 1974), 221–22; *Alta California*, Aug. 15, 1853, March 30, 1855, Dec. 31, 1856.

38. Afffidavit of George Wilkes, Bancroft Library, Berkeley; *The Address of the Majority of the Democratic Members of Both Branches of the Legislature* (San Francisco, 1854), copy, Bancroft Library; *Wilkes's Spirit of the Times*, Oct. 22, 1859.

39. *Alta California*, March 1, 1854; *California Chronicle*, March 7, 10, 1854; Williams, *Broderick*, 87–88; Andrew J. Hatch to James W. Mandeville, March 3, 1854; George W. Whitman to Mandeville, March 13, 1854; Mandeville to D. A. Enyart, March 15, 1854, Mandeville Papers.

40. Davis, *History of Political Conventions in California*, 29–34, 605–64; Delmatier et al., *Rumble of California Politics*, 19; Williams, *Broderick*, 92–98; James J. Ayers, *Gold and Sunshine: Reminiscences of Early California* (Boston, 1922), 120.

41. L. A. Gobright, *Recollection of Men and Things at Washington, During the Third of a Century* (Philadelphia, 1869), 160–64.

42. The literature on the 1856 Vigilance Committee is large. Among the more useful accounts are Doyce Nunis, *The San Francisco Vigilance Com-*

mittee of 1856 (Los Angeles, 1971); Richard Maxwell Brown, *Strain of Violence: Historical Studies of American Violence and Vigilantism* (New York, 1975), 134–43; Robert Senkewicz, *Vigilantes in Gold Rush San Francisco* (Stanford, Calif., 1985).

43. *Alta California*, Aug. 26, 1856; Burchell, *San Francisco Irish*, 129–30.

44. *Alta California*, June 29, 1856; Burchell, *San Francisco Irish*, 131; Ned McGowan, *McGowan vs. the Vigilantes* (Oakland, 1946); *Memoirs of General William Tecumseh Sherman, by Himself* (New York, 1875), 143.

45. Gerritt W. Ryckman, statement, 18–20, Bancroft Library; Ethel May Tinneman, "The Opposition to the San Francisco Vigilance Committee of 1856" (master's thesis, University of California, Berkeley, 1941).

46. *Alta California*, Nov. 2–11, 1856; *San Francisco Herald*, Nov. 5, 1856.

47. Broderick to de la Guerra, Sept. 26, 1856, de la Guerra Papers, Santa Barbara Mission Archives, microfilm.

48. Latham to James W. Mandeville, Nov. 18, 1856, Mandeville Papers.

49. A. C. Blaine to James W. Mandeville, Nov. 11, 1856; anonymous to William Gwin, Nov. 10, 1856, in Gwin to Mandeville, Nov. 11, 1856—all in Mandeville Papers.

50. J. S. Watkins to James W. Mandeville, Nov. 22, 1856; B. D. Wilson to William Gwin, Dec. 5, 1856; Gwin to Mandeville, Dec. 13, 19, 1856; Joseph Walkup to Gwin, Dec. 23, 1856; P. L. Solomon to Mandeville, Dec. 28, 1856—all in Mandeville Papers.

51. Gwin to James W. Mandeville, Dec. 22, 25, 1856, Mandeville Papers.

52. Statements of D. Mahoney, Charles S. Scott, and J. M. Pindell, Jan. 13–14, 1857—all in Milton S. Latham Papers, California Historical Society, San Francisco.

53. James O'Meara, *Broderick and Gwin* (San Francisco, 1881), 184–87. Given the details of O'Meara's account, he was most likely the "friend" who accompanied Gwin. For the letter, see also Jeremiah Lynch, *A Senator of the Fifties: David C. Broderick of California* (San Francisco, 1911), 156, 182–84; Lately Thomas, *Between Two Empires: The Life Story of California's First Senator, William McKendree Gwin* (Boston, 1969), 140–41, 173–74; Williams, *Broderick*, 221–22.

54. F. Amyx to James W. Mandeville, Big Oak Flat, Jan. 16, 1857, Mandeville Papers; C. T. Botts to R. M. T. Hunter, Jan. 15, 1857, California State Library, Sacramento; John C. Hyatt to Dr. C. M. Hitchcock, Jan. 20, 1857, Hitchcock Family Correspondence, Bancroft Library.

55. Many Chivs seemed to have a general idea of what Gwin agreed to. See, for example, W. R. Isaacs MacKay to Jefferson Davis, Jan. 13, 1857, in Lynda Lasswell Crist and Mary Seaton Dix, eds., *The Papers of Jefferson Davis* (Baton Rouge, La., 1989), 6:99–101.

56. Lynch, *A Senator of the Fifties*, 182–84; Thomas, *Gwin*, 140–41, 173–74; Williams, *Broderick*, 221–22.

CHAPTER 8

1. The standard biography of Buchanan is Philip S. Klein, *President James Buchanan* (University Park, Pa., 1962). Klein's interpretation, needless to say, differs from mine, but I have drawn on his fine book for many details. I also relied extensively on Elbert B. Smith, *The Presidency of James Buchanan* (Lawrence, Kans., 1975).

2. For excellent accounts of the Ostend Manifesto, see Amos Aschbach Ettinger, *The Mission to Spain of Pierre Soulé, 1853–1855: A Study in the Cuban Diplomacy of the United States* (New Haven, Conn., 1932), 339–412; Robert E. May, *The Southern Dream of a Caribbean Empire, 1854–1861* (Baton Rouge, La., 1973), 67–74.

3. Virginia Clay-Clopton, *A Belle of the Fifties: Memoirs of Mrs. Clay, of Alabama, Covering Social and Political Life in Washington and the South, 1853–66, Put into Narrative Form by Ada Sterling* (New York, 1905), 86, 126–37; John von Sonntag de Havilland, *A Metrical Description of a Fancy Ball Given at Washington, 9th April, 1858, Dedicated to Mrs. Senator Gwin* (Washington, D.C., 1858).

4. See, for example, Buchanan to Mrs. W. M. Gwin, May 4, 1861, in John Bassett Moore, ed., *The Works of James Buchanan* (Philadelphia, 1908–11), 11:187. See also Buchanan to Miss Lane, May 14, June 10, 1859, ibid., 10:319–20, 323–24.

5. *Washington Union*, March 6, 11, 12, 21, 28, 1857.

6. *New York Tribune*, March 7, 9–12, 21, 25, Sept. 23–25, 1857; Don E. Fehrenbacher, *The Dred Scott Case: Its Significance in American Law and Politics* (New York, 1978), 417–48.

7. Philip G. Auchampaugh, "Buchanan, the Court, and the Dred Scott Case," *Tennessee Historical Magazine* 11 (1926), 231–40; Fehrenbacher, *Dred Scott*, 311–12.

8. Forney to Buchanan, n.d., James Buchanan Papers, Historical Society of Pennsylvania, Philadelphia, microfilm.

9. Broderick to Buchanan, March 8, 11, 1857, Treasury Department Applications, RG 56, National Archives; Broderick to Buchanan, March 19, 1857, Department of Justice Appointment Papers, RG 60, National Archives.

10. Latham to Buchanan, Jan. 20, 1857, Treasury Department Applications, RG 56, National Archives; Latham to Buchanan, Feb. 14, 1857, Department of Justice Appointment Papers, Northern California, RG 60, National Archives; Paschal Bequette to Howell Cobb, Secretary of the Treasury, March 17, 1857, Treasury Department Applications, RG 56, National Archives; Charles Scott to James W. Mandeville, March 18, 1857, William Gwin to Mandeville, March 19, April 3, 5, 1857, James W. Mandeville Papers, Huntington Library, San Marino, Calif. See also Roy

S. Bloss, "Biography of William McKendree Gwin and Supporting Documents, 1856–1873," MS, 223–24, Bancroft Library, Berkeley Calif.

Generally speaking, those who claim that Gwin honored his pledge also imply that Broderick himself was largely responsible for the rift with Buchanan, in that he had made so many promises to friends that he didn't want to put his recommendations in writing. See, for example, William H. Ellison, *A Self-Governing Dominion: California, 1849–1860* (Berkeley, Calif., 1950), 294–95; James O'Meara, *Broderick and Gwin* (San Francisco, 1881), 196–98; and Jeremiah Lynch, *The Life of David C. Broderick* (New York, 1911), 163. In my judgment, the evidence doesn't support this interpretation. Broderick clearly put his recommendations in writing, and Gwin clearly did not honor his pledge.

11. Broderick to Buchanan, March 8, 1857, Treasury Department Applications, RG 56, National Archives; William Bigler to Buchanan, March 11, 1857, Buchanan Papers (microfilm).

12. *Alta California*, April 30, 1857.

13. *Alta California*, May 1, 1857; Gwin to James W. Mandeville, April 3, 5, 1857, Mandeville Papers; O'Meara, *Broderick and Gwin*, 199; Kenneth Stampp, *America in 1857: A Nation on the Brink* (New York, 1990), 78.

14. Peyton Hurt, "The Rise and Fall of the 'Know Nothings' in California," *California Historical Society Quarterly* 9 (June 1930), 111–13; John D. Carter, "Henry Stuart Foote in California Politics, 1854–1857," *Journal of Southern History* 9 (May 1943), 234–35.

15. Winfield J. Davis, *History of Political Conventions in California, 1849–1892* (Sacramento, Calif., 1893), 77; *Alta California*, July 14–16, 1857.

16. Weller to Douglas, Nov. 18, 1857, Stephen A. Douglas Papers, University of Chicago, microfilm.

17. *Congressional Globe*, 35th Cong., 1st sess., 1857–58, 1907, 2068–70, 2108, 2902, 2455–56, 2643, 2645; *Congressional Globe*, 35th Cong., 2nd sess., 1858–59, 577, 1240.

18. Of the many fine studies of the Kansas controversy, I am indebted especially to Stampp, *America in 1857*, chaps. 10–12; Robert W. Johannsen, *Stephen A. Douglas* (New York, 1973), 576–631; Fehrenbacher, *Dred Scott*, chap. 19; and James Rawley, *Race and Politics: "Bleeding Kansas" and the Coming of the Civil War* (Philadelphia, 1969).

19. Daniel W. Wilder, *The Annals of Kansas* (Topeka, Kans., 1875), 140, 146.

20. *Washington Union*, Nov. 18, 24, 29, 1857.

21. *Washington Union*, Nov. 24, Dec. 1, 3, 1857.

22. James D. Richardson, ed., *A Compilation of the Messages and Papers of the Presidents*, 20 vols. (New York, 1897), 7:3010.

23. Johannsen, *Douglas*, 586; Roy F. Nichols, *The Disruption of American Democracy* (New York, 1948), 137; Stampp, *America in 1857*, 292–93.

24. *Congressional Globe*, 35th Cong., 1st sess., 1857–58, 163–64. See also Stampp, *America in 1857*, 305–6, 326, 328; Johannsen, *Douglas*, 612; David A. Williams, *David C. Broderick: A Political Portrait* (San Marino, Calif., 1969), 181.

25. *Congressional Globe*, 35th Cong., 1st sess., 1857–58, 492, 623; Nichols, *Disruption of American Democracy*, 232.

26. *Congressional Globe*, 35th Cong., 1st sess., 1857–58, 962, app., 69–71; Drew Gilpin Faust, *James Henry Hammond and the Old South: A Design for Mastery* (Baton Rouge, La., 1982), 346–47; Etta Olive Powell, "Southern Influences in California Politics Before 1864" (master's thesis, University of California, Berkeley, 1929), 150.

27. *Congressional Globe*, 35th Cong., 1st sess., 1857–58, app., 193.

28. For Buchanan's use and misuse of presidential power, see House Report 249, 36th Cong., 1st sess., 1859–60; *The Covode Investigation*, 36th Cong., 1st sess., 1859–60, House Report 648; Mark W. Summers, *The Plundering Generation: Corruption and the Crisis of the Union, 1849–1861* (New York, 1987), 252–60; David Meerse, "James Buchanan, the Patronage, and the Northern Democratic Party, 1857–1858" (Ph.D. diss., University of Illinois, 1969).

29. Elijah J. Kennedy, *The Contest for California in 1861* (Boston, 1912), 44; Edgar Eugene Robinson, ed., "The Day Journal of Milton S. Latham," *California Historical Society Quarterly* 9 (March 1932), 14. The full exchange between Broderick and Douglas was not recorded. For other versions, see Nichols, *Disruption of American Democracy*, 177–78; Stampp, *America in 1857*, 305–6, 326, 328; Johannsen, *Douglas*, 612; Williams, *Broderick*, 178.

30. Clay-Clopton, *A Belle of the Fifties*, 86, 126–37; Havilland, *A Metrical Description of a Fancy Ball Given at Washington.*

31. *San Francisco Daily National*, July 16, 1859; Johannsen, *Douglas*, 686, 690–91.

32. *Alta California*, Sept. 30, Oct. 1, Nov. 10, 16, Dec. 18, 1858; *Congressional Globe*, 35th Cong., 2nd sess., 1858–59, 357, 417.

33. John W. Forney, *Anecdotes of Public Men*, 2 vols. (New York, 1873, 1881), 1:27–28.

34. Forney was undoubtedly much taken with Broderick. He later referred to him as "the noblest Roman of them all." See ibid., 1:316.

35. George J. Bernard affidavit, *People of California v. McGlynn*, California State Archives, file 3494, 90, Sacramento.

36. *Alta California*, Sept. 2–4, 1858.

37. Leonard Pitt, *Decline of the Californios: A Social History of Spanish-Speaking Californians, 1846–1890* (Berkeley, Calif., 1966), 34–35, 139–40, 145, 203–5.

38. The motives behind the Pico bill have long been in dispute. See, for example, Hubert Howe Bancroft, *History of California, 1848–1859*, 7 vols. (San Francisco, 1888–90), 7:254–55; Theodore H. Hittell, *History of California*, 4 vols. (San Francisco, 1885–97), 4:261; James M. Guinn, "How California Escaped State Division," *Historical Society of Southern California, Annual Publications* (1905), 223–32; William H. Ellison, "The Movement for State Division in California, 1849–1860," *Southwestern Historical Quarterly* 17 (1914), 111–24; Ellison, *Self-Governing Dominion*, 175–76; Rockwell D. Hunt, "History of the California State Division Controversy," *Historical Society of Southern California Annual Publication* 13 (1924), 44–46; Peter Wang, "The Mythical Confederate Plot in Southern California," *San Bernardino County Museum Society Quarterly* 16 (1969), 14–15; Ward M. McAfee, "California's House Divided," *Civil War History* 33 (June 1987), 122–23.

39. *Communication of Governor Latham to the President of the United States in Relation to the Division of the State of California* (Sacramento, Calif., 1860), 4; Charles A. Barker, ed., *Memoirs of Elisha Oscar Crosby* (San Marino, Calif., 1945), 62–63.

40. "Speech of the Hon. H. S. Foote, of Mississippi," *DeBow's Review* 27 (July–Dec. 1859), 219.

41. Roach to Davis, June 27, 1859, in Dunbar Rowland, ed., *Jefferson Davis, Constitutionalist: His Letters, Papers, and Speeches*, 10 vols. (Jackson, Miss., 1923), 4:59–61.

42. Donald E. Hargis, "The Great Debate in California: 1859," *Historical Society of Southern California Quarterly* 42 (June 1960), 150–57; speeches reported in *Sacramento Daily Union*, July 11–Aug. 26, 1859.

43. *Sacramento Union*, Aug. 10–11, 1859; *Alta California*, Aug. 11, 1859; *San Francisco News*, Aug. 11, 1859; William Gwin, "An Address to the People of the State of California, on the Senatorial Election of 1857, Giving a History Thereof, and Exposing the Duplicity of Broderick . . ." (San Francisco, 1859), Bancroft Library.

44. *San Francisco News*, Aug. 19, 1859; *Sacramento Union*, Aug. 18, 31, 1859.

45. *Alta California*, Sept. 9–11, 1859; *San Francisco News*, Sept. 9–10, 1859.

46. For details concerning the events leading to the Broderick-Terry duel, see Donald E. Hargis, "The Issues in the Broderick-Gwin Debates of 1859," *California Historical Society Quarterly* 32 (Dec. 1953), 313–25; Donald E. Hargis, " 'Straight Toward His Heart': George Wilkes' Eulogy of David C. Broderick," *California Historical Society Quarterly* 38 (Sept. 1959), 196–217; L. E. Fredman, "Broderick: A Reassessment," *Pacific Historical Review* 30 (Feb. 1961), 39–46; John Currey, *The Terry-Broderick Duel* (Washington, D.C., 1896); Carroll Douglas Hall, *The Terry-Broderick Duel* (San Francisco, 1939); A. Russell Buchanan, *David S. Terry of California: Dueling Judge* (San Marino, Calif., 1956).

47. "Oration of Col. E. D. Baker," in Lynch, *Life of David C. Broderick*, 229–38.

48. Oscar T. Shuck, *Masterpieces of E. D. Baker* (San Francisco, 1899); "Oration of Colonel Edward D. Baker over the Dead Body of David C. Broderick," in Currey, *Terry-Broderick Duel*, 44; Cornelius Cole to William H. Seward, Sept. 19, 1859, Cole Papers, UCLA, microfilm; Barker, *Memoirs of Crosby*, 62–63; *Alta California*, Aug. 17, 24, 1860; *Sacramento Union*, Aug. 27, 1860; Gerald Stanley, "The Slavery Issue and Election in California, 1860," *Mid-America* 62 (Jan. 1980), 38.

49. *San Francisco Examiner*, Aug. 18, 1889, clipping, Bancroft Library.

EPILOGUE

1. *Alta California*, Sept. 17–21, 1859; *San Francisco Steamer Times*, Sept. 20, 1859.

2. Allan Nevins, *The Emergence of Lincoln: Prologue to the Civil War*, 2 vols. (New York, 1950), 2:121; Drew Gilpin Faust, *James Henry Hammond and the Old South: A Design for Mastery* (Baton Rouge, La., 1982), 355.

3. *New Orleans Daily Delta*, Nov. 19, 1859; William J. Cooper, Jr., *Jefferson Davis, American* (New York, 2000), 301–2.

4. *Congressional Globe*, 36th Cong., 1st sess., 1859–60, 121–24, 128–29.

5. Ibid., 121–24; William H. Ellison, ed., "Memoirs of the Hon. William M. Gwin," *California Historical Society Quarterly* 19 (Dec. 1940), 348ff.

6. John W. Forney, *Anecdotes of Public Men*, 2 vols. (New York, 1873, 1881), 1:315.

7. These incidents became tied up with a celebrated duel between McCorkle and Gwin in 1853. The duel itself was a farce. The contestants agreed on rifles at thirty paces. The seconds forgot to bring bullets. Then, once bullets were obtained, both contestants fired and missed, not once but three times. Finally, everyone pretended it was all a misunderstanding and went home. For the details, see *San Francisco Pacific*, June and July 1853; *San Francisco Herald*, June 4, 1853; the lengthy satire in *Alta California*, June 9, 1853; Sylvester Mowry to Edward Bicknall, May 31–June 1, 1853, in Letters to Edward Bicknall, 1853–55, Bancroft Library.

8. *Communication of Governor Latham to the President of the United States in Relation to the Division of the State of California* (Sacramento, Calif., 1860), 4; Rockwell D. Hunt, "History of the California State Division Controversy," *Historical Society of Southern California Annual Publication* 13 (1924), 44–46; William F. Thompson, "The Political Career of Milton Slocum Latham of California" (Ph.D. diss., Stanford University, 1952).

9. *Congressional Globe*, 36th Cong., 1st sess., 1859–60, 1728; Winfield J. Davis, *History of Political Conventions in California, 1849–1892* (Sacramento, Calif., 1893), 128–30.

10. Davis, *Political Conventions in California*, 110, 112–14.

11. Thompson, "Latham of California," 86–90; Ward M. McAfee, "California's House Divided," *Civil War History* 33 (June 1987), 122–23; for the quotation, see Davis, *Political Conventions in California*, 106.

12. David A. Williams, "California Democrats of 1860: Division, Disruption, Defeat," *Southern California Quarterly* 55 (Fall 1973), 244, 246; Rockwell D. Hunt, *John Bidwell* (Caldwell, Idaho, 1942), 175–76; John Parkhurst, *Official Proceedings of the Democratic Convention at Charleston and Baltimore* (n.p., 1860), 74–89.

13. Williams, "California Democrats of 1860," 247–49; Murat Halstead, *Caucuses of 1860* (Columbus, Ohio, 1860), 198–99; Parkhurst, *Official Proceedings of the Democratic Convention at Charleston and Baltimore*, 148.

14. Williams, "California Democrats of 1860," 249–50; Halstead, *Caucuses of 1860*, 221.

15. *San Francisco Evening Bulletin*, June 18, 1860; *Los Angeles Star*, Aug. 11, 1860; *Sacramento Union*, Nov. 9, 1860; Etta Olive Powell, "Southern Influences in California Politics Before 1864" (master's thesis, University of California, Berkeley, 1929), 148–50; Davis, *Political Conventions in California*, 113–14.

16. *Los Angeles Star*, Nov. 10, 17, 24, 1860, May 4, 1861; Ronald C. Woolsey, "Disunion or Dissent? A New Look at an Old Problem in Southern California Attitudes Toward the Civil War," *Southern California Quarterly* 66 (Fall 1984), 187.

17. Davis, *Political Conventions in California*, 128–30; Joseph W. Ellison, *California and the Nation, 1850–1869* (Berkeley, Calif., 1927), 182–87.

18. John Haskell Kemble, *The Panama Route, 1848–1869* (Berkeley, Calif., 1943), 208–9, 255; Thomas Senior Berry, "Gold! But How Much?" *California Historical Quarterly* 55 (Fall 1976), 251–52; James M. Hill, *Historical Summary of Gold, Silver, Copper, Lead, and Zinc Produced in California, 1848 to 1926*, U.S. Bureau of Mines, Economic Paper 3 (Washington, D.C., 1929); Bray Hammond, *Sovereignty and an Empty Purse: Banks and Politics in the Civil War* (Princeton, N.J., 1970), 38–39, 74, 119, 151; Helen B. Walters, "Confederates in Southern California," *Historical Society of Southern California Quarterly* 35 (March 1953), 41.

19. The commander of Union forces in California, General Edwin V. Sumner, estimated that the "secession party" in California numbered "about 32,000 men." The U.S. military estimated that three-eighths of the citizens were from the slaveholding states. In coming up with this number, the military apparently excluded all the foreign-born, who accounted for nearly 40 percent of the state's population, and exaggerated the number of Southern-born. In any event, these figures didn't come close to matching the official numbers in the 1860 census. For the figures and the prob-

lems with them, see U.S. War Department, *The War of the Rebellion: A Compilation of the Official Records of the Union and Confederate Armies* (Washington, D.C., 1897), ser. 1, vol. 50, pt. 1, 643, 290; and Benjamin Franklin Gilbert, "California and the Civil War: A Bibliographical Essay," *California Historical Society Quarterly* 40 (Dec. 1961), 292. For a handy guide to the state's population in 1860, see Doris Marion Wright, "The Making of Cosmopolitan California: An Analysis of Immigration, 1848–1870," *California Historical Society Quarterly* 19 (Dec. 1940), 339–40.

20. Ralph S. Kuykendall, "A California States Rights Editor," *Grizzly Bear* 24 (Jan. 1919), 3–4.

21. For conflicting details, see Benjamin Franklin Gilbert, "The Confederate Minority in California," *California Historical Society Quarterly* 20 (June 1941), 154–70; Walters, "Confederates in Southern California," 41–53; Ronald C. Woolsey, "The Politics of a Lost Cause: 'Seceshers' and Democrats in Southern California During the Civil War," *California History* 69 (Winter 1990–91), 372–83; Clarence C. Clendennen, "Dan Showalter—California Secessionist," *California Historical Society Quarterly* 40 (Dec. 1961), 309–25; Peter Wang, "The Mythical Confederation Plot in Southern California," *Quarterly of San Bernardino County Museum Association* 16 (1969), 1–24.

22. Benjamin Franklin Gilbert, "Kentucky Privateers in California," *Register of Kentucky State Historical Society* 38 (1940), 256–66; James Wilkins, ed., *The Great Diamond Hoax and Other Stirring Incidents in the Life of Asbury Harpending* (San Francisco, 1913), 45–83; *Alta California*, March 16–17, 1863; James A. B. Scherer, *Thirty-first Star* (New York, 1942), 256–57; Aurora Hunt, *The Army of the Pacific, 1860–1866* (Glendale, Calif., 1950), 305–10.

23. On California and the war generally, see Gilbert, "California and the Civil War," 289–307. For details on the men who fought in the war, see especially Richard H. Orton, comp., *Records of California Men in the War of the Rebellion, 1861–1865* (Sacramento, Calif., 1890). For the California Battalion, see James McLean, *California Sabers: The 2nd Massachusetts in the Civil War* (Indianapolis, 2000); Larry Rogers and Keith Rogers, *Their Horses Climbed Trees: A Chronicle of the California 100 and Battalion in the Civil War, from San Francisco to Appomattox* (Atglen, Pa., 2001). For an exaggerated version of Colonel Baker's heroics, see Elijah J. Kennedy, *The Contest for California in 1861* (Boston, 1912).

24. For the details of this incident, see A. Russell Buchanan, *David S. Terry of California: Dueling Judge* (San Marino, Calif., 1956), 191–231; Robert H. Kroninger, "The Justice and the Lady," *Supreme Court Historical Society 1977 Yearbook* (Washington, D.C., 1976); Paul Kens, *Justice Stephen Field:*

Shaping Liberty from the Gold Rush to the Gilded Age (Lawrence, Kans., 1997), 275–83.

25. Stephen J. Field, *Personal Reminiscences of Early Days in California* (San Francisco, 1893), 70–71.

26. Ibid., 101. See also Kroninger, "The Justice and the Lady"; Kens, *Justice Field*, 74, 275–83.

Index

Index

Leonard L. Richards, professor of history at the University of Massachusetts, grew up in California and earned his A.B., M.A., and Ph.D. at the University of California, Berkeley and Davis. He has also taught at San Francisco State College and the University of Hawaii. His *"Gentlemen of Property and Standing": Anti-Abolition Mobs in Jacksonian America* won the American Historical Association's Albert J. Beveridge Award in 1970. *The Life and Times of Congressman John Quincy Adams* was a finalist for the Pulitzer Prize in 1987, and *The Slave Power: The Free North and Southern Domination, 1780–1860* took the second-place Lincoln Prize in 2001. He is also the author of *The Advent of American Democracy, 1815–1848* (1977), of *Shays's Rebellion: The American Revolution's Final Battle* (2002), and, with William Graebner, of *The American Record* (1981, 1987, 1995, 2000, 2005). He and his wife live in Amherst, Massachusetts.

A NOTE ABOUT THE TYPE

This book was set in Janson, a typeface long thought to have been made by the Dutchman Anton Janson, who was a practicing typefounder in Leipzig during the years 1668–1687. However, it has been conclusively demonstrated that these types are actually the work of Nicholas Kis (1650–1702), a Hungarian, who most probably learned his trade from the master Dutch typefounder Dirk Voskens. The type is an excellent example of the influential and sturdy Dutch types that prevailed in England up to the time William Caslon (1692–1766) developed his own incomparable designs from them.

Composed by North Market Street Graphics,
Lancaster, Pennsylvania

Printed and bound by Berryville Graphics,
Berryville, Virginia

Maps designed by Jennifer Bonin

Designed by Soonyoung Kwon